Communicating

in

the

Classroom

Communicating in the Classroom

Kathleen Kougl

Youngstown State University

WAVELAND
PRESS, INC.
Prospect Heights, Illinois

Robert E. Denton, Jr.
Consulting Editor

For information about this book, write or call:
Waveland Press, Inc.
P.O. Box 400
Prospect Heights, Illinois 60070
(847) 634-0081

To the memory of Frank J. Kougl Jr., my father, and Gerald M. Phillips, teacher, mentor and friend.

Contents

Preface

Communicating in the Classroom has been written for students who are preparing to become teachers and who may have had little formal instruction in speech communication. Although poised on the brink of the communication-intensive profession of teaching, they may not fully understand the nature and importance of effective speaking and listening in the classroom, nor how to do it.

The goal of this text is to help students understand the dynamic process of classroom communication in a personal and fundamental way that affects the choices they will make as teachers. This goal recognizes that the success of teaching and learning depends on the effectiveness of communication among the teacher and students and that subject matter is not all that is at stake, but also students' *attitudes* about self, the subject, other students, and education as well.

This goal can be achieved by helping prospective teachers develop a communicative perspective, a habit of mind that involves thinking critically about their communication: being aware of their speaking goals, their students, the situation, and the dynamics of the communication interaction; examining their communication options; and making appropriate choices. This perspective is brought to bear in *planning* what to say and how to express it, in *monitoring* what happens while communicating, and in *evaluating* what happens in a reflective way that informs their future communicative choices.

The text models the communicative perspective in its organization. Throughout each chapter, characteristics, options, and bases for choices are presented with consideration of both teachers' and students' perspectives. It is written in a conversational tone with many examples and thought-provoking questions.

The nine chapters are grouped into three parts. In Part I, "Understanding the Communication Process, Self, and Others," chapter 1 stresses the importance of effective oral communication in the classroom and explains the communicative perspective and the elements in the communication process. Chapter 2 examines the factors that are unique to each person—perception, self-concept, learning style, and expectations (especially teacher expectations)—and how they affect students' and teachers' communicative behavior.

Next, Part II deals with the building blocks of communication. Chapter 3 discusses characteristics and types of nonverbal behavior, emphasizing the impact of cultural learning, context, and perception. Chapter 4 explores the linguistic and pragmatic dimensions of verbal behavior and looks at skill training, how to handle quiet students, and how to create a talk friendly environment. Chapter 5 examines listening—its characteristics, what causes poor listening, and suggestions for how teachers can improve teacher-student listening through their input as: role model, planner, speaker, and listener.

Part III, "Shaping Oral Communication Interactions in the Classroom," applies the communicative perspective to the basic ways teachers shape communicative interactions in the classroom. Each chapter explains the *why* and the *what* of possible types of classroom communication interactions and provides practical suggestions about how to prepare, conduct, and evaluate each type. Chapter 6, "Communicating Interpersonally," examines the dynamics of influence, persuasion, and conflict, focusing on choices and outcomes. Chapter 7, "Discussion," establishes the connection between language and thought, how discussion develops critical thinking, and focuses on planning, writing effective questions, and facilitating discussion. Chapter 8, "Small Groups," establishes the connection between work in groups and cooperative learning, explains the basic elements of the group process in terms of questions that need to be answered when planning a group activity, and provides the practical details of running different types of groups. Chapter 9, "Lecturing: Giving Information," explores common myths about lecturing and provides a step-by-step approach for preparing and giving a lecture.

As a result of reading this text, I hope prospective teachers develop a communicative perspective and demonstrate more flexibility and appropriateness when speaking and listening, as students, and as teachers with their students. I think the information presented in this text can empower them to become effective and confident communicators.

Acknowledgements

Writing a book is a long, solitary journey, and I have many people to thank for their help along the way. Thank you to Neil and Carol Rowe, of Waveland Press, for the opportunity to write this book and for their continued support. Thank you to my many students and teacher friends who supplied examples that appear in the text. Thank you to the people who read and commented on portions of the text and discussed ideas with me: the late Gerald Phillips, The Pennsylvania State University; Carolyn Adger, Center for Applied Linguistics; Nancy Metzger, Mount Carmel Health Systems; Larry Bartos, teacher at Poland High School (OH); Debbie Madsen, former teacher at McKinley High School (OH); Frank Kougl, recent retiree from Patterson High School (MD). Thank you to my friends and family for their interest, generous support, and boundless patience.

Finally, a most heartfelt thank you to my editor, Jeni Ogilvie, of Waveland Press for her thoroughness, encouragement, and unfailing good humor. It was a pleasure to work with her.

Part I

Understanding the
Communication Process,
Self, and Others

Part I explains the basic process of communication and the personal factors that shape us as communicators. It introduces basic concepts and provides the foundation for the rest of the book.

Chapter 1 begins with a look at why effective oral communication in the classroom is important. It then defines communication and examines the basic elements of communication as they occur in classrooms. The chapter ends with explaining how developing a "communicative perspective" will make you a more effective communicator as a teacher.

Chapter 2 focuses on the personal factors that contribute to individual students' and teachers' unique outlooks as communicators in the classroom: perception, self-concept, learning style, and teacher expectations.

Chapter 1

Effective Communication in the Classroom

Ideas to Remember

* Communication in the classroom matters more now than ever before because the Information Age Is redefining the meaning of knowledge, learning, and teaching and the importance of oral communication skills.
* Communication is a dynamic process of interaction between people in which they assign meaning to each other's behavior.
* The dynamic components of the process are:

    The Communicators—each of whom simultaneously plays the roles of speaker and listener.

    The Message—which has content/delivery dimensions and degree of intentionality.

    Context—the physical, temporal, and social/psychological environment.

    Meaning—what meaning is assigned may be interrupted or distorted by many factors and facilitated by feedback.
* Key Ideas to Understanding Oral Communication:

    Communication is complex.

    Communication involves mutual influence.

    Communication is continuous.

3

> Communication involves content and a relationship.
> Communication is purposive.
> * Teachers need to develop a communicative perspective—think analytically when they communicate and apply the ideas from this book.

If you are reading this, you are probably enrolled in a teacher training program. If you are like most prospective teachers, you probably are—and always have been—a "good student." Perhaps you liked everything about school or just fell in love with a particular subject. Chances are you had a special teacher who inspired you to want to teach. You want to be the kind of teacher who inspires and creates the excitement you felt as a student.

You know teaching isn't easy. You read the newspapers and listen to the news. The problems in society—dwindling resources, families in crisis, poverty, drugs, violence—affect students in and out of school. Declining student performance nationwide has led to increased requirements and competency testing for high school graduation. The National Education Goals, "Goals 2000," set high standards to meet. All over the country schools, curricula, and teacher education programs are being reevaluated. You are familiar with the problems, yet you still want to teach. Let's face it: Teachers are optimists. They believe in the future, and they believe they can make a difference. If you were not an optimistic person, you would not be preparing to teach.

What comes to mind when you think of teaching? The question, "What are you going to teach?" is often asked in introductory education classes. Students respond with the name of their teaching field— English, science, math—and the professor says, "No, you are going to teach students!" Both answers are correct because students and teachers meet in a class devoted to a particular subject. Thus teaching is more than just subject matter; it is a meeting of people who come together for specific tasks called "teaching" and "learning." Educators, legislators, and the public disagree about what should be taught and how learning should be measured. Nevertheless, all would agree that communication is central to education. A national survey of secondary-school principals demonstrates the importance of communication skills in hiring and in teaching effectiveness (Johnson 1994).[1] What happens when teachers and students come together occurs through the process of communication, primarily through speaking and listening.

Why Communication Matters

Face-to-face communication has always been a central element in the life of classrooms. However, how "knowledge" is defined affects the nature of the communicating that goes on, that is, who is talking to whom for what purpose. You are coming to teaching at a time when the definition of knowledge is changing. This change affects the nature of the communicating process that is expected in the classrooms, redefining "teaching" and "learning."

Knowledge has been viewed as a product that the teacher-as-expert gives to the students to master. In the past, communication in the classroom was teacher-centered and focused on one-way information transferral from the teacher to the students. The teacher did most of the talking, while students were passive—speaking only when asked to respond: the key question asked was, "What do you know?"

In the Information Age knowledge is ever changing and expanding. It does not matter how much you know, but how you think and what you can do with what you know. Current educational thought views learning as an active process of making knowledge the students' own through critical thinking, collaboration, and problem solving. The key question is, "What does it mean?" Communication in the classroom is student-centered and focuses on discovery. Everyone talks and listens to everyone else—the teacher as intellectual guide or coach, and the students as actively engaged learners. Active inquiry is already part of curricular redesign in math, the sciences, English, and history.[2] This shift in educational thought means that *communicating becomes the way to learn*. It is no longer only a way to report what was learned.

The growing public awareness of the importance of communication is contributing to expectations for teaching more communication in the classroom. In the past, schools emphasized reading and writing for all students. If speech communication got any attention, it was limited to specialized speaking events, such as public speaking or debate, and reserved for small numbers of students. Yet speech communication has always been the means through which we conduct our personal and public lives. Walter Loban, author of a landmark study in language development from kindergarten through grade twelve, expressed the importance of speech communication in our lives in a colorful way. According to Loban (1973, p. 687), "It is said that typical Americans listen to a book a day, speak a book a week, read a book a month, and write a book a year." These estimates are considered to be as accurate now as when first expressed (Buckley 1992).

Problems in society and the rapid rate of continual change are also creating public recognition of the need for well-developed speech communication skills for life after the classroom. As business restructures the nature of work, there is a need for workers who can communicate well in order to work cooperatively as team members to set goals and solve problems. As companies downsize, retool, relocate, and new companies spring up, workers need to retrain and communicate in new jobs with new people. According to labor marketing information from the Department of Labor, Americans will have an average of six jobs and three career changes during their working years (Howell 1995). As the competition for good jobs escalates, those with well-honed communication skills will have an edge. Even beyond personal careers, as society becomes more global yet fragmented along special interest, ethnic, racial, and economic lines, there is an ever greater need for people to be able to communicate across the rifts.

Skill in speaking and listening now more than ever has become crucial to the quality of our lives. As with so many other aspects of living, the public is coming to expect that schools will develop speech communication skills. For years, teachers of all subject matter have been expected to develop reading and writing skills. Now, as a teacher, you will need to think about how you can develop your students' abilities to communicate, not only for learning in the classroom, but for life.

Teachers have always been professional communicators, but the nature of the communication that is expected of teachers has changed. In addition, there is an emphasis on getting students communicating. Thus, it is critical that you understand communication's importance to you and your students. Your understanding of the communication process and your beliefs and skills will shape how and what your students learn. What kind of talking you allow and encourage—how you integrate speaking and listening into your classroom activities—will affect how your students think and how effectively they communicate. You will even be evaluated based on the results of the communicating that goes on between you and your students. This is true no matter where you teach, what you teach, or the age or ability of your students.

Your experience of communication in classrooms thus far has been as a student. Think back to the teachers whom you thought were poor teachers. How well did they communicate? Based on them, what would you declare off-limits right now as ineffective teacher communication?

I asked these questions of students in communication classes for education majors. The most frequently mentioned items were: picking on students; assuming too much; intolerance of questions; mumbling;

lack of preparation; boring voice; poor explanations; avoiding questions; lack of concern for students; speaking too fast; lack of organization; no or little eye contact; yelling; inappropriate use of humor.

What is intriguing about this list is that it represents the experiences of people who were preparing to teach. These people were survivors. They had graduated from high school and were in college preparing to be teachers. Think about the students who had trouble with school, dropped out, or only just got by. What part did their teachers' poor communication skills play in their scholastic difficulties?

No one goes into teaching wanting to be a bad teacher. Education majors do not say, "I want to get out of college and confuse and frustrate my students." No one wants to end up on a list of bad examples, yet poor teaching happens. We have all experienced it, yet we do not believe we will ever be guilty of committing bad teaching.

Effective teaching requires effective communication and effective communication can occur only if you understand the complexities of the communication process, develop a communicative perspective toward communication in the classroom, and continually apply this understanding and perspective when you teach. This book is about helping you prepare to do so.

What Communication Is

Communication is a dynamic process of interaction between people in which they assign meaning to each other's verbal and nonverbal behavior. "Dynamic process" means that what is occurring is not static. It changes moment to moment in complex, unpredictable ways. For example, let's assume we are two people who are talking to each other. It does not matter who is speaking or listening because we constantly do both when we communicate. Turn-taking is involved. I may be listening to what you are saying, but I also may be formulating what I will say next. As I'm speaking, you may be thinking about the response you will make. At any given moment, each element in the process has the potential to influence all the other elements and to affect the ongoing process. To understand how this complex process works we need to examine the component parts: the communicators, the message, the context, and the meaning of the message.

The Communicators

That people communicate holistically is one factor that complicates this seemingly simple exchange. Each person brings all of himself or herself to any given instance of communication. In effect, everything that makes each of us a unique individual—our beliefs, values, experiences, hopes, perceptual habits, self-concept, fears, knowledge, and speaking and listening skills—affects the communication that is taking place. This mix of personal elements affects how we see ourselves in various situations, influences what we think about the others involved, and applies to everyone in the process. Think of the differences an assistant principal might encounter when observing an anxious student teacher and an experienced teacher in the classroom. Think of the unique influences the following three students would bring to interactions with you, their teacher: a student repeating your class; a student who got a "D" in your subject area the preceding year; and a student in the honor society.

Our life histories shape what we say, how we say it, and the meanings we assign to what other people say. This is true of each party in the communicative exchange—students and teacher. Think of each person in the process as an iceberg. What we see, hear, and respond to when we communicate is like the one-tenth of the iceberg that shows above the waterline. The other nine-tenths below the waterline is everything about us that shapes how and what we say. It cannot be *seen*, yet it affects the process. In other words, seemingly unrelated events also can have an effect on the communication that occurs. For example, consider the teacher who arrives at school angry because of an argument at home and yells at the class. The students do not know about the argument, but they are affected by and may respond to the yelling. The unrelated incident becomes part of the communication process between the teacher and the students.

The Message

Messages are what we say when we talk. Many people assume that messages are only the words spoken, but messages may be verbal or nonverbal. Either type of message is subject to two factors that affect its potential meaning: content/delivery dimensions and degree of intentionality.

Content/Delivery Dimensions. A message always has two dimensions: **content** (what it is about) and **delivery** (how it is expressed—how the speaker sounds, looks, and acts while expressing the content). This is true whether the message is verbal or nonverbal. It is the delivery dimension that communicates attitude or feeling about the content dimension of the message.

Let's take the example of a teacher who wants to convey the content, "Be quiet." If she says it, the message is verbal. How she says it is the delivery dimension. Does she yell it at the whole class? Say it softly to a group of noisy students working in a group? Say it loudly with a tone of exasperation in her voice? Or, she may deliver the same content as a nonverbal message by putting her finger to her lips and saying "Shhh." Even with nonverbal content, there is a delivery dimension. Does she "Shhh" loudly and glare at the offenders? Shake her head "no" and wait for quiet? Or sit casually on a desk and smile?

Degree of Intentionality. Degree of intentionality is another factor that complicates messages. People assume that others are *deliberately* sending them messages that are crafted and controlled verbally and nonverbally. They say what they mean, and they mean what they say. However, this is not necessarily accurate. As our definition of communication reminds us, we assign meaning to each other's verbal and nonverbal behavior. It does not say we do this only when an intentional message is given to us.

A message may be perceived even when none was intended. A person notices some aspect of your behavior and "assigns a meaning" to it. This meaning then becomes part of the communication process between the person and you. Imagine talking with friends and your mind wanders. Someone says, "What's wrong?" or, "Are you mad?" You were not even listening to the conversation, much less sending a message. Your friend assigned a meaning based on how you looked.

Sometimes the verbal and nonverbal aspects of a message may be intended, even when there is a discrepancy between them—the words mean one thing, the nonverbal behavior another. This is what sarcasm is all about. The words, "Good job, class," convey a positive message, but a bitter tone of voice and a cold stare indicate a negative message. Have you ever experienced this type of mixed message?

Context

The environment in which people communicate their messages is referred to as **context**. It affects what each person says and how it is expressed. The effects may be different for each person present. There are three kinds of contexts that simultaneously surround any communicative exchange: physical, temporal, and social/psychological (DeVito 1995). The effects may be minimal and subtle or complex and obvious, depending upon the situation.

Physical. The actual location is referred to as the **physical context**. Think about how the differences in the following physical contexts affect your communicating: a college classroom, the student union, your home. Try to imagine how a teacher's talk might be affected depending upon whether it was occurring in a classroom, the teacher's lounge, or the principal's office. Imagine how a student's talk might be different on the playground or in the lunchroom or in the principal's office.

Temporal. The timing of messages and how they fit into the ongoing communication process is referred to as the **temporal context**. This includes how one message is timed in terms of another message. For example, take the question, "Do we have any homework?" If asked after the homework has been assigned, the question is poorly timed. Temporal context also includes how a message is timed for the people involved. A well-timed message in this sense would be if you have people's attention and they are ready to listen to the message. Teachers report that student response varies depending on timing (for example, before or after lunch) or timing relative to other events (for example, before or after a holiday or special events in the school). Scheduling and planning can affect the appropriateness and flexibility needed for well-timed messages. The sound of a bell dictates when students must move to the next class, even if they did not comprehend the lesson they just encountered or complete their tasks. A rigid, fast paced curriculum pressures teachers to move on regardless of student responses and difficulties.

Social/Psychological. The social expectations within a situation and the emotional tone that develops involves the **social/psychological context**.

Social Expectations. This includes **norms** (ideas of what are appropriate or inappropriate behaviors) and **roles** (how a person is to do a particular job, task, or function). Society establishes implicit social expectations, while explicit policies and laws are mandated by the educational organization (school boards, state legislatures). Both affect what goes on during individual interactions in classrooms. For example, traditional implicit expectations in schools include status differences between teachers and students—an authoritative and evaluative role for teachers and compliance from students. School boards and legislatures make explicit policies and laws, such as number of school days or dress codes.

Emotional Tone. This refers to the atmosphere or psychological climate people experience. Emotional tone results from the dynamic interplay of the people communicating. It develops over time. It is how people feel about being in the situation. Defensive? Wary? Intimidated? Liked? Safe? Tolerated? Ignored? Respected? **Classroom climate** is the term for psychological context in schools. Classrooms with *positive* climates are considered more conducive to learning. A positive climate exists when learners feel accepted and supported. If learners feel judged or threatened, the climate is negative. The impact of emotional tone is that people communicate more openly when they feel accepted and supported rather than rejected or judged.

Meaning

Notice the definition of communication includes the phrase "assign meaning." It does not say communicators "give" or "receive" meaning. Yet people commonly assume that once they speak their words, the intended message is automatically received. The teacher who says, "We went over that yesterday" is an example of this assumption—that meaning is universally in the words and can be lobbed like a tennis ball over the net. The meaning may have been clear to the teacher, but whether the explanation had the same or no meaning to the students is a different consideration.

This "I said it, you got it" thinking works sometimes because words have denotative meanings available to people who speak the same language. **Denotations** point to tangible objects, events, or processes. Dictionaries provide denotative meanings. However, words also resonate with **connotative meanings**, which involve the values, attitudes, and feelings associated with a word. Often, connotative meanings are unique to an individual, a result of personal experience. Even with simple messages composed of basic words, the sender cannot know with certainty that the receiver will assign the same meaning intended by the sender. If communicating meaning were as simple as exchanging words, we would never misunderstand each other.

Meaning is something created through the dynamic process of interaction between the communicators. All communicators depend on their unique perception to create their own messages and perceive and interpret other people's messages. All the elements of communication discussed thus far collide and impact on each other to stir up possible meanings. Who the "communicators" are, what "message" (intentionally or unintentionally) is perceived, and how the "context" frames the interaction are all in motion. The participants create meaning together. Meaning does not reside in the verbal or nonverbal behavior, but in individuals' interpretations of the verbal and nonverbal behavior. *Meaning is in people.*

To understand the complexity and creativity involved in trying to get our meaning across, we need to look at the variables that may come into play.

Noise. Speech communication educators use the term **noise** for anything that interferes, distorts, or complicates the creation of meaning.

It is important to remember that all or some noises (presented in random order) can operate in *each* person involved in *any* interaction. Public school classes vary from 15 to 45 students, and class periods from 30 minutes to two hours. Imagine the multiple combinations of noises at work influencing what is *meant* for each student and the teacher.

Physical. The physical environment is full of sounds that make it hard to hear or that disrupt concentration. Schools are noisy places: bells ringing, street noise, hall noise, interruptions from the public address system and people (administrators, parents, other teachers, guidance counselors, etc.).

Physiological. Internal, bodily states within the communicators often influence their communicating. It takes energy to focus on communicating. Whether teachers or students are sick, tired, hungry or cold influences what they say and how they say it. Staying up too late at night (for example, because of watching TV or because of family arguments) makes a difference in how an individual communicates. Sick children who come to school because there is no one to stay home with them or no money for a doctor will have physiological "noise" occurring.

Psychological. Internal, personal feelings can affect how we speak and listen to each other. Positive emotions expedite the communication process, while negative emotions—anger, fear, anxiety, depression—impede it. Feelings from the past, life outside the classroom, or current happenings in the class can have an effect. For example, students often bring their feelings about their past school experience, whether successful or not, to their communicating relationship with you. Children who live in violent neighborhoods or dysfunctional families bring their anxiety and fear with them. Feelings generated daily in classroom interaction influence how teachers and students communicate with each other. Keep in mind, not only the students', but the teacher's past and present personal feelings also produce psychological noise. A teacher with personal problems or who does not like particular students will communicate differently than someone who has a more positive orientation.

Social. Communicators have values, attitudes, and expectations that are not necessarily shared or fully understood by each other. Social noise may occur because of differences in social experiences, age, ethnic, cultural, or economic background. These social differences reveal themselves through our verbal and nonverbal behavior and may range from how people dress, to expectations about how to act or treat other people, to what is real or true. Communicators assume their personal values and expectations are shared by the people with whom they communicate. When they are not, social noise intrudes into what meanings are assigned. The possibilities for social noise are endless in our multicultural society.

A classic example of social noise is the difference between the perspectives of educators and many students about the value of education. Administrators, legislators, and teachers feel that education is important. The content of curricula, class activities, and graduation requirements are designed assuming education has inherent value. Learning is a life-enriching experience, a way to get ahead and to achieve goals. Yet many students' personal worlds are filled with role models who believe their school experience was a waste of time. These people's attitudes illustrate to the students that education is irrelevant. Students who espouse this value do not take school seriously. Attendance is erratic and effort is minimal. As one urban teacher I know expressed it, "For many of our students, school is only a place to come to get their free lunch and bus passes." Those are concrete outcomes experienced by all who attend; the other values have not been internalized because they have not yet been meaningful.

Semantic. People have different meanings or no meanings for the words being used. As small children, we learned to use words that had specific concrete meanings in order to have our needs met. As we grew, we continually added new words and additional meanings for the words we already knew. Semantic noise occurs when we assume everyone knows the words we know and has the same meanings for them.

It is the experience of the people communicating, no matter what their age, which determines what words they use and what meanings they have. Common causes of semantic noise are: differences in mental development, different dialects, slang, and verbal traps. These causes will be explored in chapter 4.

Grammatical. Words are put together to make meaningful utterances in a language; each language has its own system which is governed by certain rules. Problems arise when speakers are operating with different grammatical rules or do not use the rules of the language they are speaking. These circumstances would occur with students for whom English is not the native language or who speak a dialect of English. Grammatical noise will be examined further in chapter 4.

Grammatical noise can also be generated by teachers when they overload a sentence. **Overloading** is conveying too much information through excessively complicated syntax. The spoken sentence is too long with too many qualifiers, details, and clauses. Overloading makes listening very hard. Students become frustrated and confused.

Phonetic. Phonology is the study of the sound system of a language. A phoneme is the smallest unit of sound in any language. Phonetic interference occurs when there are differences in articulation or pronunciation between what is expected and what is produced. The listener is unsure what the words are and must pause and figure them out. More will be said about phonetic noise in chapter 4.

Feedback. Feedback is another aspect of the communication process that affects what meanings are assigned. **Feedback** is a message sent in response to another message. It meets the need we all have whenever we communicate to know how we are doing. Remember, communicators are continually, simultaneously speaking or listening as they interact. Any verbal or nonverbal response from either person is feedback. A question about what was said is feedback. Nodding your head up and down and saying "uh-huh" while someone is speaking is feedback. A puzzled look or a blank stare in the eyes of someone you are talking to is feedback. These responses help us figure out what the other person is getting out of the exchange. Feedback is information that allows each communicator to evaluate how he or she is doing and then decide what to clarify, adjust, continue, correct, change, or stop. Feedback is what optimizes the likelihood of one person's intended meaning correlating with the other person's assigned meaning.

Feedback can fail to function for many reasons. Many people are concerned only about the feedback that they are *getting*; they neglect to *give* feedback because they do not realize they have a responsibility to let the message sender know how he or she is doing. Sometimes receivers lack skill in giving effective feedback or do not realize that they are not giving feedback. No matter what the cause, no feedback or inappropriate feedback interferes with the communication process. How poor feedback can affect a lesson is illustrated by the following example. A student teacher was leading a discussion. Her pattern was to call on a student, staring at the student until he or she finished speaking, and then call on another student. Other than the blank stare, which was intimidating, there was no feedback to indicate that she heard, understood, or cared about the comment. Her lack of feedback soon reduced everyone to silence. Students stopped raising their hands and would not answer when called on.

To be effective communicators teachers need to seek out feedback for themselves and provide feedback for their students. To ask students, "What questions do you have?" is a request for feedback. A smile, the thumb's up sign, or a question about what a student has said gives feedback to students.

This concludes our examination of the elements in the process of speech communication: communicators, messages, context, and meaning. In the next section, we review several key ideas to keep in mind.

Key Ideas

Communication Is Complex

Communicating is much more than exchanging spoken words. Every message, whether intentional or unintentional, involves many bits of verbal (words) and nonverbal (sensory information) behavior. The meaning of any word or nonverbal cue is not inherent or automatic. Each person in the interaction chooses, shapes, and interprets these bits of behavior in fashioning meaning. Individual perceptions of the other communicators, the content of the message, and the context in which the message is delivered and received influences the meaning each person gets.

As teachers, we need to grasp the awesome complexity of the communication process, so we do not create problems due to naive or simplistic thinking. Communication is fraught with possibilities, unknowns, interferences, and unexpected outcomes. We continually need to remind ourselves and to help our students understand that it requires effort to communicate effectively.

Communication Involves Mutual Influence

The dynamic, interactive nature of the communication process means people influence each other as they communicate. Meaning is not given, rather is negotiated, as people assign meaning to each other's verbal and nonverbal behavior. People influence each other as they communicate through giving and getting feedback. What they pay attention to and what they interpret it to mean affect what happens next. The potential is always there to make adjustments based on what feedback is received or the kind of impression people think they are creating.

The nature and degree of the mutual influence that occurs in any given situation depend upon the individuals involved. It may be conscious or unconscious, subtle or obvious, accurately or inaccurately interpreted. If we are paying any attention to someone, there will be some type of influence.

As teachers, we need to remember and to help our students understand that creating meaning is a cooperative venture. Our verbal and nonverbal behavior have the potential to help, hinder, or harm our communicating. We need to look for our students' feedback and use it to communicate more effectively with them. We also need to sensitize students to the importance of clear feedback when they communicate. We need to help them learn to give it, look for it, and interpret it as objectively as possible.

Communication Is Continuous

Communicative events have no clear beginning and ending points. Any communicative event begins before it starts and continues after it is over. All of our past communicative experiences come to bear each time we communicate. For example, our feelings, attitudes, and ideas about the person(s), the situation, the event itself, and the topic are part of our thinking about the present interaction. We anticipate what will happen prior to the event; we are affected by what actually occurs. Then we continue to think about the event after it ends. The anticipation is like running coming attractions in our head of what might happen. The post-event analysis is like Monday morning quarterbacking. We replay the mental tapes of what happened and critique them. Whatever impact the event has on us, the effect lingers and can influence how and what we communicate in the future with the same person or with other people.

As teachers, we need to remember every interaction is surrounded by communicative histories, ours and our students'. What happened to our students before we met them influences how they communicate in our classroom. What happens today as we talk and listen to each other affects what will happen tomorrow.

Communication Involves Content and Relationship

All communicative events have a content and a relationship dimension. "Content" is whatever the communicative event is about. "Relationship" is the connection that happens between people as they communicate. This connection generates feelings and attitudes about the other person. These feelings and attitudes then affect the ongoing communication process. When they are positive, there tends to be more open communicating. Whatever the feelings and attitudes are, they define the nature of the relationship—which then, in turn, affects the process.

As teachers, we need to remember that the relationships we develop with our students affect the communicating and learning that takes place. We need to think about what relationship messages we are giving to our students, and what attitudes and feelings they are displaying in response.

Communication Is Purposive

People talk or choose not to talk for a reason. We have a purpose or goal that impels us to communicate or to refrain from communicating. We may not be consciously aware of our purpose or other people's purposes, but goals drive the communication process nonetheless.

A purpose may be straightforward. specific, and short-term or involved, general, and long-term. Purposes may involve definite content or impressions. Many purposes can be operating simultaneously. These purposes may complement or conflict with each other. For example, a teacher may have the simple, specific purpose to answer a student's question. At the same time, he or she may have the more global, long-term purpose of being perceived as a good teacher. A motivated student may have as an immediate purpose making a comment in a class discussion, but a long-term goal of being accepted by others. The former purpose needs talk to accomplish it, while the latter may demand silence to be seen as "cool."

As teachers, we need to appreciate the importance and complexity of personal purposes and goals. We need to try to understand our purposes and those of our students. We need to discover ways to use students' goals to help them learn. We also need to help our students identify their own reasons for speaking or not speaking.

Understanding the complexities of the communication process and these key points are the first steps in developing a communicative perspective. The next step is to realize how these ideas come into play when you think from a communicative perspective in the classroom.

Developing a Communicative Perspective

To communicate more effectively as a teacher, you must develop a "communicative perspective." This means making an effort to think analytically about your communication. It means applying the ideas in this book to your actual speaking and listening experiences.

A communicative perspective is a critical habit of mind. It is self-reflective while at the same time attuned to the other people involved in the process. It considers the key ideas about communication and recognizes the need to be flexible.

Someone thinking with a communicative perspective examines what is occurring in the communication process and then makes choices in order to be effective. A teacher with a communicative perspective understands that what is likely to be meaningful for student A may not be for student B. What may be appropriate in one situation may be inappropriate in another. A person with a communicative perspective understands how the choices made now affect current meanings and future relationships.

A communicative perspective involves planning, monitoring, and evaluating.

1. *Planning*. This involves thinking about your message before you communicate. Trying to understand your students and their purposes, the classroom situation, and yourself as a communicator. Analyze your own speaking and listening skills and continually work to improve them. Always work at creating clear messages. Anticipate possible noises and try to eliminate them or adjust to them.

2. *Monitoring*. Adjusting your verbal and nonverbal behavior as you communicate means keeping in mind the negotiated nature of meaning. Look for verbal and nonverbal feedback and use it to ensure that your intended meanings are getting through to your students. Be alert to noises and deal with them. Work at giving clear verbal and nonverbal feedback, so your students can adjust their messages and have their meanings come through.

3. *Evaluating*. Analyzing outcomes after the communication ends is a necessity for future interactions. Reflect on what happened based on your purposes and your perception of your students' purposes. Use what you learn from this assessment in your future communicating.

Notes

[1] Principals were asked to consider the criteria they used when hiring teachers. The most important grouping of criteria was "communication," which included: interpersonal communication, poise, oral communication skills, enthusiasm, listening skills, and writing skills. (Selection items rank ordered by mean, greater than 7.99: enthusiasm, oral communication skills, competence in area of specialization, interpersonal communication skills, and listening skills).

"Teacher effectiveness" items indicated that communication skills, classroom preparation, and classroom management were equally important. The researcher concluded that the principals see teachers as needing to be balanced and capable when using a variety of skills. (Effectiveness items rank ordered by mean, greater than 8.0): ability to motivate students, enthusiasm, interpersonal communication skills, preparation for class, classroom control, positive climate, oral communication skills, ability to actively involve students, ability to adapt to individuals, competence in area of specialization, questioning skills, and disciplinary skills.

[2] See "New Designs for Teaching and Learning, A Special Report on Education." *Wall Street Journal*, Section B, 7/11/92. *National Standards for U.S. History*, report by the National Center for History in the Schools, UCLA, released October 1994. The National Council of Teachers of Math released national standards in 1989. "A Winning Formula," *Teacher*. September, 1994 (17–19) reports on a K–6 program in line with these standards. *Geography for Life: National Geography Standards 1994*. These voluntary standards were developed by the American Geographical Society, Association of American Geographers, National Council for Geographic Education and the National Geographic Society. They were released in October, 1994.

References

Buckley, Marilyn. December, 1992. "Focus on Research: We Listen a Book a Day; We Speak a Book a Week: Learning from Walter Loban." *Language Arts* 69:622–26.

Corder, Jim. 1981. *Handbook of Current English*, 6th edition. Glenview, IL: Scott, Foresman & Co.

DeVito, Joseph. 1995. *The Interpersonal Communication Book*, 7th edition. New York: HarperCollins.

Eisenson, Jon and Mardel Ogilvie. 1983. *Communicative Disorders in Children*, 5th edition. New York: MacMillan.

Howell, Lynne. Personal conversation January 26, 1995. Ms. Howell is a Counselor at Career Services, Youngstown State University.

Johnson, S. January, 1994. "A National Assessment of Secondary-School Principals' Perceptions of Teaching-Effectiveness Criteria." *Communication Education* 43(1): 1–16.

Loban, Walter. 1973. "The Green Pastures of English." *Elementary English* 50(5): 683-90

Suggested Reading

"When Teaching 'Works': Stories of Communication in Education," L. Rosenfeld, Editor. October, 1993. *Communication Education* 42(4): entire issue.

Thirteen outstanding teachers write narratives about their most memorable instructional moment of communication. The moments cover all levels, take place in and out of the classroom, and occur when the authors were students, as well as teachers. They are humorous, touching, profound. All are thought-provoking about what it means to teach and to learn. Make sure to read the four critical analyses that follow the stories.

"Why Communication? Why Education? Toward a Politics of Teaching," by Roderick Hart. April, 1993. *Communication Education*. 42 (2): 97–105.

This essay examines what it means to teach in the 1990s, why education is more important than it has ever been, why teaching communication skills is a political matter, and why the implicit politics of communication as a field attracts detractors. It concludes with a stirring reminder of what communication is all about.

Chapter 2

Communication Starts with "I"

Ideas to Remember

* Perception, self-concept, learning styles, and teacher expectations intertwine in complex ways and affect what and how we communicate.
* The perceptual process, which enables us to make sense out of our experience, involves three stages: selection, interpretation, and behavior.
* Self-concept is the multi-faceted, complex collection of the self-perceptions we have about ourselves at any given point in time.
* It is important to understand how self-concept is formed and the impact it has on how we behave, how we interpret other people's behavior, and school achievement.
* Three dimensions of students' learning styles—cognitive, affective, and physiological—must be considered to understand behavior.
* Teachers can form expectations about the future behavior of their students.
* Teachers can produce expectation effects on student outcomes when they act in response to the expectations that they have formed about students.

* The Brophy-Good Model explains how the expectation communication process works.

* Teachers communicate differential expectations (high and low) in many verbal and nonverbal ways.

* Variables associated with the teaching context affect teacher expectation effects: grade level, differences between elementary and secondary school, time of year, subject matter, and the nature of the learning environment.

* Teacher characteristics, whether they are proactive, reactive, or overreactive, affect teacher expectation effects.

In this chapter we begin examining "communicators" from their unique, personal perspectives. Communicating starts with oneself, whether teacher or student. It starts with "I." We, and each of our students, communicate outward to each other from a "self." This self operates with certain ways of perceiving experience, with a distinctive learning style, and with expectations about the way the world works. Our impulse to communicate springs from our unique sense of self, and we communicate from our personal frame of reference. To communicate more effectively in the classroom, we need to understand this frame of reference, ours and our students'.

Each of us is like a narrator in a story who shapes the events in the story and establishes a point of view, a vantage point for the telling of the story (Lee and Gura 1992, p. 208). It is the narrator who selects and arranges the details and tells us what they mean. It is the narrator's characteristic way of *seeing* that we must understand to appreciate the story being told. We are the narrators in our own life stories, but to understand another's life story, we need to study what has shaped the point of view of the person living it. As humans, our perception shapes our perspective, what we believe about others as well as ourselves, and the expectations we build.

Perception, self-concept, learning style, and expectations intertwine in complex ways when we communicate. It is through the perceptual process that we develop a sense of self and build expectations for behavior. How we learn affects our perception, how we act in the classroom, and the expectations others form about us. How we feel about ourselves affects our behavior and our expectations. Each element plays a part in the five key ideas about communication discussed in chapter 1. We enter communicative exchanges with our self-concept, perceptual habits, learning styles, and expectations already formed and functioning. We are frequently not conscious of what they are, yet they continually influence our communicating.

The mix of all these individual student and teacher selves, perceptions, learning styles, and expectations affects our communication in the classroom. They continually exert influence when we communicate, no matter who is speaking or listening, when no one is speaking or listening, and when there is no intended message. They shape our "messages" and interpretations of "meaning." If you are lecturing, students' perceptions, learning styles, and expectations determine what meaning they get from your words. If your students are leading their own discussion, their sense of themselves, perceptions, learning styles, and expectations will affect what they say and do. You, as an observer, will listen to their discussion through your own self-concept, perceptual habits, and expectations for them and yourself. Even when there is no intended message, students and teachers perceive and interpret a look on a face, a tone of voice, or silence.

Since the potential impact of perception, self-concept, learning styles, and teacher expectations on our communication is so great, we need to understand what each involves, the effects of each, how they interrelate, and how to use this information constructively when communicating with our students. Our experience begins with perception.

Perception

Perception is the fundamental process through which we make sense of the world as we encounter it. According to William James, we begin life with the world as, "a big, booming, buzzing confusion." (James; as cited in Adler and Towne 1993, p. 82). We spend the rest of our lives filtering and interpreting what our senses reveal to create a meaningful picture of the world. As we grow, we take in data through our five senses—sight, smell, taste, touch, and hearing. Like information processors, we take in raw information, process it, and decide what it means. We give meaning to the things and people around us through this perception process. Our need for consistency and order imposes structure on these subjective experiences of perception (Bassett-Smyth 1979). We develop "reality maps" or images of the world as we experience it (Roberts et al. 1987, p. 3). These personal versions of reality represent how we view the world and serve as guides to our behavior.

Perception, then, is an individual and unique experience for each of us. What we call reality is actually our perceptual version of what is out there. This is why witnesses to an accident have differing versions of what happened. Unique, individual, and varying interpretations of events occur all the time in classrooms. To understand why this happens, let's examine the three stages involved in the perceptual process.

Selection

Perception is always selective. Each of us is bombarded continually with an avalanche of information or *stimuli* demanding attention, such as sensory information from our environment, bodily signals, and thoughts. Attention is a limited commodity. From all the available possibilities, we select what to heed and filter out what to ignore.

There are many possible factors that might cause a person to attend to one thing rather than another. Keep in mind people are not usually aware of which factor is operating either for themselves or other people. What is selected for attention varies from person to person, and with each person from moment to moment. This subjectivity means each of us attends to some things, ignores and omits others, and edits what we see, feel, or hear.

Stimuli—objects, events, people, details—are attended to because of:

- *Sensory acuity*. People may be more sensitive to one kind of sensory information than another, so they pay more attention to that kind of information. For example, people who are more visually acute notice line, form, color, and composition more than other people might.
- *Motivation*. If something has value to you, then you have the incentive to pay attention to it.
- *Intensity*. If something is bigger, brighter, louder, then it draws attention.
- *Repetition*. Anything that is repeated calls attention to itself.
- *Novelty*. The new, different, or distracting draws attention.
- *Change*. Something that represents a change provides variety and contrast.
- *Need*. According to Maslow (1970), humans have a hierarchy of needs: physiological (food, water, warmth); safety (security, freedom from fear); social (affection, sense of belonging); esteem (achievement, recognition, mastery, reputation), and; self-actualization (self-fulfillment). Information related to meeting an unmet need assumes importance.
- *Background*. Our experiences, culture, language, beliefs, and expectations direct what we pay attention to.
- *Self-Concept*. Exerts a continuous and crucial selective effect on everything we see and do (Combs 1982).

Interpretation

Once a stimulus gets attention, then a search for meaning begins through our long-term memory. This search involves the **schemata** (networks of connected ideas or relationships) and cognitive categories or concepts that make up a person's reality map. The objective is to find where the stimuli fit, to find a match between the stimuli and the information already stored in the brain.

Through our experiences with people, events, and objects we create our categories or concepts. Certain attributes are highlighted and become our definition—what we know and believe about that category. Over time and with experience, we may pick up additional attributes for the category. If more attributes are added, the category becomes richer in meanings. Also, the more attributes a category has, the more likely it becomes interrelated to other categories in complex schemata.

It is important to remember what the categories and schemata are and how their definition depends on the individual. We do not all have the same definitions. For the ones we do have in common, we do not necessarily have the same information in them. As we discussed in chapter 1, "meaning" is in people. Take for example, a child forming the category for the object "father." Young children pick up on the attribute of maleness. They call any male "daddy," including mailmen, uncles, and, even strangers in the supermarket. With more experience, children add another attribute to the category, such as the grown-up male who lives at my house. At this point, children may get upset when other children refer to their fathers as "daddy." Eventually, children realize it is not a proper name and use it appropriately. Depending on the nature of the family life, a child also will add connotative meanings. A child whose father is absent or abusive will add different attributes than a child whose father is present or caring.

Keep in mind that these categories, concepts, and schemata refer to the constructs that make up the structure of our mental world. They form a mental grid of what we know and believe about our experience. It includes our information about individuals, events, relationships, and behavior. As long as we are living, we are continually adding new categories and revising our meanings for the old ones. Consider how you have revised categories in the past five years. Take, for example, the category "teacher." How has its meaning changed for you since junior high? What does it mean to you now that you are preparing to become a teacher?

What categories we have and what is presently in each of them affects how long it takes to search for a match for incoming stimuli. If a category is simple and used frequently, then the search time is short. If a concept is unusual or complex, the search time is longer. If no category exists, then the search time extends until the nearest similar category is located.

When we make the match and assign meaning, it may be unrelated to other people's perceptions. Our meaning may be different from the meanings other people assign to the same stimulus. Our meaning may not be the meaning intended by the speaker. We may create meaning when none was intended. Our meaning may not only be different but wrong in harmful ways.

Behavior

The meaning of a perception is how it causes us to act. As Combs (1982) expresses it, all behavior is a function of the person's perceptual field at the instant of acting. It is the meaning of the perceptions for the person that determines what happens. We behave according to how things seem to us. Remember, our behavior includes our verbal and nonverbal communication. Our behavior is then perceived by the people with whom we are communicating, and the cycle continues.

To Sum Up

You can see how the perception process (selection, interpretation, and behavior) affects the communication process. Through the perception process we define persons, events, behavior, and information, and we build expectations about our world. "Our perceptions define our version of reality, and this reality is expressed through our communication" (Bassett and Smythe 1979, p. 54–55).

We bring our individual accumulated histories of stored information and use them as a guide whenever we communicate. Whenever communication is occurring, all the participants are continually engaged in perceiving (selecting-interpreting-behaving). What occurs during communicating is, in turn, perceived by others (selected, interpreted) and affects how they behave in response.

Try to improve the quality of the perceptual process when you communicate with your students:

1. Strive to remember the idiosyncratic nature of perception. Each of us has a different perceptual version of every event. None represent "truth," not even yours, as teacher.

2. Be introspective about your perceptual process. Think about what the basis is for your selectivity and interpretation and the behavior which results from it.

3. Seek information about your students' perceptions, so you understand what they are and what they mean from your students' point of view.

4. Explain your perceptions, so your students understand what they are and what they mean from your point of view.
5. Explain perceptual process to your students, so they understand "point of view" and how it affects communication. Encourage them to be open to perceiving more and understanding other people's alternative interpretations.

The perceptual process is how we form our reality map that we use to make sense of our experience. At the heart of this map, central to how we perceive our world, is our self-concept (Roberts et al. 1987). It acts as a source of unity and as a guide to behavior (Beane and Lipka 1986). Since our self-concept plays such an important part in how we perceive, we need to understand what it is, how it forms, and how it affects students' behavior in the classroom.

Self-Concept

Self-concept is how we see ourselves. It is our private mental image of ourselves derived from all of our experiences. According to Hamachek (1987), it is a private synthesis of the feelings and ideas we have developed about our abilities, attributes, potential, and behavior. Self-concept is the collection of self-perceptions we have about ourselves at any given point in time.

The term "self-concept" looks simple, but it is really multi-faceted and complex. It involves at least four separate but interrelated aspects: a physical self-concept, a social self-concept, an emotional self-concept, and an intellectual self-concept. Each of these aspects may have many dimensions. For example, the physical self-concept may involve our perceptions of our physical appearance, physical ability, etc. (Silvernail 1985). These aspects interrelate and can affect each other, either positively or negatively. For example, a student whose physical self-concept is poor may be inhibited from taking risks with the social self or expressing the emotional self (Hamachek 1987).

Taken together, these aspects form a person's *general* or *global* self-concept. Self-concept, then, operates like an umbrella covering many different kinds of information about the self.

To understand self-concept, it is also important to understand **self-esteem**. The terms are often used interchangeably and occur together, but they refer to different kinds of information about the self. *Self-concept describes self-perceptions, while self-esteem evaluates them.* It indicates the degree of satisfaction and feelings of worth associated with the self-perceptions. Self-esteem is a personal assessment of the worth or competence of the things we do, who we are, and what we achieve (Hamachek 1987).

The following example illustrates the distinction in meaning between self-concept and self-esteem. "I am a student" is a descriptive statement, so it is part of the self-concept. "I am a poor student" makes a judgment about the description, so it is a statement about self-esteem.

Formation of the Self-Concept

The establishment of a self-concept begins at birth, develops slowly, and evolves over time through social interaction with others. What happens when we communicate with others is critical in the evolution of our self-concept. Communicating with others and our perception of their responses to us forges our self-concept.

According to Beane and Lipka, most theorists agree that the self is dynamic. "It seeks stability, consistency, and enhancement, yet is in constant interaction with the environment and is subject to modification or refinement" (1986, p. 15). Interactions throughout our lives carry the potential for gleaning information about ourselves that feeds into our self-concept. Hamachek says students' self-concepts expand and take shape during the elementary years. The self-concept can also be "reshaped, redirected, and modified—for better or worse—during the junior and high school years" (1990, p. 339).

Beane and Lipka (1986, p. 17) provide the following figure to illustrate how the self-perceiving process works:

Figure 2.1   The Process of Self-Perceiving

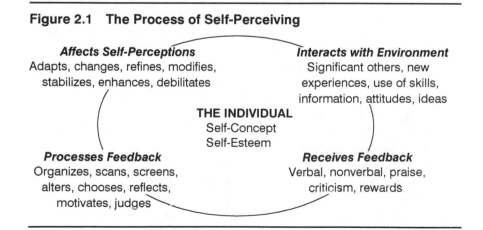

Affects Self-Perceptions
Adapts, changes, refines, modifies, stabilizes, enhances, debilitates

Interacts with Environment
Significant others, new experiences, use of skills, information, attitudes, ideas

THE INDIVIDUAL
Self-Concept
Self-Esteem

Processes Feedback
Organizes, scans, screens, alters, chooses, reflects, motivates, judges

Receives Feedback
Verbal, nonverbal, praise, criticism, rewards

At the center is the individual with a self-concept who constantly "interacts with the environment" and "receives feedback." The term **significant others** refers to people who are important to the individual, whose opinions matter. Feedback from a significant other has special significance for an individual.

Notice the variety of options the individual has for "processes feedback." Epstein (1973) suggests the self acts like a scientist in using these devices to test, adapt, refine and evaluate itself. However, the self is unscientific because it is not objective. The self is perceptual, personal, and subjective. It selects what it wants to believe based on its own definition. This personal subjectivity of the self can be seen at work in people suffering from anorexia nervosa, the eating disorder. Viewed objectively, they are skinny and underweight, but they believe they are overweight and will avoid eating by any means. Feedback that contradicts this view of themselves is ignored.

Once the feedback is processed, then it "affects self-perceptions" in some way. The self-concept could be strengthened, refined, or remain unchanged. In the example of the people with anorexia, the self-concept would remain unchanged.

Let's look at how this process of self-perceiving operates from birth through adolescence. Keeping in mind figure 2.1 will help you understand the self-perceptions of your students. Think about it in context of the physical, cognitive, and social changes that your students are going through. The process is the same throughout life, but the age and developmental level of your students will affect their individual experiences.

As infants and young children, it is our primary caregivers who respond to us. These interactions establish the basic foundation of the self. By age four or five children acquire many labels for themselves. Hamachek (1987) points out that these labels carry a positive or negative charge. He says it is one thing to be called a "girl," but the message is different with "just a girl" or "dumb girl." Parents with positive self-images and environments that are warm, affectionate, and respectful promote a healthy self-image (Silvernail 1985).

As the media, educators, and people in the helping professions point out, many children do not receive support in establishing this initial sense of personal adequacy. A number of causes contribute to this unfortunate situation: poor parenting skills, families that are dysfunctional due to drugs or alcohol, too little time spent with the children, and child abuse. A February 2, 1993, CBS *Eye on America* report on preschool education stated that one-third of the children were unready for school and so emotionally insecure that they could not relate to others. The report said that 30 percent of parents never read to their children and 40 percent never taught them letters or numbers. The report explained that such activities help children develop a sense of self. The report showed a class of preschool children who had so little sense of their physical selves that they could not identify their body parts. One child, when asked where her nose was, pointed to her elbow.

In middle childhood, children experience a wider social world of peers and adults, although parents are still the most significant others. Self-perceptions are opened to feedback from teachers, classmates, and others. Self-thinking centers on self-competence (How well do I do . . . ?) and acceptance outside the home. Interactions with peers provide points of comparison that give children ideas about themselves: Am I liked? Am I as good an athlete as my friend? In later childhood, the peer group becomes part of significant others. Teachers and other adults who provide feedback in areas important to the child may also become significant others (Beane and Lipka 1986).

With adolescence the social comparisons continue and the significance of the peer group increases, particularly in terms of dress, behavior, and values. There is tension between the self-perceived need for peer acceptance and the need to retain the security of the family. The social, physical, emotional, and mental changes that occur during adolescence bring on an increased introspection about the self and a reworking of the sense of self.

Each time we attempt to **master a new role** (to meet the requirements of a particular situation appropriately), we learn something about ourselves from the responses we get. A new role might involve a job (student, teacher, employee), a task (leading, tutoring, discussing), a social situation (meeting strangers, making friends at college), or a social role (spouse, parent, group member, date). The clearer the role is and the more assistance and practice we get learning it, the more likely we will develop a positive self-perception about ourselves in that role.

Whenever we try to meet other people's expectations for us, their reactions to our efforts affect how we view ourselves. People in relationships always have expectations for each other: parents-children; friend-friend; boss-employee; students-teachers. The expectations may be simple or complex, verbally or nonverbally expressed. Often the expectations are assumed to be clear, yet the people involved have different ideas about what they are or what they mean. Regardless of the degree of clarity or agreement about meaning, there are always consequences to how well or how poorly we measure up to the expectations. Whoever sets the expectations also gives the feedback about performance.

A person's role and expectations, as sources of information about the self, are especially important for you to think about as you prepare to teach. What have you learned from all your teachers about what the role of teacher means? You have years of experience as a student meeting the expectations of teachers. Their responses to your efforts form part of your self-concept. Think about what expectations your teachers had for you. How have their responses to your efforts influenced your self-concept? Recognize that your experiences have the potential to influence how you will define your role as teacher and the expectations you set in your own classroom.

All of our beliefs about self are organized in a hierarchy. At the apex are the beliefs that are the essence of whom we believe ourselves to be. We hold these beliefs with great conviction and change them only under great pressure. As we move down the hierarchy, away from the core beliefs, self-perceptions are organized according to their value to us and our confidence in their accuracy. These self-perceptions change more easily.

Impact of the Self-Concept

Self-concept, then, forms through our perception of our communicative interactions. It affects how we perceive the world and how we communicate. Self-concept impacts our behavior in three major ways: how we behave, how we interpret other people's behavior, and how we achieve in school.

How We Behave. Self-concept functions like a mental blueprint. We behave as consistently as possible with our self-concepts, who we perceive ourselves to be (Brooks and Emmert 1976). The need for internal consistency causes people to behave in ways that confirm or reinforce what they already believe about themselves. This holds true whether the self-perceptions are positive or negative. What students believe about their ability affects how they behave. Table 2.1 lists behaviors that distinguish between students with high and low self-concepts.

Self-beliefs can have a **boomerang effect**. A boomerang is an angular throwing club that can be thrown so it returns to its starting point. As it applies here, you start with a belief and act in such a way so as to bring back evidence that the belief is correct. The initial belief can be positive or negative. For example, people who believe they are poor students miss classes, do not do homework, and avoid studying. They earn failing grades. The grades are proof that confirms being a poor student. The boomerang effect is like a self-imposed, self-fulfilling prophecy. The belief becomes a prophecy, which comes true by the behavior chosen.

Table 2.1 Behaviors Associated with Students Who Have a High and Low Self-Concept of Ability

Students with a high, positive self-concept of ability tend to be:	Students with a low, negative self-concept of ability tend to be:
1. Intellectually active: probe, ask questions, get excited about learning new things	1. Intellectually passive: do not ask questions, unenthusiastic about learning
2. Motivated to do as well as possible to get good grades; actively looking for ways to be successful	2. Motivated to do as well as possible to avoid poor grades; actively looking for ways to avoid failing
3. Involved in class discussions, not afraid to express themselves	3. Quiet during class discussions; seem afraid to express their ideas
4. Attribute their successes to hard work, effort, ability	4. Attribute their success to luck, fate, or some outside source
5. Attribute their failures to bad luck, a fluke, outside forces	5. Attribute their failures to lack of ability, know-how or low intelligence
6. Set realistic goals	6. Set unrealistic goals
7. Willing to ask for help; can admit not knowing without embarrassment	7. Not willing to ask for help; have trouble admitting they do not know something
8. Do work when it is to be done	8. Procrastinate doing their work

Hamachek 1987, p. 280

How We Interpret Other People's Behavior. Our self-concept becomes a filter for the way we interpret other people's behavior in general and their behavior directed toward us in particular.

According to psychologists, people project their own view of themselves onto other people. We interpret other people's behavior in light of how we interpret our own. According to Hamachek (1987) in reviewing 30 years of research on self-concept, people who think highly of themselves tend to think highly of others, and people who have a negative view of themselves tend to have a negative view of others. As Ralph Waldo Emerson expressed this idea, "What we are, that only can we see" (Emerson; as cited in Hamachek 1987, p. 80). This tendency to view others as we view ourselves is illustrated by the kind of statements students with a low self-concept tend to make about themselves and other people (Bassett and Smythe 1979, p. 37):

- Self-critical statements: "I've never been able to do that."
- Criticism of others: "He just got a lucky break."
- Pointing out the failures of others: "Her problem is . . ."
- Negative expectations about competition: "What's the use, I haven't got a chance."
- Unwillingness to accept blame: "It's not my fault."
- Inability to accept praise: "You don't really mean that."

When we interpret other people's behavior directed toward us personally, we engage in **biased scanning**. We are *scanning* other people's verbal and nonverbal cues for confirmation of what we believe about ourselves. Figure 2.1 indicated the devices available to the self for processing feedback from others. The general rule is that information consistent with our self-concept is accepted, while inconsistent information is ignored, rejected, or reinterpreted (Bassett and Smythe 1979). We do this with negative or positive beliefs about the self. For instance, if a student believes he or she is smart, then the teacher calling on him or her may be interpreted as an offer for the opportunity to shine. A student who believes the opposite may interpret the same teacher's behavior as an attempt at embarrassment.

School Achievement

Hamachek (1987), reviewing research on the self-concept and achievement patterns, concludes, "Children's feelings about their ability to do school work (their sense of competence) are rooted in their early school experiences, and these determine . . . both the intensity and direction of their emerging self-conceptions of ability" (p. 266). He says the window of opportunity for developing a strong academic self-concept occurs during K–6.

During this period failure and success experiences affect students' self-perceptions about themselves as learners. Failure experiences define their academic ability and affect their sense of personal worth. According to Hamachek (1990), success experiences:

- make subsequent success seem more possible;
- lead to a sense of competence and accomplishment; set a precedent;
- provide a buffer for any later failures;
- help develop a positive mental self-image.

Researchers report a significant and positive relationship between self-concept and academic achievement. "High self-concept is concomitant with high achievement, low self-concept with low achievement" (Silvernail 1985). Hamachek (1990, p. 324) states many studies show that successful students are characterized by self-confidence, feelings of adequacy, and personal competence, while less successful students are characterized by feelings of uncertainty, low self-regard, and inferiority feelings.[1]

Such reports suggest that high self-concept causes high achievement, but it does not. A high self-concept may be a necessary and important quality for a student to have in order to achieve, but it does not guarantee academic achievement. For example, it is possible to have a high concept of ability but lack the motivation to work. It is also possible to have a good general self-concept because of successful achievements in other aspects of the self-concept, such as social (relationships) or physical (athletics) and still do poorly in school.

A question everybody asks is, "Which comes first, a high self-concept or school achievement?" Although there is much research to support either possible answer to the question, the actual answer is that self-concept and achievement are interactive and reciprocal forces. This means that each one has the potential to affect the other in a positive or negative way, but one does not cause the other.

How self-concept and school achievement (or lack of achievement) influence each other depends on how individual students interpret their experience. As we saw in table 2.1, students with low or high self-concepts of their ability attribute their successes and failures differently. High ability students attribute their success to intrinsic factors they can control (effort, work), and their failures to extrinsic factors beyond their control (bad luck). In effect, they give themselves credit for their successes and distance themselves from their failures. Low ability students attribute their successes and failures in reverse. Successes are due to extrinsic factors they cannot control (fate, good luck), while failures result from intrinsic factors inside themselves (lack of knowledge or ability). They do not take credit for their success, but blame themselves for their failures.

Interpretation is the key, and there are many other possible scenarios. Let's examine a couple of different combinations of how people attribute success and failure and how this attribution affects their confidence in their ability. Students with poor self-concepts who have successes, which they attribute to personal efforts, feel more positive about their ability. In fact, there is evidence that suggests people who lack confidence in their ability feel the most satisfied when they complete something they did not think they could do (Feathers 1969). On the other hand, students with high self-concepts who explain their failures are due to intrinsic factors might lose confidence in their ability.

The important thing to remember is that high self-concept and school achievement are mutually reinforcing. A positive change in one encourages a positive change in the other.

To Sum Up

Up to this point, we have examined the process of perception and the role self-concept plays in our perception and communication. Our self-concept is a set of self-expectations we develop in our interactions with others through social comparisons, meeting the expectations of others, and acquiring new roles. How students perceive themselves will affect how they behave, how they interact in the classroom, and their achievement.

Although our focus has been on students, it is important to consider how this information applies to you personally and how your self-concept will affect your students. Your self-concept, too, will affect how you behave, interact in the classroom, and what you achieve. Teachers with a high self-concept serve as role models for students. "Teachers who have realistic conceptions of themselves, who are accepting of themselves and others, and who accent their positive attributes will help students make realistic assessments and begin to view themselves in a positive light" (Silvernail 1985, p. 41). If you have a positive self-concept, then you can help your students develop more positive self-concepts.

Since self-concept is so fundamental to our lives in the classroom, we need to discover how our students see themselves and how to help them view themselves more positively.

1. Observe student interactions and listen to what they say about themselves to understand how they view themselves.
2. Point out specific abilities, skills, strengths, accomplishments.
3. Help students set realistic, obtainable goals, so they can experience the connection between effort and success.
4. View students in a positive way and project favorable expectations for them.
5. Give personalized, constructive feedback.
6. Get to know your students and develop constructive teacher-student relationships.
7. Encourage participation, so there are more opportunities for favorable outcomes.

At the point in their lives when we meet our students, they are armed with their perceptual learnings and self-concepts. What they believe about themselves and their worlds affects the style and substance of their communication with us. Students also come with learning predispositions, which affect how they learn and their behavior in the classroom. It is important to understand what learning styles are and how they can influence teachers' perceptions and expectations for their students.

Learning Styles

Students' learning styles affect which strategies teachers choose and students' responses to those strategies—what students learn. According to the National Association of Secondary School Principals (NASSP 1979; as cited in Keefe 1987, p. 5), "**Learning style** is a composite of characteristic cognitive, affective, and physiological behaviors that serve as stable indicators of how learners perceive, interact with, and respond to the learning environment." In other words, learning style is a person's characteristic *set of behaviors* when learning. Notice the emphasis on "behaviors." We infer a person's learning style based on our observation of his or her behavior. Learning styles are consistent ways of functioning that persist regardless of the teaching method used or content experienced (Keefe 1987).

Three Dimensions of Learning Style

Let's look at the three dimensions of learning style to give you an idea of what behaviors are involved. Keep in mind that the term "learning style" is used with different meanings. People may use it to refer to a particular element of learning style or to mean a composite profile, which incorporates many elements of learning style. Although each dimension has many elements, I have selected ones with special interest to teachers.

Cognitive. The **cognitive dimension** consists of "information processing habits representing the learner's typical mode of perceiving, thinking, problem-solving, and remembering" (Messick 1976; as cited in Keefe 1987, p. 7). Elements relating to this dimension include:

Perceptual Modality Preference. This is a preferred reliance on one of the three sensory modes for understanding: (1) visual or spatial (reading and viewing)—learns by seeing and watching demonstrations; (2) auditory (hearing and speaking)—learns through verbal instructions from others and self; and (3) kinesthetic/tactile or psychomotor (learns by touching and doing)—learns by being directly involved. According to Richmond and Gorham (1992), some people have a single modality strength, others have two, still others have all three.

Field-Independence (FI) vs. Field-Dependence (FD).   This is the degree to which people "overcome the effects of distracting background elements (the field) when they try to differentiate the relevant aspects of a situation" (Dembo 1991, p. 83). Independents perceive things as distinct from the field, while dependents tend to be influenced by any embedding context.

- Independents differentiate among experiences in an analytical and systematic way. They work in a sequential, inductive manner (start from details and work toward concept). Independents determine their own goals and reinforcements, "can structure situations," and are "less affected by criticism," (Garger and Guild 1984; as cited in Dembo 1991, p. 85).
- Dependents see experiences as fused in a global, holistic way. They work in a deductive manner (start with concept and proceed to details). Dependents require externally defined goals, reinforcements, organization and are "more affected by criticism," (Garger and Guild 1984; as cited in Dembo 1991, p. 85). They are more socially oriented than independents and like working with peers. The majority of elementary children are global, but students may become more analytical the older they get and the longer they stay in school (Dunn and Dunn 1993).

Conceptual Tempo. Individuals differ in the amount of time they need to get down to work and to complete a learning task. They work more or less reflectively (slowly with precision, considering alternatives) or more or less impulsively (quickly with abandon, giving the first answer that occurs to them) (Keefe 1987).

Cognitive Complexity vs. Simplicity. This is also known as *abstract vs. concrete*. A high complex cognitive style is multi-dimensional and handles diverse, contradictory information, while a low complex cognitive style seeks order, pattern, and similarities (Keefe 1987).

Affective. The **affective dimension** has emotional and personality characteristics that have to do with attention, motivation, interests, willingness to take risks, responsibility, and locus of control (Cornett 1983). Elements of the affective dimension include:

Conceptual Level (CL). Students differ in how much structure they require in order to learn best. Students who need structure need definite and consistent rules, specific guidelines, short-term goals, and immediate feedback. They often have trouble functioning in groups and discussions. Students needing less structure like to go off on their own, make decisions (about alternatives for assignments, timetables), and like discussions and group work (Richmond and Gorham 1992).

Persistence or Perseverance. Students who are high in persistence will work on a task until it is done no matter how hard or uncomfortable. Short attention spans and inability to work at a task for any length of time are signs of low persistence.

Locus of Control. People vary in their perceptions of causality for their behavior on a "continuum from internality to externality" (Keefe 1987). Those with an *internal* locus of control believe they are responsible for their own behavior. They accept praise for their success and blame for their failure. People who believe control is *external* feel something (luck) or someone (another person) is responsible for their behavior.

Physiological. The **physiological dimension** includes elements relating to the students' responses to the environmental conditions in which learning occurs (Richmond and Gorham 1992), such as:

> *Time-of-Day Rhythms.* Individuals differ in the time of day during which they learn best.
>
> *Need for Mobility.* Students vary in their need for change in posture and location.
>
> *Environmental Elements.* Students differ in their preferences for and responses to light, sound, and temperature.

How Understanding Learning Styles Aids You

Knowing your and your students' learning styles helps you in several ways:
1. You can consider how learning styles reflect cultural-social background and adjust your instructional choices accordingly. Teachers tend to teach the way they learn, unless there is a conscious reason to do otherwise (Cornett 1983).

    According to Gay (1978), in the United States there is frequently a dichotomy between the preferred learning styles of students with different cultural backgrounds, and the preferred instructional style of teachers. Many cultures reflect a "shared-function" orientation in their role relationships (p. 50).

In such cultures traditional values emphasize group cooperation, collective (group) identity, and deference to authority. Such an orientation favors a learning style involving more social-centered (group) and cooperative techniques, learning by modeling and imitation, and global aspects of conceptual learning. Teachers' instructional styles tend to be analytic, field-independent, reflecting mainstream cultural values, such as individual asssertiveness and success, inductive reasoning, and competition.[2]

2. You can understand how differences between your teaching style and your students' learning styles can affect behavior and learning. When teachers perceive students as misbehaving, not trying, or lacking ability, what they may be responding to is differences in learning styles. For example, an analytical, reflective math teacher may view as defiance a student's refusal to write down every step. A global, impulsive student may intuit the answer and call it out. Dunn and Dunn (1993) state that young children, underachievers, at-risk, and drop-out students are predominantly tactile/ kinesthetic learners. Traditional instruction is primarily auditory, secondarily visual. Examine whether the learning styles of good students happen to match your teaching style.

3. You gain the means to compensate for differences in learning styles. A teacher who appreciates students' different learning styles can plan flexible uses of time, provide alternative ways to demonstrate learning, and supply the assistance needed for success. For example, a teacher planning a lecture can give each student a written outline of the main points. The outline helps everyone listen and concentrate but is especially helpful to visual learners.

Accommodating Different Learning Styles

Learning style experts recommend that ideally learning styles should be dealt with on a system-wide basis where all students are tested on a standardized instrument. Richmond and Gorham (1992) describe three ways such information has been used:

Matching. Students are taught in their own preferred styles. It has proven successful for high-risk students with records of failure. Matching has been used successfully in Madison Prep in New York's Lower East Side.

Bridging. Teachers teach in their preferred way. Style-based materials are available when students encounter difficulty. Students go to a learning center and access supplemental materials designed for their style. Bridging is used in Community Consolidated School District #47 in Crystal Lake, Illinois.

Style-Flexing. Lessons are structured so individual learning styles are both accommodated (matched) at one point and challenged (stretched) at another (McCarthy 1981).

When a school-wide approach is impossible, Keefe (1987) suggests individual teachers should diagnose certain dimensions of their students' learning styles and modify their instruction. If no money is available for testing, he suggests teachers observe their students with diagnostic questions in mind. For example, to determine modality preferences he suggests questions such as, "What kind of learning activity does the learner handle the best? What kind of activities do not hold attention?" He says a teacher alert to students' modality strengths can be flexible in grouping, use a variety of materials, and vary the teaching style. Cornett (1983) suggests discussing with students how, when, where, and what they learn best.

Cornett (1983) also suggests a way for students to develop both an understanding of their own learning styles and of style flexibility. Students discuss productive and unproductive study/learning situations. These situations may be either personal or hypothetical. Students' conclusions become learning strategies that they then use. Cornett says this has been used successfully with elementary students with weekly discussions continually adding new ideas (1983).

If teachers can plan strategies that accommodate their students' learning styles, students will experience more success and develop more positive images of themselves as learners. When students enter your classroom, they are entering another situation where they must figure out and adequately perform a role (what it means to be a good student in your class) and meet your expectations. How you perform your role, express your expectations, and react to them will be perceived by them and will influence their behavior and self-concept. For this reason, it is important to look at how teacher expectations affect students. Let's examine what teacher expectations are, how they are formed, and how they are communicated.

Teacher Expectations

For over two decades much educational research has been done on the effects of teacher expectations. There are two key terms to understand (Good and Brophy 1994, p. 83):

Teacher expectations—inferences that teachers make about the future behavior or academic achievement of their students based on what they know about their students now.

Teacher expectation effects—effects on student outcomes that occur because of the actions that teachers take in response to their expectations.

There are two types of teacher expectation effects: sustaining expectation effects and self-fulfilling prophecies. Most people have never heard of **sustaining expectation effects (S.E.E.)**. They are subtle, frequent, and prevent change in student behavior (Cooper and Good 1983). S.E.E. occurs when teachers respond on the basis of their existing expectations for students rather than to changes in student performance. According to Salomon (1981), these effects reinforce and sustain existing behaviors, while other behaviors are ignored or explained away. If a weak student performed well, the teacher either would not notice or put it down as a fluke. In effect, the teacher's behavior implies "don't confuse me with the facts."

Self-fulfilling prophecy occurs when an erroneous expectation leads to behavior that causes the expectation to become true (Good 1987). The teacher acts in ways consistent with a belief about a student, and eventually the student's behavior is affected. The expectation becomes reality. The teacher's active rather than passive role is what distinguishes this from S.E.E. Self-fulfilling prophecies are visible and dramatic because they create change in student performance, although they may occur infrequently in classrooms (Cooper and Good 1983).

Self-fulfilling prophecy is based on the work reported in the late 1960s in Rosenthal and Jacobson's *Pygmalion in the Classroom* (See suggested reading list). Teacher expectations for student achievement were manipulated to see if the high expectations would be fulfilled, which they were. Initial euphoria at the results was followed by exaggerated claims being made based on the results, then criticism of the original study, and then continued interest in teacher expectation effects and related topics. In the decades since the original study, research has continued. There is consensus that teacher expectations can and sometimes do affect the teacher-student interaction and student outcomes, but the processes involved are more complex than originally believed (Good and Brophy 1994).

It is important to keep in mind that it is not an expectation that causes a self-fulfilling prophecy. A self-fulfilling prophecy is an outgrowth of the teacher's behavior inspired by his or her expectation. This behavior is perceived by students who then are more likely to respond in the expected ways.

Brophy-Good Model—Expectation Communication Process

The classic model of how the expectation communication process works in the classroom was developed by Brophy and Good (1970; as cited in Good and Brophy 1994, pp. 88–89):

1. Early in the year, the teacher forms differential expectations for student behavior and achievement.
2. Consistent with these differential expectations, the teacher behaves differently toward different students.
3. This treatment tells students about how they are expected to behave in the classroom and perform on academic tasks.
4. If the teacher's treatment is consistent over time, and if the students do not actively resist or change it, it will likely affect their self-concepts, achievement motivation, levels of aspiration, classroom conduct, and interactions with the teacher.
5. These effects will generally complement and reinforce the teacher's expectations, so that students will come to conform to these expectations more than they might have otherwise.
6. Ultimately, this will affect student achievement and other outcome measures. High-expectation students will be led to achieve at or near their potentials, but low-expectation students will not gain as much as they could have gained if taught differently.

In thinking about this model, keep in mind that the self-fulfilling prophecy effects occur only when *all* of the elements in the model occur. Good and Brophy point out that one or more elements are frequently missing (1994). For example, a teacher may not have clear expectations about every student or may change expectations continually. Alternatively, expectations may be consistent but not communicated consistently. In such a case, Good and Brophy say the expectations would not be fulfilled even if they turned out to be correct. Finally, students could prevent expectations from becoming self-fulfilling through resistance or countering their effects. For example, I have had many female students now training to become math teachers tell me that when they were in high school, their math teachers ignored them in class, told them they were incapable of doing math, and discouraged them from taking advanced courses. The students refused to accept their teachers' expectations, and refuted the expectations by outperforming them. The students mentally tuned out their teachers, viewing them as an *insignificant others*.

In looking at this model in terms of sustaining expectations, Good (1987, p. 34) states that it is only necessary for teachers to engage in behaviors that ". . . maintain students' and teachers' previously formed low expectations (e.g., low achieving students receive only drill work, easy questions, etc.)."

Now that we know what teacher expectations involve and how they form, let's turn to how teachers communicate their positive and negative expectations.

How Teachers Communicate Differential Expectations

Rosenthal (1974; as cited in Good and Brophy 1994, p. 95) focused on positive self-fulfilling prophecy effects and identified four ways teachers could maximize student achievement :

1. Create warm social-emotional relationships with their students (climate).
2. Give them more feedback about their performance (feedback).
3. Teach them more and more difficult material (input).
4. Give them more opportunities to respond and to ask questions (output).

Good and Brophy (1994) point out that teachers are more likely to be affected by information leading to negative expectations than by information leading to positive expectations. Reviews of the literature (Brophy, 1983; Brophy and Good, 1974) suggest the following behaviors indicate differential teacher treatment of high and low achievers (Good and Brophy, 1994, pp. 95–96):

Interpersonal Interaction

1. Generally paying less attention to lows or interacting with them less frequently
2. Seating lows farther away from the teacher
3. Interacting with lows more privately than publicly, and monitoring and structuring their activities more closely
4. Less friendly interactions with lows, including less smiling, and fewer other nonverbal indicators of support
5. Less eye contact and other nonverbal communication of attention and responsiveness (forward lean, positive head nodding) in interaction with lows

Questioning/Answering

6. Calling on lows less often to respond to questions, or asking them only easier, nonanalytic questions

7. Waiting less time for lows to answer a question before giving the answer or calling on someone else

8. Giving lows answers or calling on someone else rather than trying to improve their responses by giving clues or repeating or rephrasing the question

9. Briefer and less informative feedback to questions of lows

10. Less acceptance and use of lows' ideas

Feedback

11. Inappropriate reinforcement: rewarding inappropriate behavior or incorrect answers by lows

12. Criticizing lows more often for failure

13. Praising lows less often for success

14. Failing to give feedback to the public responses of lows

Instruction

15. Demanding less from lows: accepting low-quality or incorrect responses

16. Differential administration or grading of tests or assignments—lows would not get the same benefit of doubt as highs

17. Less use of effective but time-consuming instructional methods with lows when time is limited

18. Impoverished curriculum: overly limited and repetitious input, emphasis on factual recitation rather than on lesson extending discussion, emphasis on drill and practice rather than application and higher-level thinking tasks

---

Good and Brophy (1994) suggest several points to keep in mind when thinking about these forms of differential treatment. First, they do not occur in all classrooms. "Teachers differ considerably in how much they differentiate in their treatment of students toward whom they hold different expectations" (p. 96). Second, differential treatment is not automatically inappropriate when it occurs. It is appropriate at times and can represent the individualizing of instruction rather than negative expectations. For example, lower achievers may need more structuring of assignments and closer monitoring of their work. Third, differential treatment may also be a response to what students are doing. If lows do not volunteer, the teacher may have trouble getting them to respond as frequently as higher achievers.

However, when the degree of differentiation is large and involves many of these behaviors, then the behaviors are danger signals. Many of the forms of differential treatment have direct effects on the students' learning opportunities. Indirect effects on students' self-concepts, motivational levels, performance expectations, or attributions would also occur through teacher behavior (Good and Brophy, 1994). Review table 2.1 to see how these indirect effects can translate into behaviors for students with high and low concepts of ability. Students who internalize the teacher's expectations will either live *up* to them or *down* to them.

Ultimately, the strength and direction (positive or negative) of teacher expectation effects that are likely to appear vary with the nature of the classroom context and the kind of person the teacher is. This point has special bearing for you as you consider your role as teacher, so let's turn our attention to how context variables and teacher characteristics affect expectation effects.

Context Variables and Teacher Expectation Effects

Context variables refer to the context for teaching. Context involves the grade and subject you teach, the effect of time of year, and the classroom climate you create through your instructional choices. Think about these conclusions in light of what you are preparing to teach (Good and Brophy 1994, pp. 100–101):

> *Grade Level.* Expectation effects are greater in the earlier grades before achievement, academic self-concepts, and attribution patterns are established. This finding may also apply to situations where students are new to an institution and their teachers, such as the beginning of middle school and senior high.
>
> *Differences between Elementary and Secondary School.* Elementary and secondary levels differ in how differential treatment manifests itself. On the elementary level, expectations are communicated qualitatively (frequent interaction with all students, but teacher may treat highs and lows differently). On the secondary level, expectations are communicated quantitatively (teachers interact more with highs who contribute more).
>
> *Time of Year.* Greater expectation effects occur early in the year (Brophy and Good 1974). Students and teachers settle into routine interaction patterns (Cooper 1985). As the year passes, teachers pay less attention to differences between individuals or sub-groups and more attention to the progress of the class as a whole (Cooper and Good 1983).
>
> *Subject Matter.* There are larger expectation effects on reading achievement than on math achievement (Smith

1980). The greater variety of grouping and instructional practices used in teaching reading provides more opportunities for differential treatment.

The Nature of the Learning Environment. The greatest negative expectation effects occur in classrooms that are characterized by the following: uniform goals, narrow range of activity structures, norm-referenced achievement standards, competitive atmosphere, public performance evaluation, emphasis on achievement differences in how high and low achievers are treated (Rosenholtz and Simpson 1984; as cited in Good and Brophy 1994, p. 101).

Teacher Characteristics and Teacher Expectation Effects

Brophy and Good (1974) examined how a teacher's characteristics relate to expectation effects and placed teachers along a continuum from proactive to reactive to overreactive teachers.

Proactive	Reactive	Overactive

Think about where your former teachers lie on the continuum. Consider where you want to be placed on the continuum:

- *Proactive* teachers are guided by their own beliefs about what is appropriate in setting individual and class goals. They work actively with all students, rather than differentiating on the basis of performance, and they are the least hampered by perceptual selectivities or rigid beliefs about students (Bassette and Smythe 1979). With realistic goals and the needed skills, they are likely to move their students toward fulfilling the expectations associated with the goals. Proactive teachers are the most likely to have positive expectation effects on their students.

- *Reactive* teachers hold their expectations lightly and adjust to feedback and trends. They have minimal expectation effects on their students and maintain existing differences between high and low achievers.

- *Overreactive* teachers develop rigid, stereotyped perceptions of their students based on prior records and first impressions of their behavior. Their selective perception operates to aggravate the differences between high and low achievers (Bassett and Smythe 1979). They treat their students as stereotypes and are the most likely to have negative expectation effects. Overreactive teachers are likely to be authoritarian, dogmatic, rigid, and conventional.

Subsequent research has supported these distinctions in teacher expectation effects. However, research has also shown that most of the sizable teacher expectation effects on student achievement are negative ones, that is, low expectations lead to lower achievement than might have occurred otherwise (Good and Brophy 1994).

To Sum Up

Teacher's expectations for their students affect their behavior towards their students and subsequently affect students' self-perceptions, achievement, and motivation. "Expectations are powerful, self-perpetuating attitudes for students as well as teachers because expectations guide both perceptions and behavior" (Hamachek 1987, p. 290).

How can we avoid negative expectation effects and promote positive expectation effects? Good and Brophy (1994, pp. 110–112) suggest the following guidelines:

1. Recognize that the formation of expectations is a natural, inevitable result of interacting with students, even if other sources of information are avoided.
2. Seek accurate information about students because it can be helpful in adjusting instruction to meet students' specific needs.
3. Expectations should be appropriate for students' current capabilities and followed up with instruction that promotes improvement and success.
4. Be aware of your expectations and monitor their effect on your behavior.
5. Keep your expectations for students current and flexible.

Maintaining Awareness of Each "I"

We must continuously seek to be aware of and understand the fundamental elements that shape each of our unique perspectives, which we bring to bear every time we communicate. Who we are and what we expect have been shaped by our interpersonal relationships to significant others. As teachers, we may become significant others for some of our students.

We have come full circle. Perception enables us to develop expectations about ourselves (self-concept) and about how the world works. Our self-concepts, perceptual habits, and learning predispositions (learning styles) affect how we behave in the classroom. We perceive each other's behavior and form expectations for each other. As teachers, our expectations for our students can affect our behavior toward them, what they learn, and their self-concepts.

In the end, there are no easy answers to how to help your students have a great self-concept, how to be 100 percent accurate in your perceptions, how to accommodate all learning styles all the time, and how always to have high expectations for everybody, including yourself. Developing a communicative perspective means understanding the options and trying to make effective choices for each individual.

Notes

[1] See also:

Boggiano, A. K., D. Main, and P. Katz. 1988. "Children's Preference for Challenge: The Role of Perceived Competence and Control." *Journal of Personality and Social Psychology* 54:134–41.

Byrne, B. 1986. "Self-Concept/Academic Achievement Relations: An Investigation of Dimensionality, Stability, and Causality." *Canadian Journal of Behavioral Science* 18:173–86.

Johnson, D. 1981. "Naturally Acquired Helplessness: The Relationship of School Failure to Achievement Behavior, Attributions, and Self-Concept." *Journal of Educational Psychology* 73:174–80.

Marsh, M. 1984. "Relations Among Dimensions of Self-Attribution, Dimensions of Self-Concept, and Academic Achievements." *Journal of Educational Psychology* 76:1291–308.

Roger, C., M. Smith, and J. Coleman. 1978. "Social Comparison to the Classroom: The Relationship Between Academic Achievement and Self-Concept." *Journal of Educational Psychology* 70:50–57.

[2] Gay cites the following sources:

Brembeck, C. and W. Hill (editors). 1973. *Cultural Challenges to Education.* Lexington, MA: Lexington Books

Gladwin, T. 1974. "Cultural and Logical Process." In J. Berry and P. Dasen (editors), *Culture and Cognition: Readings in Cross-Cultural Psychology.* London, England: Methuen and Co. (pp. 27–37).

Kagan, S. and M. Madsen. 1971. "Cooperation and Competition of Mexican, Mexican-American, and Anglo-American Children of Two Ages under Four Instructional Sets." *Developmental Psychology* (July), pp. 32–39.

Shinn, R. (editor). 1922. *Culture and School: Socio-Cultural Significances.* San Francisco: Intext Educational Publishers.

References

Adler, Ronald and N. Towne. 1993. *Looking Out/Looking In*, 7th edition. Forth Worth, TX: Harcourt Brace Jovanovich.

Bassett, Ronald and Mary-Jeanette Smythe. 1979. *Communication and Instruction.* New York: Harper & Row.

Beane, James and R. Lipka. 1986. *Self-Concept, Self-Esteem, and the Curriculum*. New York: Teachers College Press.

Brophy, Jere. 1983. "Research on the Self-Fulfilling Prophecy and Teacher Expectations." *Journal of Educational Psychology*, 75:631–61.

Brophy, Jere and T. Good. 1970. "Teachers' Communication of Differential Expectations for Children's Classroom Performance: Some Behavioral Data." *Journal of Educational Psychology* 61:365–74. Cited in T. Good and J. Brophy, *Looking In Classrooms*, 6th edition (New York: Harper-Collins 1994).

———. 1974. *Teacher-Student Relationships: Causes and Consequences*. New York: Holt, Rinehart, & Winston.

Brooks, W. D. and P. Emmert. 1976. *Interpersonal Communication*. Dubuque, IA. Cited in R. Bassett and M. Smythe, *Communication and Instruction* (New York: Harper & Row, 1979).

CBS. *Eye on America*. February 2, 1993.

Combs, Arthur. 1982. *A Personal Approach To Teaching—Beliefs That Make a Difference*. Boston: Allyn & Bacon.

Cooper, H. 1985. "Models of Teacher Expectation Communication." In J. Dusek, Editor, *Teacher Expectancies*. Hillsdale, NJ: Erlbaum.

Cooper, H. and T. Good. 1983. *Pygmalion Grows Up: Studies in the Expectation Communication Process*. New York: Longman.

Cornett, C. 1983. *What You Should Know About Teaching and Learning Styles*. Bloomington, IN: Phi Delta Kappa Educational Foundation.

Dembo, M. 1991. *Applying Educational Psychology in the Classroom*, 4th edition. New York: Longman.

Dunn, R. and K. Dunn. 1993. *Reaching Secondary Students Through Individual Learning Styles: Practical Approaches Grades 7–12*. Boston: Allyn & Bacon.

Epstein, S. 1973. "The Self-Concept Revisited: Or a Theory of a Theory." *American Psychologist* 28:404–16. Cited in J. Beane and R. Lipka, *Self-Concept, Self-Esteem, and the Curriculum* (New York: Teachers College Press, 1986).

Feathers, N. 1969. "Attribution of Responsibility and Valence of Success and Failure in Relation to Initial Confidence and Task Performance," *Journal of Personality and Social Psychology* 13:129–44. Cited in D. Hamachek, *Encounters with the Self* (New York: Holt, Rinehart, and Winston, 1987).

Garger, S. and P. Guild. 1984. "Learning Styles: The Crucial Differences." *Curriculum Review* 23:9–12. Cited in M. Dembo, *Applying Educational Psychology*, 4th edition (New York: Longman, 1991).

Gay, G. 1978. "Viewing the Pluralistic Classroom as a Cultural Microcosm." *Education Research Quarterly* 2:45–9.

Good, Thomas. 1987. "Two Decades of Research on Teacher Expectations: Findings and Future Directions." *Journal of Teacher Education* 38(4): 32-37.

Good, Thomas, and Jere Brophy. 1994. *Looking In Classrooms*, 6th edition. New York: HarperCollins.

Hamachek, Don. 1987. *Encounters With the Self*, 3rd edition. New York: Holt, Rinehart, and Winston.

Hamachek, Don. 1990. *Psychology in Teaching, Learning, and Growth,* 4th edition. Boston: Allyn & Bacon.

Keefe, J. 1987. *Learning Style: Theory & Practice.* Reston, VA: NASSP.

Lee, Charlotte And Timothy Gura. 1992. *Oral Interpretation,* 8th edition. Boston: Houghton Mifflin.

Maslow, A. 1970. *Motivation and Personality.* New York: Harper & Row. Cited in Arthur Combs, *A Personal Approach to Teaching—Beliefs That Make A Difference* (Boston: Allyn & Bacon, 1982).

McCarthy, B. 1981. *The 4Mat system: Teaching to Learning Styles with Right/left Mode Techniques.* Cited in Richmond & Gorham, *Communication, Learning, and Affect in Instruction* (Edina, MN: Burgess, 1992).

Messick, S. and Associates. 1976. *Individuality in Learning.* San Francisco: Jossey-Bass. Cited in J. Keefe, *Learning Style: Theory & Practice* (Reston, VA: NASSP, 1987).

National Association of Secondary School Principals (1979). *Student Learning Styles—Diagnosing and Prescribing Programs.* Reston, VA: NASSP. Cited in J. Keefe *Learning Style: Theory & Practice* (Reston, VA: NASSP, 1987)

Richmond, V. and J. Gorham. 1992. *Communication, Learning, and Affect in Instruction.* Edina, MN: Burgess.

Roberts, Charles, Renee Edwards and Larry Barker. 1987. *Intrapersonal Communication Processes.* Scottsdale, AZ: Gorsuch Scarisbrick.

Rosenholtz, S. and C. Simpson. 1984. "Classroom Organization and Student Stratification." *Elementary School Journal* 85:21–37. Cited in T. Good and J. Brophy, *Looking In Classrooms,* 6th edition (New York: Harper-Collins, 1994).

Rosenthal, R. 1974. *On the Social Psychology of the Self-Fulfilling Prophecy: Further Evidence for Pygmalion Effects and Their Mediating Mechanism.* New York: MSS Modular Publications. Cited in T. Good and J. Brophy, *Looking In Classrooms,* 6th edition (New York: HarperCollins, 1994).

Salomon, G. 1981. "Self-Fulfilling and Self-Sustaining Prophecies and the Behaviors That Realize Them." *American Psychologist* 36:1452–453. Cited in H. Cooper and T. Good, *Pygmalion Grows Up* (New York: Longman, 1983).

Silvernail, David. 1985. *Developing Positive Student Self-Concept,* 2nd edition. Washington, DC: NEA.

Smith, M. 1980. "Meta-Analysis of Research on Teacher Expectation," *Evaluation in Education* 4:53–55. Cited in T. Good and J. Brophy, *Looking in Classrooms,* 6th edition (New York: HarperCollins, 1994).

Suggested Reading

The Six Pillars of Self-Esteem, by Nathaniel Branden. 1994. New York: Bantam.

> This book deals with answers to four questions about self-esteem: What is it? Why is it important? What can we do to raise our self-esteem? (Chapters focus on practicing self-acceptance, self-responsibility,

self-assertiveness, living purposefully, and personal integrity.) What roles do others play in influencing self-esteem (Chapters focus on nurturing children's self-esteem, self-esteem in the schools, at work, psychotherapy, and the culture.)

Pygmalion in the Classroom, by Robert Rosenthal and Lenore Jacobson. 1968. New York: Holt, Rinehart and Winston.

Since this landmark study in self-fulfilling prophecy is cited frequently, you might want to read it. Describes how self-fulfilling prophecies operate in education, social science research, medicine, and everyday life.

Communication, Learning and Affect in Instruction, by Virginia Richmond and J. Gorham. 1992. Edina, MN: Burgess.

Chapter 8 deals with student self-concept and chapter 12 examines teacher self-concept. There are suggested strategies for developing self-concept.

Part II

The Building Blocks of Communication

In part I, we examined the elements in the dynamic process of communication: communicators, message, context, and meaning. We looked at how perception, self-concept, learning style, and teacher expectations interrelate and affect the communicative behavior of students and teachers.

Communicating more effectively as a teacher involves developing a **communicative perspective**. To think from this perspective is to understand that communication involves making choices about what to say and how to say it. Effective communication is about making appropriate choices for the people you are talking to, the context, and the message. Having a communicative perspective allows you to plan, monitor, and evaluate your choices when you communicate with your students.

To help you develop your communicative perspective and make more appropriate choices, part II takes a closer look at the building blocks involved in the communication process. The next three chapters will deal with nonverbal behavior, verbal behavior, and listening.

Nonverbal behavior is presented first because (1) it occurs first developmentally—humans communicate nonverbally before they are able to use words and (2) throughout our lives nonverbal behavior has an enormous impact on how we interpret words—attitudes and feelings are revealed through nonverbal behavior. Listening is presented last because it deals with both nonverbal and verbal messages and meanings.

Chapter 3

Nonverbal Behavior

Ideas to Remember

* Nonverbal behavior sends messages about attitudes and feelings and affects student-teacher communication and relationships.
* Nonverbal behavior is learned, culturally determined, contextual, and inevitable.
* It is important to understand each type of nonverbal behavior and its potential for influencing classroom communication:
    Physical environment (color, lighting, temperature, decor)
    Spatial arrangements
    Physical appearance
    Kinesics (eye and facial behavior, body movement)
    Paralanguage (vocal quality and vocal variety)
    Proxemics (interpersonal space, vertical space, and territoriality)
    Haptics (tactile behavior)
    Chronemics (how time is perceived and structured)
* The types of nonverbal behavior interact and contribute to how you accomplish the various dimensions of teaching: self-presentation, rules and regulations, instruction, feedback, and affect.

Recall the definition of communication from chapter 1:

> Communication is a dynamic process of interaction between people in which they assign meaning to each other's verbal and nonverbal behavior.

Remember also from chapter 1 that verbal (what we say) and nonverbal (everything other than the words) behavior are both part of intentional and unintentional messages. We continually perceive others' verbal and nonverbal behavior and assign meanings to them. We mutually influence each other's communication in a dynamic way. In our case, the "we" are teachers and students in classrooms.

For most people, teachers included, communication means words. Hickson and Stacks (1993) point out that verbal communication is consciously learned, while nonverbal communication is unconsciously picked up. School reinforces the emphasis on words. K–12 curricula focus on spelling, composition, reading, and writing. We carry over the verbal emphasis to our thinking about oral communication. Due to professional training and responsibilities, teachers are even more word-centered than the average person. Words are our stock and trade in the classroom.

Yet our words are continually surrounded by nonverbal behavior to which our students pay attention. Anthropologist Ray Birdwhistell estimates that 60–70 percent of the meaning of a message is nonverbal (1970). Other researchers contend that teachers' messages are 82 percent nonverbal (Grant and Hennings 1971). Stop and think about these figures in terms of your own experience as a student. How many times have you scrutinized the nonverbal cues of teachers, such as facial expressions and tone of voice, to figure out what they mean? Verbal and nonverbal behaviors are inseparable in creating and interpreting meaning. As teachers, we need to redress the imbalance of emphasizing words only and pay attention to nonverbal behavior, too.

Impact of Nonverbal Behavior

It is important to realize that nonverbal behavior has the power to send messages about attitudes and feelings. These kinds of messages can dramatically affect your communication with students. People, teachers included, are usually not consciously aware of their nonverbal behavior. As a result, they are often oblivious to what attitudes and feelings they are expressing. Yet students pick up on these emotional cues—positive or negative—and react to them. This illustrates the perceptual process in action: selecting, interpreting, and behaving.

Our nonverbal behavior has the potential to influence student feelings, attitudes, and behavior towards us, our subject, other students, and themselves. Think about different attitudinal and feeling messages resulting from a teacher's nonverbal behavior and how these messages might be interpreted by students. Droning through directions says the assignment is not important, and students will not take it seriously. Yawning in a student's face and looking away while he or she talks says, "You bore me," and the student will stop talking. Taking time to help a student who is confused says, "You matter to me." The student will ask for help again when he or she does not understand.

Think about the teachers cited in chapter 2 who expected certain students to be low achievers. Their attitudes toward these students were expressed nonverbally by talking to them less, seating them farther away, smiling at them less, making less eye contact with them, and demonstrating less responsiveness. Do you think these teachers consciously chose to send these negative nonverbal messages? They were probably unaware their nonverbal behaviors were saying: "I do not expect much from you. I do not like you." Students may accept or resist the message, but students who internalize or accept the message stop trying.

We also need to recognize the reciprocal: students' nonverbal behavior will unknowingly reveal their attitudes and feelings. What nonverbal behaviors we notice and the meanings we assign to them will affect our feelings, attitudes, expectations, and behavior towards our students. The more we understand about nonverbal communication, the better able we will be to understand the meaning expressed by our students' nonverbal behavior. It will help us become better receivers of their messages.

The first step to be effective nonverbally in the classroom involves raising your awareness of the nonverbal behavior you experience every day. Consciously think about what you do nonverbally when you are communicating and notice how people respond. Become observant of other people's nonverbal behavior and analyze your perceptual responses. What do you select to pay attention to? What do you tell yourself it means? How do those meanings affect your communicating?

The next step is learning more about nonverbal communication and applying what you learn to your communication. This chapter is about helping you do both. The skills you develop now will help you to send constructive nonverbal messages to your students and to avoid negative ones.

This chapter begins with defining the characteristics of nonverbal behavior. Next, it examines the types of nonverbal behavior from a pragmatic standpoint: how to help you make effective choices in your classroom. What does each type involve? What possibilities and challenges does each type present? The chapter ends with an explanation of how all the types of nonverbal behavior work together to help you perform the role of teacher.

Characteristics of Nonverbal Behavior

It is essential to begin with the distinguishing characteristics because they form the foundation for understanding nonverbal behavior. Failure to grasp these fundamental ideas contributes to many communication misunderstandings and problems in the classroom. Not appreciating these basic ideas about nonverbal behavior can lead to social and psychological noise, misinterpretation and mislabelling of students, and difficult student-teacher relationships.

> Nonverbal behavior is learned, culturally determined, contextual, and inevitable (Based on Bassett and Smythe 1979).

Nonverbal behavior encompasses all aspects of oral communication except the words. Nonverbal information about the person communicating, the context, the message, or the meaning can be sent and received through our senses—seeing, hearing, touching (haptics), tasting, smelling; through any action (kinesics)—movement, gestures, posture; or through attributes—physical appearance. Contextual refers to the environment and includes physical context—location, decor, temperature, physical distance between people (proxemics)—and temporal context (chronemics)—time of day, time of season, time of year, etc. Message and meaning information involves how the message is delivered, which includes vocal aspects (paralanguage)—tone of voice, volume, rate of speaking—and visual aspects (facial and eye expressions). Later in the chapter, we will go into more detail about each type of nonverbal behavior.

Learned

Nonverbal behaviors and what they mean are learned simultaneously with all other aspects of our native language. You can see this learning occurring in its simplest form with infants. They cry instinctively when they are hungry, wet, or hurt. They *learn* this brings someone to hold them, to look at them intently, and to speak to them in soothing tones.

Parents who say their babies understand what they are saying to them are noting their baby's responsiveness to vocal tones, touch, and facial expressions.

The learning of nonverbal communication intertwines with language learning, is rapid, and goes on throughout our lives. By age one children use distance, eye contact, gestures, touch, intonation patterns, vocalizing, and smiling to communicate (Rom and Bliss 1983). Children ages three–five begin adopting nonverbal behavior according to the situation. They use appropriate eye contact, respond appropriately to the facial expressions of others, and integrate their verbal and nonverbal strategies (Allen and Brown 1976).

Nonverbal behavior can be misleading. People get into trouble when they assume everybody has learned the same thing. They assume the meaning they have for any particular nonverbal behavior is the same meaning everybody else has. This assumption is false because we learn nonverbal behavior within the confines of groups (families, communities) that are culture bound.

Yet, even sharing the same culture does not ensure the exact same meanings. There are individual differences in people's ability to execute and to interpret nonverbal behaviors. Some people are better at expressing or interpreting nonverbal behaviors due to professional training; we expect psychologists, actors, and clergy to be adept at nonverbal communication. Some differences in ability are due to age, development, or social learning. The ability to "evaluate emotional states from verbal and nonverbal communication" develops approximately between the ages of twelve and eighteen (Allen and Brown 1976, p. 184).

Psychologists at Emory University have concluded that problems of social rejection often stem from ineffectual nonverbal communication. Some children fail to learn appropriate nonverbal communication. Researchers call this nonverbal deficit *dyssemia* (From Greek: *dys* = difficulty; *semes* = signals or signs) and compare it to the verbal deficit dyslexia (*dys* = difficulty; *lexia* = words). Dyssemic children may have difficulty either expressing or receiving nonverbal cues from one or more types of nonverbal behavior. A child with an expressive problem would understand others' cues but would produce an inappropriate response. For example, a child would understand a smile but might glare back. A receptive problem is mis-reading the cue. For example, smiles are interpreted as anger. "Life for these children must be a continual jumble of unforeseen reactions and confusing counterreactions" (Nowicki and Duke 1992, p. 19).

Culturally Determined

Cultural groups define the meaning of any specific nonverbal behavior. **Culture** in this sense refers to people who identify themselves as a group because of some combination of the following ties: language, religion, ethnicity, geography, and history. The group develops norms of conduct, social roles, and expectations that define what is acceptable or appropriate behavior.

The term "culture" refers to variously defined groups. Social scientists speak in a global sense of Western and Eastern cultures. Culture is often defined by national boundaries, as in French culture or the Japanese culture. Groups within a country may define themselves as having a separate cultural identity, such as the indigenous people in Canada or Native Americans in the United States. Also, groups within a country may define their culture as related but different from the mainstream culture, as African Americans do in the United States. Culture defined by religion, as in Islamic culture, transcends national borders. Ethnic designations, such as Hispanic, embrace many different national cultures, such as Cuban, Spanish, and Mexican.

What we need to remember is that a person's referent group defines what are appropriate nonverbal behaviors and what those behaviors mean. The nonverbal meanings people learn as children in their families and communities are reflections of that culture. It is easier for young children to interpret the nonverbal behavior of people from the same cultural background or language community (Woolfolk and Brooks 1985). Think about the cultural referent group in which you were raised. What nonverbal behaviors and meanings are unique to your group?

Failure to understand the cultural relativism of nonverbal behavior and its meaning leads to communication problems. People tend to assume that their group's nonverbal meanings are the *only* meanings. Problems arise when they use their nonverbal behaviors and meanings with people from other cultural groups. For example, American teachers frequently use the "O.K." sign, thumb and forefinger forming a circle, to mean "good job." In France and Turkey it means, "You're worth zero." In Greece and Turkey, it is a vulgar sexual invitation (Ekman, Friesen, and Baer 1984). Middle-class American teachers expect direct eye contact from students. However, indirect eye contact with people in authority is a norm in many cultures, including Oriental cultures, many Native American tribes, and African Americans. A teacher might pat a student on the head meaning "good for you." For a Thai student this is an insult (Cooper 1995). Given the multicultural backgrounds of students today, be aware of the potential for different meanings for nonverbal behavior in your classroom.

Contextual

Even if we learn what a specific nonverbal behavior means in a particular culture, we still cannot define it by one meaning. What it means would depend on the **context**—where it was used, with whom, and how it was timed.

Take a smile as an example. A smile is one of the few nonverbal cues believed to have a universal meaning. A smile means friendliness, yet context can give it very different meanings. A teacher reprimands a student, and the student smiles. A stranger smiles at you as you cross the deserted school parking lot after dark. You are trying to make a serious point in a argument, and you smile.

Consider a frown. Woolfolk and Brooks (1985) illustrate how the meaning of a frown can be different for students, depending on the context. In the context of a demanding assignment for high-ability students, a teacher's frown might mean high standards and a belief that the students can do better. In the context of a remedial lesson with slower students, the teacher's frown may mean impatience and low expectations.

With nonverbal behavior, you need all of the surrounding nonverbal cues to interpret correctly what the behavior means in this particular instance of communication.

Inevitable

Our definition of communication and the nature of the perception process make nonverbal behavior inevitable. If one person assigns meaning to something about another person, then communication has happened, even though there may have been no intentional message. If a person selectively perceives some nonverbal aspect, interprets it, and uses the interpretation as a basis for a response, then communication occurs.

Test out this inevitability factor in an experiment with your friends or family. Sit very still and make an effort to suppress any possible nonverbal cues. Someone will assign meaning to how you sit, the lack of expression on your face, the look in your eyes, and your silence.

It is axiomatic that *we cannot not communicate*. If someone fixes his or her attention on you, then the nonverbal aspects of you, your words (if there are any), and the context will mean something to that person.

To Sum Up

Consider the distinguishing characteristics of nonverbal behavior as signposts pointing toward constructive attitudes about nonverbal communication in the classroom.

- *Learned*. You and your students have not all learned the same meanings for nonverbal cues or have the same skill in using them.
- *Culturally Determined*. The meanings we do learn are based on our reference group. Your meanings are not necessarily those of your students. Be alert to the differences in nonverbal behaviors and meanings.
- *Contextual*. Do not pull a nonverbal cue out of the context in which it occurs and interpret it in isolation.
- *Inevitable*. Remember that nonverbal behavior is a constant in the perception process. Everything potentially means something and can affect the communication process.

All nonverbal behaviors share these defining characteristics. To deepen our understanding of nonverbal behavior, let's look next at the specific types of nonverbal behavior.

Types of Nonverbal Behavior

As we examine each type of nonverbal behavior, keep these important ideas in mind:

1. The meanings associated with each type are learned, culturally determined, contextual, and inevitable.
2. Although one type might have more impact than another at a given moment, all types operate simultaneously and continually within the classroom setting.
3. Teachers and students perceive nonverbal information holistically and personally. What *each* person selectively perceives, interprets, and then responds to depends on the individual.

Let's look at the categories of nonverbal behavior from a practical point of view. What is involved? What are the potential meanings and messages? As we go through each type, recall how your teachers handled it and how you were affected. Imagine yourself teaching. What choices would you make? Why? How might your students react to your choices?

We will consider each type in the order it might impact students as they enter a classroom for the first time: physical environment, physical appearance, kinesics, paralanguage, proxemics, haptics, and chronemics.

Physical Environment

Color, lighting, temperature, decor, and spatial arrangements are elements in the room that impact the senses when students enter a classroom. These separate aspects of the **physical environment** contribute to the overall impression of the kind of space it is and how students feel about being in it. Is it psychologically inviting or, as the British say, "offputting"? Teachers usually have no control over some of these factors, such as color, lighting, and temperature. The best you can do is to be flexible about the circumstances you are given. Recognize limitations and enlist student help in creating ways to cope with it. Teachers can affect decor and spatial arrangement by the decisions they make. Remember that all five aspects potentially affect students.

Color, Lighting, and Temperature. Color, lighting, and temperature affect mood and behavior. (Todd-Mancillas 1982). We all like to be in bright, pleasant, and comfortable rooms.

Color. Elementary age students respond better to rooms with warm colors (yellow, peach, and pink), while secondary students respond better to cool colors (blue and blue green). William Todd-Mancillas cites (1982) studies that show color affects achievement, school pride, and a reduction in vandalism. For rooms painted battleship gray or hospital green, consider brightening the walls with student work. We will explore this idea when we discuss "decor."

Lighting. Inadequate lighting, either too little or too much for a task, produces eye strain, fatigue, irritability, and contributes to poor concentration. If the lighting is inadequate or uneven, consider adding area lamps for more light (if feasible). Another possibility is doing activities in the best available light. Assign students to do work that requires good light, such as reading and written work, in the brighter spots in the room. Discussions and group work could be done effectively in dimmer areas.

Temperature. Students preoccupied with being cold or hot experience physiological noise. The optimum classroom temperature for learning is 66–72 degrees (Todd-Mancillas 1982). Humidity needs to be factored into any consideration of temperature. A high temperature with low humidity may *feel* cooler than a lower temperature with high humidity.

   In a building with inadequate heating or cooling, make whatever adjustments you can. I have a friend who teaches in the new wing of an old school. The original furnace services both buildings, and it is turned off on the weekends to save money. After it is turned on again on Monday, it takes until Wednesday for the heat to creep around to the far end of the new wing and warm his classroom. He lets his students wear their coats in class.

Decor. You already know the effect of decor. Teachers and students prefer being in classrooms they find attractive. Virginia Richmond (1992, p. 161), summing up many studies, says teachers and students respond in the following ways, ". . . prefer to work more on the subject matter, . . . learn more, feel better physically and mentally, and have more effective communication outcomes." She mentions several additional positive effects on teachers that are worth noting. Teachers ". . . feel better at the end of the day, . . . are more energetic, like their students more, see their students as less of a threat to them . . ." (Richmond 1992, p. 161).

It is no surprise that people like being in an aesthetically pleasing environment. The issues are figuring out what people find pleasing and creating it. Dealing with these issues involves answering two questions, "Who does the defining?" and, "How do we pay for it?"

Ideally, teachers and students would have a role in decisions about furniture and equipment selections, perhaps even architectural decisions. The reality is you are hired, and you and your students must live with your room assignment. Most of the decor decisions—walls, windows, furniture—are already made, but decisions about decorations are individual. Inviting students to offer opinions can be a positive experience. When people are allowed to participate in decisions concerning them, it is empowering. It gives them a sense of ownership and pride about the decisions. Using student input turns "the" room into "our" room. It is an exercise in joint problem solving. "We have to spend a lot of time together in here, so how can we make this room more attractive for all of us?" If students like plants, perhaps they can bring favorites from home. If students vote for art work, then they can create it.

Most teachers decorate their rooms, at least partially, by displaying their students' best work. From a teacher's point of view, it serves as a model of good work and rewards effort. Consider how students whose work never makes it might feel about such a decorating decision. Consider what answers and subsequent feelings might result from asking students if they wanted their work displayed and, if so, which work and how? Suggest alternatives, such as every student's best work will be displayed and letting students decide what it is.

Teachers who share classrooms with other teachers have little opportunity to personalize decorations for their students. Creating a sense of "our" space is especially important in large, impersonal high schools where students move from one classroom to another and often feel anonymous. Work out what is possible with the other teach-

ers with whom you share the room. What area can you use? A wall?
A bulletin board? Part of a bulletin board? A corner of the room?

Spatial Arrangement. How the furniture is arranged determines
what communicative relationships are possible and affects the teaching-learning process. The traditional straight-row seating arrangement originally evolved to make optimum use of natural light from
windows (Sommer 1969). Students were to listen to the teacher who
was in front of the class and speak when spoken to. This arrangement
is frequently used today out of habit or tradition. Whatever the reason
for the choice, the communicative outcomes are the same. The teacher
is in control of the talk and of student-student interaction.

Seating arrangement decisions should be based on the learning
objective and on what kind of interaction you need to accomplish it.
There are several seating arrangements. None is any better than the
others. It is a matter of choosing which one arranges the students most
appropriately for what you want them to do. This means you might
use one seating arrangement one day and a different one on another
day. It means you might use one arrangement for the beginning of the
class and another for the rest of the period.

Changing spatial arrangements also has the positive side benefit of
being motivating. Recall from chapter 2 the different bases for selectively attending to a stimuli. "Novelty" and "change" apply here. You
catch the attention of students accustomed to rows simply by using
any other arrangement. You arouse their curiosity. It signals something different is going to happen.

Let's look at the options according to what learning objectives they
support and the kind of communication they promote.

1. *Straight-Row*. Appropriate when you want to minimize stu-
    dent-student interaction. You might want to do this to promote
    teacher-student interaction (as with a lecture) or to promote indi-
    vidual work (as with test taking or independent seat work). This
    arrangement is also appropriate any time you need the whole
    group listening to a single source. This might occur with a guest
    speaker or students making individual or group presentations to
    the rest of the class.

2. *Modular* (grouping the desks in clumps). Appropriate when you
    want to maximize student-student interaction in small groups and
    minimize teacher-student interaction. You might want to do this
    to have students work cooperatively in groups to solve a problem
    or to do a project.

3. *Horseshoe* (desks arranged in a U with someone in the open end
    of the U). Appropriate for student-student interaction with some-
    one supplying a central, directive focus. For example, you might

want all your students to discuss something (an issue, an event) together, but you want to lead the discussion.

4. *Circular*. Appropriate when you want to maximize student-student interaction and minimize teacher input. Promotes co-equal participation by all members of the circle because everyone can see and hear easily. If the teacher sits in the circle, she or he is another participant and not the leader. Alternatively, the teacher might sit outside the circle and listen to the discussion.

A variation on this pattern is having two circles, one within the other. The students in the inner circle discuss an issue among themselves, while the rest of the class forms the outer circle and listens. This is called the "fish bowl effect" with the students in the middle feeling like they are in a fish bowl. The inner circle has its discussion. Then students in the outer circle could comment on the discussion, adding their own ideas. You might use an arrangement like this to get different group perspectives on a subject or to let groups observe how other groups discuss issues or solve problems.

Physical Appearance

Once students enter the room, they notice the teacher and each other. As a teacher, you watch them come in and sit. All eyes scan the room. First impressions form. When we meet new people, we direct perceptual energies toward them. We notice and evaluate each other according to our personal standards of what is appropriate, attractive, repulsive. These impressions, which may not be conscious, affect the way we then interact with each other. Put simply: we approach people whose physical appearance we like; we avoid people whose physical appearance we do not like.

There is bad and good news about this normal cycle of personal perception. The bad news is that we initially operate on a surface level, often dealing with stereotypes. We form impressions about and interact based on **object characteristics**, including physical characteristics (skin color, hair color, body type, cleanliness, odor), attractiveness, clothing, and artifacts (accessories like glasses, jewelry). Some people, including students and teachers, get ideas about what is important and necessary about physical appearance from the entertainment media and advertising. They evaluate themselves (physical and social self-concepts) and the worthiness of others based on ideas from television, films, and commercials, where females are held to a standard of looking like models (thin, shapely, beautiful, and sexy) and males must be tall, muscular, macho, and handsome.

Students failing to fit the image (too fat, too short, not good looking, wearing the wrong clothes) may have problems. They may have a nagging dissatisfaction with self, lack self-confidence, and feel socially devalued by others, for example, if they are not being chosen for friendships or dates. Young people can easily become obsessed with wanting to have a certain image, and the results can be dramatically negative. The percentage of school-age girls on diets and the incidence of eating disorders (anorexia and bulimia) has increased; girls as young as eight years old are affected. Students who buy expensive jackets with logos of sports teams, athletic shoes, and gold chains, can become victims of assaults, robberies, and sometimes murder by other young people.

Yet physical appearance does not impact behavior only among peers. Richmond (1992) says teachers communicate differently with students whom they think are attractive or unattractive. The difference results in "more" communication for the attractive students and "less" for the unattractive students. According to Richmond, the attractive students get more attention, one-on-one communication, individualized instruction, and personal interest than do unattractive students. They are rarely seen as causing problems and are more likely to be excused rather than punished. Unattractive students are perceived as chronically misbehaving. (The one exception to the "less" norm is that some teachers are more likely to give unattractive students attention by calling them names and ridiculing them about their appearance.) Teachers' nonverbal behaviors also differentiate between more for attractive students and less for unattractive students. The differences are striking when put in chart form:

Teacher Behavior Toward Attractive Students	Teacher Behavior Toward Unattractive Students
Looks at them more, more eye contact	Looks at them less, less eye contact
Smiles more	Fewer smiles
Gestures more to them	Gestures less to them
Touches more	Touches less
Stands closer to them	Physically avoids them
Uses more plesant vocal tone	Uses less pleasant vocal tone

The good news about the perception process is, as time passes, attention usually shifts to a deeper level. With continued contact, people base impressions on **personal characteristics**. These include the attributes that make them unique, such as personality and attitudes. We see past the surface and notice what is on the inside. This perceptual refocusing to personal characteristics is a natural function of getting to know people better. It is another good reason to pay attention to interpersonal communication with students, a subject we will explore in a later chapter.

As teachers, we need to recognize our own biases when it comes to physical appearance and not let them affect how we treat students. We need to look beyond outward appearance to identify distinguishing characteristics. We need to appreciate the powerful need for identity, status, and peer approval that drives the choices students make about their physical appearance. Teachers should strive to be nonjudgmental about their students' fashion statements, viewing the choices as expressions of wanting to be accepted by peers.

I once had a student teacher who declared he only liked good looking students. Despite this bias, his nonverbal communication was effective with all students, no matter what they looked like. I mention him as an example of someone who successfully understood his personal biases about physical appearance. He monitored his behavior so his biases did not intrude into his communication with students.

We also need to think about how our physical appearance will be perceived by our students. We, too, deal with certain givens of sex, height, weight, race, hair, and eye color. Students will have their preferences and make their judgments. However, our role as teacher and the expectations that go with it will affect both the physical appearance choices we make and how students perceive us. Teachers are expected to dress differently and more formally than students. In other words, teachers should look like teachers. What this actually means depends on the individual school. As a student teacher or a new teacher, observe what the other teachers wear to decide what is appropriate in that school.

Student teachers and young, new teachers also need to consider how young they look as they make the transition from college student to classroom teacher. Clothing and grooming choices appropriate for college may be inappropriate when teaching. For example, the current fashionable short skirt lengths suitable for social occasions may be provocative to male students. Student teachers on the secondary level often are or look about the same age as their students. Dressing more formally separates you visually from the students and helps define your role for them.

Kinesics

After we form overall impressions of people, then specific "animating" details catch our attention. We notice how they move and handle themselves physically, which is kinesic behavior. **Kinesics** is the study of human body movements (from the Greek *kinesis* meaning motion). It includes hand gestures, posture, walk, head position and movements, facial expressions, and eye movements.

We continually scan this wide range of kinesic behavior for information about our communication interactions. In and out of classrooms, kinesic behavior is used to judge people's feelings and attitudes about themselves, other people, the subject at hand, and the situation. People who use appropriate kinesic behavior, are usually judged in positive terms—warm, interested, or enthusiastic. When teachers use kinesic behavior, for example, students of all ages respond with more positive attitudes toward the teacher, the subject, and achievement.

How Body Movements Function

Ekman and Friesen (1969) categorize the potential meanings of the types of body movements in terms of how they function: emblems, illustrators, regulators, adaptors, and affect displays.

1. *Emblems* have direct specific verbal translations. Their meaning is culture specific (known by people within the referent group). They are used intentionally instead of words. One example in the United States is the "thumbs up" sign to mean "good job."

2. *Illustrators* are movements which amplify a verbal message by adding a visual dimension. They are often used in giving directions (pointing the way to go), when describing size, shape, or motion (holding your thumb and fingers two inches apart while saying how thick the book is), or to emphasize words or sentences (slapping the table while telling someone how mad you are).

    According to Richmond (1992), students from kindergarten through fourth or fifth grade use a lot of illustrators to show what they have trouble saying orally. As they mature and their command of oral language develops, they use fewer illustrators, but the ones they use are more complex.

3. *Regulators* are kinesic behaviors used to maintain or control verbal interactions. Called "turn-taking cues," they indicate when to speak, when not to speak, when others want to speak, and the desire not to speak. When leading a discussion, teachers use regulators to indicate who is to speak (gesture, eye contact, smile), to

signal listening and encourage continued talking (eye contact, attentive posture, head nodding, moving toward, or leaning forward), and to note the end of turn or change of subject (looking away, moving away). Students signal "I don't want to speak" by avoiding eye contact with the teacher.

4. *Adaptors* are kinesic behaviors which have idiosyncratic meanings for an individual—they meet some need. They serve no purpose in an interaction, but they help an individual cope. People are generally unaware of their own adaptors, although they notice those of others. Students of all ages use adaptors to manage stressful, novel, or boring moments (chew their fingernails, twist their hair, or fiddle with objects on their desks). Teachers report they observe more adaptors before holidays, breaks, recess, exams, or special events (Richmond 1992).

   Teachers' adaptors distract students (pacing; fiddling with objects like pens, paper clips, jewelry; jiggling change in pockets). Students may get the impression that the teacher is nervous, insecure, or bored.

5. *Affect displays* express a person's emotional state, reaction, or mood and its intensity. Although we look to the face and eyes for cues about what another person is feeling, we *feel* emotions throughout our bodies. Whether we are happy, angry, or bored, it shows in our face and eyes, posture, gestures, and walk. Most affect displays are spontaneous and unintentional and may even contradict what is said.

Types of Kinesic Behavior

With these functions in mind, let's look more specifically at the types of kinesic behaviors. Although we need to consider them separately, keep in mind that we perceive them holistically, as a package.

Eye and Facial Behavior. In the mainstream culture in the United States, we look to the face and the eyes for meanings when we communicate. Mehrabian, a nonverbal scholar, concluded that 93 percent of the emotional meaning of a message was communicated nonverbally. Of that 93 percent, he said 55 percent was expressed via the face (1981). In schools, teachers and students look at each other's faces a lot.

Eyes. People speak of eye contact as if it were a light switch. It is either on or off; you have it or you don't. Actually, eye behavior is more complex than that. There are many types of eye behavior, and we use eye behavior to accomplish different tasks.

The types of eye behaviors give us a vocabulary with which to talk about eye contact. Each type relates communicators in a different way. Five types are discussed by Richmond (1992) and a sixth is identified by Goffman (1971). These descriptions will help you understand your own eye behavior and aid you in interpreting your students' eye behavior.

1. *Gaze* (a person looks at something or someone) indicates interest or attention.
2. *Stare* (a prolonged gaze) often means power or control, such as "Stop doing what you are doing!"
3. *Mutual gazing* (two people looking at each other) indicates mutual interest or attention.
4. *Gaze aversion* (intentionally avoiding or averting eye contact) means an unwillingness to communicate.
5. *Gaze omission* (unintentional aversion of eye contact) results when one communicator does not realize that another is seeking contact. Confusion between this type and the previous one can lead to misunderstandings. Often, the "other person," whether teacher or student, assumes the omission is intentional.
6. *Civil inattention* (two people acknowledging each other's presence and then averting their gazes) is a term coined by Erving Goffman (1971), the sociologist, for a behavioral ritual in which people are aware of each other's presence but choose not to interact. It permits little moments of privacy in crowded environments, such as hallways and lunchrooms.

We use these types of eye behavior to regulate the flow of communication, monitor feedback, express emotions, and reflect cognitive activity (Knapp and Hall 1992). Most of these functions we have already discussed, and you are familiar with what they involve in the classroom. We regulate the flow of communication with gaze (initiate), mutual gaze (listen), gaze aversion (nonparticipant), and withdrawal of gaze. We monitor feedback to gauge the responses we are getting. Teachers use more eye contact with students they find attractive or for whom they have high expectations. As teachers, we are willing to believe that gaze and mutual gaze mean students are listening. We try to interpret the expression in a gaze or an averted gaze to understand what a person is feeling.

One last aspect of eye behavior is interesting (and somewhat more technical). "Reflect cognitive activity" refers to the fact that both speakers and listeners tend to look away when they are trying to process difficult or complex ideas (Knapp and Hall 1992). These involuntary lateral eye shifts to the left and right are called CLEMS (conjugate-lateral eye movements). We look away to the left and/or to the right while we are thinking, and then back to the center when we are done. Knapp and Hall cite several studies which concluded that 75 percent of the time individuals' CLEMS are predominantly in the same direction. CLEMS are important to understand for what they are (signs of concentration) and for what they look like (daydreaming, trying to cheat, lack of attention).

Facial Expression. Although it is hard to separate the eyes and the face when it comes to interpreting meaning, there are points about facial expression that need to be made. The face is a complex channel of expression because of the number of emotions it is capable of revealing and how fast facial expressions can change (Adler and Towne 1993). When we speak of emotions playing across the face, we recognize this complex, ephemeral quality.

In many cases it is difficult to "read" the meaning of facial expressions, since facial expression of emotion and the interpretations of their meaning can vary with every individual and are affected by age, gender, and culture. Although most people are not conscious of what their faces are doing at any given moment, they are quick to notice and to judge other people's facial expressions. It is easy to leap to conclusions about students' expressions and allow interferences from psychological noise. For example, a teacher thinks some students are not listening during a lecture so immediately bombards them with questions to catch them not paying attention. It is important to exercise caution. Try to be aware what your face is expressing and to appreciate the individual differences among students' facial expressions.

People's facial expressions may be involuntary or managed in some way that they have learned is appropriate for the topic, situation, gender, or others involved. This facial management may be done consciously or unconsciously. According to Ekman, Friesen, and Ellsworth (1982), there are four basic **social facial management techniques**. Applying these techniques in the classroom can help you manage your facial expressions when necessary and to understand your students' facial management.

1. *Intensifying.* We exaggerate or heighten our facial reactions to meet the expectations or needs of others. A teacher might do this in response to a long awaited achievement of some goal: mastering a concept, finishing a project, attendance. Young children tend to do this with every strongly felt emotion.

2. *Deintensifying.* We downplay or minimize our facial behavior to maintain smooth interpersonal relationships or because it is socially expected. People with lower status may deintensify their facial expression in the presence of higher status people. For

example, your students may do this when talking to you or you might do it when talking to your superintendent.

3. *Neutralizing.* We avoid showing any facial expression. This is the proverbial "poker face." A teacher might do this to avoid swaying the outcome when helping a student make a decision or leading a class.

4. *Masking.* We conceal or camouflage what we are feeling by substituting facial expressions that are more acceptable under the circumstances. We mask to protect ourselves or others. Students might mask their anger when being reprimanded. A teacher might mask a humorous response to a student's naive comment.

Research indicates students respond best to teachers who are approachable, caring, and friendly (Andersen and Andersen 1982). A smile is only one way to indicate your positive feelings about a student. Since a smile is a universal sign of positive feelings, there is no reason to think your students will regard it as an abdication of authority. Students in all grade levels are sensitive to smiles as a sign of positive feelings and warmth (Andersen and Andersen 1982). However, smiles, like any other nonverbal cue, need to be used appropriately to help convey your meaning.

Teachers need to pay attention to whom they are smiling, because students will notice if there are patterns and assign meanings to where they fit into them. Research cited in the previous chapter said teachers smile less at students for whom they have low expectations. Earlier in this chapter the point was made that teachers smile less at unattractive students.

Richmond (1992) suggests there is a gender difference in the use of smiles in the United States. Due to socialization patterns, men internalize feelings (mask, neutralize) and women externalize feelings (intensify). She says the result is female teachers tend to smile too much and male teachers too little. Her rule of thumb for all teachers: "When you want to be taken seriously, put on a serious, calm expression. When you want to be considered . . . likable, and approachable, put on a smile" (pp. 79–80).

Body Movement. Posture and body orientation and gestures are included in **body movement**. All three supply cues about a person's attitudes and feelings. As with other kinesic cues, we are usually unaware of what our movements are signalling, but we do notice and give meaning to other people's movements.

Posture and Body Orientation. An erect, well-aligned posture with weight equally distributed between both feet is a "good" posture for a teacher for several reasons. First, it creates the impression that you are prepared and ready to go. It "looks" professional. Teachers, who slouch and drape themselves over the furniture, do not look involved. Sloppy posture is not the same as relaxed posture, which is discussed later in this section.

Second, teachers spend a lot of time standing and moving around a classroom. From this stance, it is easy to move and change direction without tripping over your feet and looking awkward. This stance also conserves physical energy, making it possible to stand for long periods of time. Throwing all your weight to one foot, or balancing on one foot is more tiring.

Third, and critical for teachers, good posture gives you better breath support for speaking. An erect posture allows you to inhale deeply and your diaphragm to push the air out of the lungs up through the windpipe. Slumping and slouching squeeze the lungs and the diaphragm together making it harder to get enough breath for deep diaphragmatic breathing. Inadequate breath support can lead to speaking problems, such as breathiness, not being able to speak loudly enough, and throat strain.

There are two dimensions of posture and bodily orientation that are revealing about attitude and feelings: tension-relaxation and open-closed. We need to consider both in terms of our own and our students' posture. According to Mehrabian (1981), the **tension-relaxation dimension** indicates a person's comfort in a situation. People assume loose, relaxed postures in nonthreatening situations; when they feel threatened, the posture is tight and tense. If you are tense, students may think you are insecure or angry or that you dislike them. As a supervisor of student teachers, I observe how body tension changes during the term. At first, student teachers are tense but relax as they become more comfortable and confident.

The **open-closed dimension** suggests people's feelings about communicating in a given instance. An *open* posture would indicate attentiveness or interest. Postural signs of openness are turning or leaning toward the other person, arms by the sides or in some relaxed position, legs in a natural, relaxed position, and head nodding as a response. A *closed* posture indicates indifference or hostility. Postural signs of being "closed" are turning away, leaning away, crossed arms, crossed legs, and a lack of head movement. An open posture makes a teacher seem more approachable, inviting questions, comments, and presence. Recall that teachers use closed posture with students they do not expect much from academically. Students may exhibit a closed posture for many reasons: apathy, low expectations for themselves as learners, or because of noise. Noise may be social (uncomfortable interpersonally with you or other students), physical (cold room), or psychological (insecure, fearful).

Gestures. These refer to hand and arm movements. **Gestures** play a major role in the functions of kinesic behavior. Emblems are speech-independent gestures. Gestures frequently perform the illustrator and "regulator" functions.

Gestures play an important role in a teacher's effort to capture and maintain attention whenever talking in the classroom. Gestures used judiciously are one way to accomplish many of the bases for selective attention listed in chapter 2. Since gestures are visual, students see them. Gestures can provide intensity, repetition, novelty, and change. In general, a teacher who uses gestures is perceived as being enthusiastic about the subject and interested in the person with whom he or she is speaking. If a student perceives gestures as signs of involvement and caring, then listening and talking to the teacher become motivating.

A key word in the preceding paragraph is "judicious." Each of us has a repertoire of gestures that we have learned and use habitually, as well as unconsciously. As a teacher, you need to analyze your gestures for whether they distract or help you communicate more effectively.

I had a student who raised his arms up and out in a large, open gesture and then moved his arms around from that position. Picture an orchestra conductor at work, and you have the right image. Nothing is wrong with the gesture. It was emphatic and dramatic. The problem was he used it all the time—when he gave speeches, during discussions, and in conversations. He used it so much that other students would smile and suppress laughter whenever he talked. If he used this gesture as much when he taught, his students probably would laugh out loud. It was natural and comfortable for him, but distracting for everybody else. He had to practice restraining its use to those times when he wanted to be dramatic.

Paralanguage

Once teachers and students begin speaking to each other, they notice each other's voices. Before we pay attention to the words, we listen to *how* something is said. We tune into the paralinguistic characteristics, the sounds of the voice that vocally communicate meaning. *Para* means beside, alongside, or beyond. **Paralanguage** involves the sounds that communicate meaning beside, alongside, and beyond the language.

People form vocal impressions and make judgments about each other based on these aspects of the voice. We have our preferences for what makes a voice attractive to us—one to which we like to listen. We infer attitudes and feelings of the person speaking: about themselves, what they are talking about, and toward us. We also stereotype a combination of vocal characteristics as our definition of whether someone sounds smart, stupid, educated, feminine, masculine, etc.

This normal labelling is often unconscious but, nevertheless, affects our perceptions of the person and how we communicate with him or her. As teachers, we need to avoid building expectations for students based solely on their vocal behavior. It is important to understand students' vocal behavior so you can interpret their meaning when they speak. It is also important to analyze how your voice affects people now with an eye to how it might affect your students someday. Your voice is one of your major tools as a teacher. The more sophisticated your use of your voice, the more help it will be in communicating effectively.

A teacher's voice is instrumental in two crucial ways: setting the emotional tone in the classroom and affecting learning. A teacher's paralinguistic cues help each student gauge whether he or she is emotionally safe. "How" a teacher sounds gives signals to students about themselves as learners with consequences to their self-esteem. Does the teacher care about the class or only about collecting a paycheck? Does the teacher like students or not? Is it safe to ask a question or make a comment?

Teachers' paralanguage affects learning in a number of ways. Voices that are warm, lively, and expressive aid listening, comprehension, and retention (Richmond 1992). The voice can aid in getting and holding students' attention. Since vocal cues are aural, students hear them. Paralinguistic cues can be used to provide novelty, intensity, change, and motivation.

Vocal Quality. The characteristic sound of a person's voice as defined by timbre, tonality, and resonance is known as **vocal quality**. If you think of the voice as a musical sound, then good vocal quality is a rich, pleasant sound. Vocal quality is produced (like any musical sound) by what you do with the instrument. In the case of vocal quality, the instrument is your vocal mechanism.

Sound for speech starts with a controlled, exhaled breath from the lungs which goes up the windpipe (trachea) and then through the vocal cords (larynx). The vibrating cords produce sound. The sound continues up through the three resonating cavities where it is reinforced and amplified: the throat (pharynx), mouth (oral cavity), and the nose (nasal cavities). Vocal quality is the resulting sound.

How the elements are manipulated determines your characteristic vocal quality. Good vocal quality results from using all the elements in an efficient, relaxed manner. "Breathiness" is running out of breath. "Nasal" is forcing too much sound through the nasal cavities. "Denasal" is not using the nasal cavities. "Strident" is too much tension.

"Throatiness" is trapping the sound in the throat cavity. "Husky" is abuse of the vocal mechanism in some way.

Whatever your vocal quality is, it will affect your students' perceptions. A pleasing vocal quality invites listening, while other vocal qualities have less favorable reactions. A strident voice sounds demanding and tense. Nasal voices sound whiny and argumentative.

Vocal Variety. The term used to describe the interaction of pitch, volume, rate, and pauses is referred to as **vocal variety**. "Good vocal variety" is the judgment made when the result is an interesting, expressive voice.

Pitch. A person's **pitch** is the customary lowness or highness of the voice. It is produced by the frequency of vibration of the vocal cords, which is determined by their thickness, length, and tension. Male vocal cords are thicker and longer with little tension, so they vibrate slower and produce a lower pitch. Female cords are thinner and shorter with higher tension, so they vibrate faster, resulting in a higher pitch. Everyone's pitch becomes lower as they age because the vocal folds increase in length and thickness. At any age, smoking, drinking, and inhaling foreign substances can thicken the cords and change the pitch.

A person's pitch is not one tone, but a range of several pitches that operate like a personal musical scale. **Optimum pitch** is a person's individual pitch range, the comfort zone of pitches. If you force your pitch beyond this optimum, either too high or too low, then you irritate the vocal cords. This produces strain, and, over time, could lead to nodes or growths on the vocal cords.

Forcing your pitch range is not good, but varying your pitch within its range is what adds emphasis, emotion, and attitudinal color to your words. Changes in pitch can clarify your meaning and the response you want. In English, a rising intonation indicates a question, while a steady level indicates a statement or opinion. Teachers with expressive voices are perceived as enthusiastic and interested. A teacher lacking pitch variety is monotone, sounding bored and boring.

If there are limits to your pitch range, then you need to compensate with the other vocal variety elements and to use other kinesic behavior to achieve expressiveness. I had a student with a hearing loss, which limited his ability to produce different pitches. He developed expressiveness through using a lot of variety in his rate, volume, use of pauses, and facial expressions.

Volume. The loudness of the voice is its **volume**. If your students cannot hear you easily and comfortably, then they will not listen. There is no one all-purpose volume level. An unvarying volume level has an effect similar to monotone pitch. Some teachers maintain a consistently high volume level, thinking it will hold students' attention. Students tune it out. They hear the sound, but they are not listening. Students' volume levels are a reflection of their cultural learning and may be different from the teacher's cultural norm. For instance, students with normal (for their group) but too loud (for the teacher) volume are often perceived as aggressive and discipline problems. Young children often speak too loudly for small classrooms. Of course, loudness at any age may be used to attract attention or be a sign of a hearing problem.

"Good" volume is loudness that is varied appropriately according to your ability, situational and audience factors, and your speaking goal. A speaker needs to figure out how much volume is required for a particular situation. Loudness depends on pitch. Male voices tend to carry more than female voices due to their deeper pitch. Male teachers should take this into account when determining appropriate volume.

Situational and audience factors involve the size and shape of the space you are in, the number of students you are speaking to, what else is going on simultaneously, and physical noise. If you are in a large, crowded classroom making announcements or lecturing, you need to be louder. If you are working with a small group of students in a room of any size, then your volume needs to be at a conversational level. If you are talking privately with one student while the others work, then you need to lower your volume to a whisper. Physical noise, like lawn mowers outside the windows or the normal undercurrent of shuffling feet, dropping items on the floor, and scraping chairs and desks requires an upward volume adjustment.

Remember your speaking goal when deciding volume level. As you speak, you need to vary your volume to make your emphasis clear. A high volume used for a brief period of time gains attention. Raising volume slightly signals that what is being said is important. Getting louder or softer can maintain or regain attention.

Rate. The speed at which a person speaks is **rate**. It affects whether students listen to you and their perception of your attitude about them and the subject. The faster the rate in instructional situations, the harder it is to comprehend. If a rate is too fast for new or complex information, students may misunderstand what they manage to catch or they may stop listening. A teacher who customarily talks too fast may be perceived as impatient, annoyed, and not caring about the subject or the students. A slow rate makes it easier to keep up. However, if the rate is too slow, students' minds wander. Teachers with characteristically slow rates may come across as lethargic or patronizing.

As with volume, variation and appropriateness of rate are the keys to effectiveness. A *mono* rate, whether it is too fast, too slow, or moderate, becomes numbing to students because of its sameness. Rate varied for emphasis aids attention and comprehension. A teacher who uses rate changes successfully seems more interested and is more interesting.

Determining how to vary your rate appropriately depends on your usual rate, student factors, and your speaking goal. Each of us has developed a characteristic rate of speaking, and we will use it in the classroom if we do not stop and think about possible consequences. If your basic rate is extreme, either fast or slow, the effect on your family is minimal because they probably have the same rate. However, you need to think about the obstacle your rate may present to your students. Analyze your habitual rate and plan necessary changes for specific purposes.

Student factors to consider include background, age, learning abilities, listening skills, and what is going on in the classroom. Younger students, students with poor listening skills, and students who learn more slowly may need a slower rate. Older students benefit from a faster, peppier rate. Students for whom English is a second language are helped by a slower rate. Students who are stressed or overexcited are calmed by a slower rate.

Thinking about your speaking goal involves answering two questions: What are you talking about? What kind of response do you want? If you are talking about familiar or personal subjects, then you want to use a quicker, conversational rate. If you are talking about new or complex subjects, then you need a slower rate. Giving directions slowly increases the odds that students will understand them. Slowing down also signals something is important and provides thinking and response time. For example, if you were asking a thought-provoking question, a slower rate would give students time to understand the question and formulate a response. Slowing down when lecturing helps highlight what is a main point and assists note taking.

Pauses. Breaks or **pauses** are imposed between spoken words, speech phrases, sentences, and ideas. These little silences of varying length organize oral words like punctuation organizes written words.

You must recognize that both speakers and listeners need pauses. Speakers need to inhale for breath so they can speak, think their next thought, and decide how to express it. Listeners need pauses to keep up with the speaker, think about what is being said, and formulate a response. Understanding this need for pauses is important because you and your students are continually speaker and listener simultaneously. Remembering this helps you figure out how to handle your own pauses and also how to interpret those of your students.

Teachers talk a lot so that when they choose silence, students know it means something. Teacher silence can have a powerful effect like the title of a Swahili folktale states, *A Little Silence Makes a Great Noise*. Use pauses so they highlight your intended meaning. Using pauses effectively depends on controlling their placement and length.

Where you put your pauses frames your words and signals their significance to listeners, while the length of the pause indicates what response is wanted. Consider the teacher who asks a question during a discussion. If she pauses and waits for an answer, then students know she wants them to participate. If she does not pause or pauses very briefly, then students know their answers are not really wanted. Remember from the last chapter that teachers pause longer when they have high academic expectations for students. In a lecture, short pauses right before or after a statement say "this is important." Long pauses signal a transitional shift for students.

The best pauses are silent. However, people usually fill up pauses with extraneous material. These **fillers** can be vocalizations (um, ah) or verbal (O.K., like, you know what I mean). People are rarely aware when they are using fillers. They use them out of habit or when nervous, insecure, or worried about listener response. People think pausing may be interpreted as forgetfulness, that they have finished speaking, lack of planning, or being a poor speaker.

Teacher fillers are distracting to students. I have heard students talk about daily betting pools on high school teachers' number of O.K.s or ums. Once students start counting your fillers, they are not listening to what you are saying.

Proxemics

After we are together awhile, we start reacting to how far or close we are to each other. Edward Hall, an anthropologist, coined the term **proxemics** (from the Latin *proximus* for nearness) to describe the study of the ways people use and communicate with space and distance in their physical environment. How we handle space says something about how we feel about ourselves, our needs, and how we see our relationships to the others in the space. In an unconscious yet fundamental way, physical closeness translates into psychological closeness, and spacing defines the nature of the relationship. This idea is illustrated by teachers who stand closer to attractive students or place farther away the students from whom they do not expect much.

To understand the meanings and possible messages space communicates, you need to understand interpersonal space, vertical space, and territoriality. Finally, we need to relate proxemics to what has been said about spatial arrangements and kinesics.

Interpersonal Space. People develop a sense of their personal space requirements. **Interpersonal space** deals with how we handle horizontal space, the distance between us and others on a horizontal plane. This circular space around each person's body operates as a vantage point from which they organize their perceptions and as a barrier to regulate their interactions with other people. Think of it like an invisible bubble surrounding you which shrinks and expands depending upon personal and situational circumstances. You and each of your students have this personally defined space bubble.

Personal Characteristics. This category includes personality, age, gender, and background. Students who are introverted, shy, or nervous need more space (Richmond 1992). Students who are extroverted, have a high need for affiliation, possess an internal locus of control, or have positive self-esteem tend to need less distance (Richmond 1992). At any age we interact closer with our peers than with older people. In classrooms we stand closer to people we like. Cultural spatial norms are learned slowly. Young children are sensitive to the use of space, but it takes until the age of twelve for the adult cultural norms to be internalized (Malandro, Barker, and Barker 1989). Up until then, children frequently invade other people's personal space. In the United States females of any age interact with less distance than males.

Background creates different expectations for what spatial differences should be maintained. North Americans and northern Europeans interact at greater distances than do Latin Americans and southern Europeans. Remember these are generalizations; there are variations in spacing expectations depending on the country, and there are variations between groups within a country (Hickson and Stacks 1993).

Situational Characteristics. Norms, task or need, relationship to other persons, and location comprise situational characteristics. Hall (1983) outlined the four **interpersonal distancing zones** that exist in North American culture. Remember, the distancing norms in other cultures may be very different. Each zone defines and encourages different kinds of interactions and relationships. Notice the range within each zone; individuals will adjust their behavior according to their comfort level.

1. *Intimate Distance* (touching to within eighteen inches). We allow people with whom we feel close in this zone: family, close friends, and people we love. When others intrude on this space, we feel uncomfortable and experience stress. Some situations create intrusions (elevators, crowded hallways, lines), but the situations are predictable and short-lived. We cope in ritualized ways (not

making eye contact and avoiding touching). Some roles require that people be within this zone to do their job, such as doctors, dentists, and teachers. As teachers, we need to realize how often we are within this range—for example, while watching over students' shoulders or helping them with a question or problem.

2. *Personal Distance* (eighteen inches to four feet). In this space we allow people with whom we feel comfortable and are familiar: friends, co-workers, peers.

3. *Social Distance* (four to twelve feet). This is the distance where impersonal interactions occur and business is conducted. This is a comfortable range for strangers or people we do not know well. Interactions feel more formal within this range.

4. *Public Distance* (twelve feet to the physical limits of the space). At the near end, you feel protected by space; at the far end, others are perceived as part of the setting, not as individuals. Interactions are formal and more impersonal.

Task, need, and relationship interrelate in classrooms to affect distancing. Teachers set the tasks which define distancing requirements (working independently, in pairs, in small groups, listening as a whole class). Teachers approach students to supervise, answer questions, and give directions. Students approach teachers to get attention, to ask for help, to demonstrate affinity for the teacher, and sometimes to feel secure.

Analyze your personal space needs and those of your students. What are the points of complementarity and conflict? How will students interpret your feelings toward them if you flinch or draw away when they stand too close to you?

Vertical Space. The height between us and others on a vertical plane is **vertical space**. Height, as a result of physical growth, is relative. Teachers are usually taller than students. Most teachers stand much of the time, while students remain seated, because the height gives them eye contact with everyone in the room.

Height can convey different meanings, depending on your point of view. Think how your height might affect your communicating with your students and decide how to manipulate the speaking planes accordingly. Adults towering over them can be intimidating to small students. Students, particularly the less talkative, confused, and those lacking confidence may be less likely to ask questions. You can reduce the intimidation factor by getting on the same level when helping them with seat or group work (kneeling or sitting next to them). On the secondary level, there will be students taller than you, especially for the women. You, too, may need to manipulate the levels for your comfort.

For example, you could sit next to or stand over the students, which puts you on the same speaking plane.

Territoriality. The basic human (and animal) instinct to define ownership of a space and to defend it is called **territoriality**. This impulse in humans is part of establishing and maintaining personal identity and status. Both teachers and students establish territories and defend them. Understanding territoriality can help give you insight into conflicts between students and between you and your students. Higher-status individuals, like teachers, always have the right to invade the territory of lower-status people, like students (DeVito 1995). This does not mean, however, that the lower-status individuals will not resent or react to the intrusion. As teachers, we need to be sensitive to what is territory and understand how territories are staked out and defended.

We think of territory as a physical space. Erving Goffman, the sociologist, says in our society we need to extend this concept to include situational and egocentric territory (1971). He lists eight **territories of the self** that people claim as personal territory. As you read through the list, remember that these territories apply to teachers and students. How each type manifests itself will depend upon the people involved (age, gender, background), and the situation. As you go through the list, think of personal examples for each type of self-territory (Goffman 1971, pp. 29–41):

1. *Personal Space.* The space immediately surrounding an individual at any given moment, particularly the space directly in front. This space is portable. It is where a person is at the moment. If entered, there is a feeling of threat. To be "in your face" violates this space.

2. *Stall.* Well-bounded space to which people lay temporary claim on an all or nothing basis, such as parking spaces and telephone booths. Stalls have external, easily visible, defendable boundaries, like desks and chairs. A stall may have a continuing recognized claim. If a person becomes associated with a space over a period of time, he or she is said to have "tenure" (Richmond 1992, p. 120). Others will defend the person's right to the space even when she or he is absent. "That's Emma's chair. She isn't here today."

3. *Use Space.* The space around a person needed for a particular activity. Examples of use space are the space between people conversing, or between a viewer and an activity (TV screen, bookshelf, sign), or the area around an activity (dancing, swinging a bat).

4. *The Turn.* A person's temporal space or order among other people. A decision rule or norm governs turn activity. Teachers usually announce the turn criteria. It could be gender (girls first),

alphabetical, or evaluative (neatness of desks, or readiness for an activity). Taking someone else's turn is a violation.

5. *The Sheath.* Skin and clothing. Goffman says a person's body functions as "a preserve in its own right, the purest kind of egocentric territoriality" (1971, p. 38). Hairdo, body ornamentation, clothing, and make-up are ways we tend this most personal space.

6. *Possessional Territory.* Objects identified with the self, such as personal effects like umbrellas and handbags, or situational objects temporarily claimed like magazines. Goffman says that dependents who are present, like children or boy- or girlfriends, are possessional territory. When teachers refer to "my class," they are stating a possessional claim. Teenagers regard their significant others as possessional territory.

7. *Information Preserve.* The information about self to which a person expects to control access. There are several varieties: biographical facts, contents of letters, diaries, purses, pockets, the contents of the mind. Teachers have control over their own informational preserves but frequently make demands on students' preserves on behalf of the school. What a person lays claim to as personal information changes with age.

8. *Conversational Preserve.* The right of a person to exert some control over when and by whom one can be summoned to talk. It also includes the right of people engaged in talk to have their circle protected from entrance or overhearing. Teachers control these rights in classrooms but need to consider how they summon students to talk and how they interrupt private conversations from the students' point of view.

Staking out Territory. Staking out or claiming territory is done by markers. **Markers** announce a territory belongs to or is reserved for someone. According to Goffman (1971), there are three types of markers: central, boundary, and ear (as in branding animals on their ears).

1. *Central markers* may be personal artifacts others recognize as yours (backpacks, purse, coat) or impersonal objects (books, lunch trays). A person could be a central marker for his or her group, such as when claiming a cafeteria table.

2. *Boundary markers* mark the lines between adjacent territories, such as armrests between auditorium seats or aisles between desks. The boundaries for people (possessional territory) are indicated by touching behavior, walking or standing variously entwined. "Offensive displays" serve as boundary markers (Richmond 1992, p. 119). These occur when someone uses intimidating behavior to ward off others (stares, aggressive postures and gestures).

3. *Ear markers* are initials or names on something you claim. Ear markers are most relevant to the self territories of stall (labels on desks and lockers), sheath (initials or names on jackets, jewelry), possession (names or initials on clothing of yours that you wear, or have your significant other wear, tattoos).

Encroachment on Territory. The militaristic connotations suggest the strong feelings and often violent reactions involved when a person's territory is threatened. What a teacher perceives as a non-event, "So he used your pencil," may lead to retaliation out of all proportion from the teacher's point of view, such as hitting, shoving, or fighting. Perspective is everything when it comes to defining what is a territorial attack and what constitutes defense. Lyman and Scott (1967) discuss different degrees of encroachment on territory, two of which have special interest to teachers: violations and invasions.

A **violation** occurs when someone uses territory without permission. It may be unintentional ("I didn't know it was yours."). It may even be temporary ("I'll give it right back when I am done."). However, the owner of the territory always feels presumed upon ("I didn't say you could use it.").

An **invasion** occurs when boundaries are crossed for the purpose of taking over someone else's territory. Invasions are deliberate and permanent. Examples are breaking into line, flirting with someone's significant other, and taking someone else's seat. The daughter of a friend experienced an invasion when she and three friends were mugged for their team jackets, while eating lunch in front of their school.

Defense of Territory. Which defense a person chooses depends on age, gender, peer expectations, the nature of the attacker, what is at stake, available weapons, and opportunity. Lyman and Scott (1967) also discuss different types of defense, three of which occur frequently in school: withdrawal, insulation, and turf defense.

Withdrawal is a retreat from the attack. A decision to withdraw is made if the stakes are small or the cost too high. The other person may be much bigger, have higher status, or carry a weapon. Frequently in classrooms, teachers enforce this type of defense. "It doesn't matter which chair you sit in. Sit over there."

Insulation is the erecting of barriers to stop the attack. These barriers could involve the use of markers, offensive displays, or physical barriers, such as piling up books or other objects between you and the attacker.

Turf defense is physically repelling the invaders. The stakes are high. A teacher friend says at his school the fights between students are about boyfriends or girlfriends (possessional territory). Considering himself lucky because fists (rather than guns or knives) are still the weapon of choice, he notes interesting differences between how the boys and girls fight. The boys circle around, follow a version of the Marquise of Queensbury Rules, play to the gathering audience, and give him the impression that they want to be separated. The girls, having no childhood practice with sparring, fight with no-holds-barred (gouge eyes, tear out hair) and are more dangerous to separate.

How Do Proxemics Relate to Spatial Arrangement, and Kinesics? Distance and movement between the teacher and students affect their interpersonal relationship. How, then, does spatial arrangement come into play with these interpersonal dynamics?

Proximity to the teacher matters. A series of studies indicates closer distances result in more positive attitudes (Mehrabian and Ksionzky 1970). Students seated nearer their teachers have more conversational interactions with them and are allowed greater latitude in their behavior (Brooks, Silvern, and Wooten 1978). Proximity to the teacher makes it easier to ask questions, make comments, talk informally, and feel psychologically closer to the teacher. It is important to create opportunities to be near all the students at some time.

Traditional row arrangements were thought to create an **action zone**, a T-shaped area which extends across the front and down the middle of the room, where most of the interaction between teachers and students takes place. This idea was predicated upon the teacher as stimulus (the action in the classroom is where the teacher is), teacher location (in the front of the room), row seating, and student self-selection of seating, such as motivated, verbal students choose to sit front and center. Even with a row arrangement, teachers can get closer to more students by moving along the sides and the back of the room. Some teachers divide the rows in half and create a wide path straight down the center of the room, thus creating another runway for teacher movement among students. Other teachers go up and down the rows during seatwork time to assist each student.

Current thinking is that every classroom has an area where participation is greatest, but it is not always front and center (Woolfolk and Brooks 1985). Where the participation is greatest on any given day is affected by such factors as students' *initial* predisposition to talk, location relative to the teacher, the task, who the student must talk to, and student comfort levels. Be wary of pigeon-holing students' level of participation as low, moderate, or high without considering these factors. When you change the seating arrangement, you set these factors spinning in a dynamic way.

For example, take a student who is a low participator when in his or her usual seat in the back row. Seat the student with a small module of classmates working on a discussion problem, and he or she may be a high participator. Why? The student may be more comfortable speaking out in a small group than in front of the whole class. Certainly, in a small group there are more chances to speak. The task may be more engaging than questions from the teacher. The peer interaction on the task is stimulating. This subject of composition of group participants will be pursued in the chapter on small groups.

Think of the different seating arrangements as presenting opportunities for you to move around and get close to individual students. When students are working in modules, then you can move among the groups, pausing to assist and support. If you are part of the circle, you can choose to sit next to different students. The point is to think of whatever seating pattern you use as an opportunity for you to make yourself physically available to all of your students.

Haptics

Once we are close enough to be within what Hall (1983) calls "intimate distance," then we are close enough to touch. **Haptics**, from the Greek, "to fasten," is the study of tactile behavior. Weitz (1974, p. 203) suggests we think of haptics as "zero-proxemics" because when people touch, there is no space between them.

Touch has enormous power to communicate positive and negative emotional meanings, such as like-dislike, control-submission, and caring-apathy. It includes physical contact, such as grasping, stroking, hitting, hugging, holding, and guiding another's movements. What any instance of touching means depends on the people involved and their culture, age, gender, and the circumstances.

Influences on Touching Behavior. Cultures are classified by the frequency of tactile behavior. Picture a continuum with *high-contact cultures* at one end and *low-contact cultures* at the other end. Andersen (1993) cites research placing various cultures along this continuum. High contact cultures include: most Arab countries; the Mediterranean region including France, Greece, and Italy; Jewish people from Europe and the Middle East; eastern Europeans and Russians; and Indonesians and Hispanics. Low-contact cultures are most of northern Europe, including England, Scandinavia, Germany; British-Americans; and the Japanese. Australians and North Americans are moderate in cultural contact, although North Americans tend toward the low end. In all cultures babies begin life as high touchers because it is their first means of learning and relating to others. From this point, cultures branch out into their own norms and expectations for kinds of touches, and *who* touches *whom*, *when*, and *where*.

In the United States, from this high touch beginning, the trend is toward limited touch under restricted conditions. Infants and toddlers receive the most touch that they will ever receive in their lives. As children move through kindergarten through sixth grade, the amount of touch they give and receive steadily declines (Willis and Hoffman 1975). Cultural norms are learned slowly and absorbed around twelve. In adolescence the amount of physical contact falls to about half of that of early elementary grades, yet it is still more touch than people experience as adults.

In short, in the United States touch becomes restricted to our intimate relationships (intimate or sexual touch), ritualized for greetings, farewells, and signs of friendliness and support (handshakes, brief hugs, pats on the back), and functional (impersonal touches connected to a task, such as doctors, dentists, shoe salespeople).

Touch as a permissible way to communicate feelings becomes restricted as we get older, and more emphasis is put on paralinguistic cues and facial expression to convey emotional meanings. Because of these normative restrictions, the United States has been described as "touch deprived," that is, people do not get enough touch to meet their psychological needs. The number of child abuse cases in recent years also has made the United States more touch phobic. Nursery school-age children through elementary students receive instruction in "good touch" and "bad touch."

Against this backdrop, you need to consider the variation in touch behavior you are likely to encounter in any classroom:

- The great melting pot of backgrounds in the United States makes for much variation among individuals even when families have been in this country for generations.
- Immigrant students might display even wider variation, especially if they are from "high touch" cultures.
- "Touch avoiders," people who do not like to give or receive touch, account for 20 percent of the population (Richmond 1992, p. 148). In situations where touch is expected, they hesitate or refuse to touch. Indications are withdrawing, turning-away, closed posture, tense posture, or averting gaze. Males are more touch avoidant than females.
- "Skin hunger" is the term used to describe children who have received too little physical or tactile contact to meet their psychological, social, and physical needs (Richmond 1992). They often have problems with socialization, adjustment, and development. Signs of this syndrome are following the teacher around, touching the teacher, touching other students, and needing a lot of reassurance that they are doing well.

What Is Good Teacher Touch? Good teacher touch is appropriate. One way to define appropriateness is by location, duration, and intensity. The touch should be on a neutral part of the body, specifically the hand, forearm, shoulder, or upper back. The touch should not last long, and it should be light.

Another way to define appropriateness is according to the students involved. Younger students through early adolescence need and initiate more touch with the teacher. Students may touch the teacher while speaking to him or her, reassuring themselves that they have his or her attention. Young students may want to hug and kiss the teacher or to be hugged. For children, not touching means dislike. Teachers in the early grades need to be careful to touch all of their students (not only the clean ones or the brightest ones), otherwise, the untouched ones may be hurt (Richmond 1992, p. 150). My cousin went up to her second grade teacher to hug her. The woman turned and walked away. At seven she could see that the teacher hugged all the other children, but would not hug her.

As older students learn the adult norms for tactile behavior, they will expect to be treated as adults. This transition makes for a long blurry period when teachers need to be sensitive to how touch may be interpreted by the student. The teacher's intended supportive touch could be misconstrued by a student as having personal meaning. Students admire teachers, get crushes, and fantasize, so a touch may mean much more from their point of view. Since adult touching becomes largely restricted to the arenas of the intimate and sexual in the United States, teenagers coming to terms with their own sexuality amidst a barrage of mixed media messages may be unsure of what is appropriate touch. Lacking a vocabulary for functional or friendly touches, any touch could have intimate overtones for them. To reduce the possibility of misunderstandings, touching should be done only when others are around. Avoid patterns, such as only females or only males, in your choices of whom to touch.

Chronemics

What happens during our time together becomes meaningful for both teachers and students. These meanings, however, are filtered through what we have learned from our cultures about the meaning and value of time. **Chronemics** (from the Greek *chronos* for time) is the study of how we perceive and structure time. When students and teachers have different expectations for appropriate time behavior, problems arise. Teachers often view violations of their own time norms as intentional messages of disrespect, apathy, or hostility. Students may perceive the teacher's time behavior as pointless, nitpicking, or vindictive.

Edward Hall (1983) views cultures as falling into one of two categories in their use of time: **monochronic** (*mono*—one), which emphasizes doing one thing at a time, and **polychronic** (*poly*—many), which stresses many things occurring at once. Each perspective has different norms about activity, structuring time, the value of time, and punctuality.

Monochronic Time	Polychronic Time
Events are compartmentalized; things are done one at a time.	Events are simultaneous; several things happen at once.
Activities are oriented to tasks, schedules, and procedures.	Activities are oriented to people and interactions.
Prioritizing is important; importance decides order and amount of time.	Completion of transactions is the focus.
Punctuality by the clock matters.	Schedules and appointments are viewed flexibly.
Time is a tangible commodity; (saved, spent, wasted, or killed).	Time is intangible, a reference point.

The United States' time is monochronic, and its influence is obvious in the ways schools are traditionally structured and run. Classes are of a set length and meet at specific times. Clocks define tasks ("You have ten minutes to finish your reading."). Bells signal when it is time to start and stop a class. The norms are so much ingrained that teachers and administrators assume them and note only their omission. Teachers punish students for being late, not completing assignments on time, taking longer to complete in-class assignments, wasting time, and not concentrating on the task at hand. Students with a polychronic sense of time are likely to be judged negatively and experience frustration at not understanding why deadlines and schedules matter.

Many of the experiments with the restructuring of schools and learning loosen the rigidity imposed by a monochronic framework. Longer periods and variable periods allow more flexible scheduling. Different learning methods take the focus off the task being done in a set time period and place it on what is being learned, such as independent learning and mastery learning. The use of cooperative learning groups, teams, and other types of small groups shift the focus to people interacting in complex, synergistic ways to learn together.

How do you handle different perspectives on time in the classroom? There is no need to choose sides. Recognize the benefits and limits each perspective brings to the tasks and relationships in the classroom. Be flexible in trying to reap the advantages and avoid the disadvantages of each perspective in the given case.

Time norms are implicit. Your norms may be different from those of many of your students. Create *ours* in an explicit way. Keep focused on your task and people objectives when planning. Explain how time will be defined and why it needs to defined that way for each task or activity. If deadlines and schedules matter, then be precise in making the expectations clear.

It must be emphasized that "amount of time" communicates meaning about relationships and tasks in both time perspectives. Polychronic time is people intensive with completion of interactions between them important. Monochronic time is task-oriented with people's importance indicated by time given, allotted, or withheld from them. The amount of time you spend or let your students spend on a task will translate in their minds as, "This is or is not important." Giving or withholding time from a student will likely be perceived as an intentional, personal message, such as the teacher "likes me-doesn't like me" or "thinks I'm smart-thinks I'm dumb."

Recall from chapter 2 that if teachers have high expectations for students, they give them more time. The cues are subtle: calling on them more often, waiting longer for them to answer, working with them to improve an answer, and interacting with them more. Be aware to whom you give your time. It comes down to, "Whom do you encourage to speak and to whom do you listen?" If you notice patterns, then ask yourself, "What do the patterns mean?" The students will notice if you "play favorites," and it will impact their behavior. Students who are not called on or who are cut off will stop speaking.

How Nonverbal Communication Functions in the Classroom

Although we examined separately each type of nonverbal behavior in order to understand it, it is important to remember that all the types are always potentially available—collectively, simultaneously—to contribute to meaning. Think of the types of nonverbal behaviors as individual dabs of paint on an artist's palette from which you, the artist, choose to create the kinds of messages that are needed in the classroom. In this section, we examine how the types of nonverbal behavior function in accomplishing the following dimensions of the teacher's role: self-presentation, rules and regulations, instruction, feedback, and affect.

Self-Presentation

How you present yourself in a given role—in this case, as teacher—is referred to as **self-presentation**. What do parents, students, and society expect from teachers? How do you define what it means to be a professional teacher? How do you see yourself in the role of teacher? Realize that however you answer these questions now, your definition will change as you are changed by the experience of teaching. How you see yourself as a teacher will be different after student teaching and after you have your own classes.

Consider how nonverbal behaviors project what it is a person believes about teaching. The choices about physical appearance make a visual statement about formality-informality. Posture and body orientation suggest attitude (positive or negative) about teaching and your confidence and ease in teaching. Decisions about spatial arrangements and movement around the classroom suggest how you see your relationship to students. For example, always using a row arrangement and choosing to stay in front of the room connote formality and the role of teacher as information giver. Varying the spatial arrangements and moving around the room suggest a more informal relationship with students and the role of teacher as facilitator. How teachers use instructional time says something about the effort they think planning deserves. Someone who works at being expressive vocally and is animated comes across as enthusiastic about the subject and about teaching.

Rules and Regulations

The procedures a teacher develops for managing students during instructional activities are referred to as **rules and regulations**. They are norms for how business is accomplished between a particular teacher and students. They come about through teacher mandate, school policies, and students' needs and responses to what goes on in the classroom. Sometimes they are formal and explicit regarding, for example, late work, absences for tests, or make-up work. Teachers announce procedures, post signs, and give handouts to be signed by the students and their parents. Often, however, norms are informal and implicit. They are not necessarily ever verbalized, but they operate to keep daily classroom life on an even keel. Examples are how people treat each other, turn-taking, and speaking and listening behaviors.

Whether or not rules and regulations are taken seriously by students often depends on the teacher's nonverbal behavior. Nonverbally, a teacher can clarify and enforce regulations or make them appear arbitrary and meaningless. Let's take as a norm, "not talking while another student has the floor." There are many ways to communicate this nonverbally depending on the age of the students and the situation. A short list includes: eye contact to the offending student with a shake of the head "no"; a finger to the lips with a frown; a stare; eye contact to the offending student with an upraised palm in a stop gesture; movement toward the offending student with a touch on the shoulder while maintaining eye contact with the speaking student. To ignore the interrupter would probably result in the student who has the floor talking louder or thinking you do not care about the interruption. Ignoring does not clarify what the norm is for the speaker, the interrupter, or the rest of the class.

Instruction

The input or instigation phase of teaching the subject matter is referred to as **instruction**. It involves giving information (explaining, directing, or lecturing) and stimulating thought (asking questions, probing responses, leading discussions). The content of instruction involves verbal communication, which must be clear and interesting to students. How well or poorly the content is delivered nonverbally determines whether and how students respond. Effective nonverbal behaviors can support, clarify, add emphasis, and create interest.

Paralanguage, kinesics, proxemics, and chronemics are especially important. An expressive voice can catch and hold attention, create dramatic tension, and emphasize what is important. Pauses signal time to start or end, thought time, and transitions. Eye contact with students helps maintain their attention. Illustrator gestures help clarify meaning and add emphasis. Movement adds drama and holds attention. Moving closer to students helps them maintain attention. Handling time effectively—reserving enough time for the level of difficulty, for example—for any instructional activity increases the likelihood that students will comprehend it, see its importance, and become engaged in it.

Feedback

In chapter 1, feedback was defined as a message sent in response to another message. Communicators judge how they are doing by responses from the person(s) with whom they are communicating. Based on how they interpret the feedback, communicators adjust their communication (continue, amend, change directions, amplify, stop).

For clear and productive communication in the classroom, teachers need both to get feedback from and to give feedback to their students. Students need to know that they are being heard, understood, and respected. They need reassurance from the teacher that what they are saying is not wrong or stupid. Teachers need to know if what they are saying is making sense. The size of most classes and the length of periods make seeking and giving verbal responses to each student on a daily basis difficult. Nonverbal behaviors permit frequent opportunities for checks on students' responses and for giving individualized feedback to students.

Teachers get feedback by scanning students' nonverbal behavior and interpreting it. Whether students are working in groups, pairs, or listening as a whole class, nonverbal cues give feedback about what they are doing. If students in a group have tense postures, are getting louder, are talking faster and "in each other's face," then it's time to check on the group. When lecturing, watch the expression in the eyes, posture, and adaptor gestures for signs of attention, confusion, and boredom. If you expect students to be taking notes and they are not, notice what are they doing instead. If you notice students glancing at each other sideways, trying to see what their neighbor has written down, or whispering together, then it's time to adjust something, such as slowing down and pausing.

Teachers' nonverbal feedback to students needs to be constructive and supportive in order to be useful. Constructive feedback messages deal with what is. They may be positive (encouraging more responses similar to what is being expressed) or negative. To be supportive, feedback must be delivered in a way that does not undermine students as people and encourages them as learners. Supportive feedback cues include: eye contact; direct body position; moving toward or standing close; head nodding; positive paralinguistic cues (slower rate, appropriate volume, pauses, inflected expression); appropriate touch; and, giving time.

Affect

"Affect" deals with the emotional domain. **Affect messages** are the emotional and attitudinal overtones of our communication. They are frequently unconscious, unintentional, although highly accurate reflections of our feelings and attitudes about people and events. Every interaction in the classroom potentially sends signals about how the people involved feel about each other. Teachers' affect messages influence how students feel about themselves and how they behave as well as shape their relationship with the teacher.

Teachers reveal both positive and negative affect through their non-verbal behaviors. Positive affect messages indicate liking, approval, respect, or preference. Nonverbal behaviors with this positive meaning are characterized by "approach" (move closer to, seat closer) and "more" (time, eye contact, smiles, head nods, paralinguistic expressiveness, gestures, and movements). Students who receive such messages perceive the teacher as more approachable and interested in them personally.

Negative affect messages indicate dislike, disapproval, rejection, or indifference. Nonverbal behaviors radiating negative meanings can be described by avoidance (keeping distance from students, perhaps using the desk as a barrier) and the words "less" or "none" (eye contact, time, movement). Such messages mean to students that the teacher is emotionally distant or absent and uninterested in them.

What Do I Do with This Information?

Nonverbal behaviors impact on the emotional and academic relationship between teachers and students. You and your students will perceive them, interpret them, and act based on the meanings you glean from them.

Understanding what nonverbal behavior is, its types, and how nonverbal behavior contributes to teaching involves your making a number of conscious choices. What you do nonverbally is subject to your control. Monitoring your nonverbal behavior for its impact on all of your students is a choice that must be backed up with effort. Trying to understand the meaning of your students' nonverbal behaviors from their point of view is a commitment requiring patient persistence. The decision to ignore nonverbal behavior in the classroom is also a choice. It is up to you to decide what contributions you will make through nonverbal behavior in your classroom and what insights you will gain from observing students' nonverbal behavior.

References

Adler, Ronald and N. Towne. 1993. *Looking Out/Looking In*, 7th edition. Fort Worth: Harcourt Brace Jovanovich.

Allen, R.R. and Kenneth Brown, editors. 1976. *Developing Communication Competence in Children: A Report of the Speech Communication Association's National Project on Speech Communication Competencies.* Skokie, IL: National Textbook Company.

Andersen, P. 1993. "Explaining Intercultural Differences in Nonverbal Communication." In L. Samovar and R. Porter, editors, *Intercultural Communication: A Reader*, 7th edition. Belmont, CA: Wadsworth.

Andersen, P. and J. Andersen. 1982. "Nonverbal Immediacy in Instruction." In Larry Barker, editor, *Communicating in the Classroom*. Englewood Cliffs, NJ: Prentice-Hall.

Bassett, Ronald and Mary-Jeanette Smythe. 1979. *Communication and Instruction*. New York: Harper & Row.

Birdwhistell, R. 1970. *Kinesics and Context*. Philadelphia: University of Pennsylvania Press. Cited in M. Hickson and D. Stacks, *Nonverbal Communication—Studies and Applications*, 3rd edition (Madison, WI: WCB Brown & Benchmark, 1993).

Brooks, D., S. Silvern, and M. Wooten. 1978. "The Ecology of the Teacher-Pupil Classroom Interaction." *Journal of Classroom Instruction* 14(1): 39–45.

Cooper, P. 1995. *Communication in the Classroom*, 5th edition. Scottsdale, AZ: Gorsuch Scarisbrick.

DeVito, Joseph. 1995. *The Interpersonal Communication Book*, 7th edition. New York: HarperCollins.

Ekman, P. and W. Friesen. 1969. "The Repertoire of Nonverbal Behavior: Categories, Origins, Usage, and Coding." *Semiotics*, 1:49–98.

Ekman, P., W. Friesen, and J. Baer. 1984. "The International Language of Gestures." *Psychology Today* 18 (May): 64–69. Cited in R. Adler and N. Towne, *Looking Out/ Looking In*, 7th edition (Fort Worth: Harcourt Brace Jovanovich College Publishers, 1993).

Ekman, P., W. Friesen, and P. Ellsworth. 1982. "Conceptual Ambiguities." In P. Ekman, editor, *Emotion in the Human Face*, 2nd edition. Cambridge, England: Cambridge University Press. Cited in L. Malandro, L. Barker, and D. Barker, *Nonverbal Communication*, 2nd edition (New York: Random House, 1989).

Goffman, Erving. 1971. *Relations in Public: Microstudies of the Public Order*. New York: Basic Books.

Grant, B. and D. Hennings. 1971. *The Teacher Moves: An Analysis of Nonverbal Activity*. New York: Teachers College Press. Cited in P. Miller, *Nonverbal Communication*, 2nd edition (Washington, DC: National Education Association, 1986).

Hall, Edward. 1983. "Monochronic and Polychronic Time." From *The Dance of Life: The Other Dimension of Time*. New York: Doubleday. In L. Samovar and R. Porter, *Intercultural Communication: A Reader*, 7th edition (Belmont, CA: Wadsworth, 1993).

Hickson, M. and D. Stacks. 1993. *Nonverbal Communication Studies and Applications*. Madison, WI: WCB Brown & Benchmark.

Knapp, Mark and J. Hall. 1992. *Nonverbal Communication in Human Interaction*, 3rd edition. Fort Worth: Holt, Rinehart, and Winston.

Lyman, S. and M. Scott. 1967. "Territoriality: A Neglected Sociological Dimension." *Social Problems* 15:236–49. Cited in J. DeVito, *The Interpersonal Communication Book*, 7th edition (New York: HarperCollins, 1995).

Malandro, L., L. Barker, and D. Barker. 1989. *Nonverbal Communication*, 2nd edition. New York: Random House.

Mehrabian, A. 1981. *Silent Messages: Implicit Communication of Emotions and Attitudes*, 2nd edition. Belmont, CA: Wadsworth.

Mehrabian, A. and S. Ksionzky. 1970. "Models for Affiliative and Conformity Behavior." *Psychological Bulletin* 74:110–26. Cited in P. Andersen and J. Andersen, "Nonverbal Immediacy in Instruction." In Larry Barker, editor, *Communicating in the Classroom* (Englewood Cliffs, NJ: Prentice-Hall, 1982).

Nowicki, S. and M. Duke. 1992. *Helping the Child Who Doesn't Fit In.* Atlanta: Peachtree Publishing.

Richmond, V. 1992. *Nonverbal Communication in the Classroom.* Edina, MN: Burgess.

Rom, A. and L. Bliss. 1983. "The Use of Nonverbal Pragmatic Behavior by Language Impaired and Normal-Speaking Children." *Journal of Communicative Disorders* 16(4): 251–56. Cited in P. Miller, *Nonverbal Communication*, 2nd edition (Washington, DC: National Education Association, 1986).

Sommer, R. 1969. *Personal Space: The Behavioral Basis of Design.* Englewood Cliffs, NJ: Prentice Hall. In P. Miller, *Nonverbal Communication*, 2nd edition (Washington, DC: National Education Association, 1986).

Todd-Mancillas, W. 1982. "Classroom Environments and Nonverbal Behaviors." In Larry Barker, editor, *Communicating in the Classroom.* Englewood Cliffs, NJ: Prentice-Hall.

Weitz, S., editor. 1974. *Nonverbal Communication: Readings and Commentary.* New York: Oxford University Press. Cited in M. Hickson and D. Stacks, *Nonverbal Communication Studies and Applications* (Madison, WI: WCB Brown & Benchmark, 1993).

Willis, F. and G. Hoffman. 1975. "Development of Tactile Patterns in Relation to Age, Sex, and Race." *Developmental Psychology* 11:866. Cited in V. Richmond, J. McCroskey, and S. Payne, *Nonverbal Behavior in Interpersonal Relations*, 2nd edition (Englewood Cliffs, NJ: Prentice Hall, 1991).

Woolfolk, A. and D. Brooks. 1985. "The Influence of Teachers' Nonverbal Behaviors on Students' Perceptions and Performance." *Elementary School Journal* 85(4): 513–28.

Suggested Reading

"Never Smile Until Christmas? Casting Doubt on an Old Myth," by J. Andersen and P. Andersen. 1987. *Journal of Thought* 22(3): 51–61.

   Discusses what is wrong with this advice frequently given to new teachers and describes what nonverbal cues send messages that signal warmth and availability for communication.

Nonverbal Communication: The Unspoken Dialogue, by J. Burgoon, D. Butler, and W. Woodall. 1989. New York: Harper & Row.

   This text presents a thorough survey of nonverbal communication. It includes chapters on managing conversations and persuading others nonverbally.

The Unspoken Way: Haragei, by M. Matsumoto. 1988. New York: Kodansha.

A look at the rules of nonverbal behavior in Japanese society and business.

Chapter **4**

Verbal
Behavior

Ideas to Remember

* Verbal behavior affects who we are and our communicative choices by shaping perception, affecting self-concept, and expressing expectations.
* People absorb the underlying assumptions and attitudes of their referent group about language form and usage.
* Verbal behavior operates simultaneously on the linguistic and pragmatics levels.
* Understanding verbal behavior in the classroom is complicated by several factors involving the differing skill levels between teachers and students, and the linguistic and pragmatic variations in English by region, ethnic groups, and socioeconomic levels.
* If teachers lack knowledge about verbal behavior, the potential exists for inappropriate teacher expectations, ineffective teaching, poor interpersonal relationships with students, and negative effects on students.
* The characteristics of language are:
   Words are symbolic.
   Meanings are in people.
   Language is learned.
   Language use is rule governed.

Language use is goal driven.

* The linguistic dimension of verbal behavior is structured in three ways: phonology, the meaning of words, and grammar.

* The pragmatic dimension of verbal behavior involves role behavior, communication skills, and the purposive nature of language use.

* All possible individual acts of communication can be grouped according to five major functions: informing, controlling, expressing feeling, imagining, and ritualizing.

* Teachers need to observe quiet students to distinguish whether they have adequate communication skills and choose not to talk, or avoid talking because they have inadequate skills.

* When students lack skills, they need to develop their skills through a skills training program and develop more positive attitudes about communicating.

* It is important to create a talk friendly environment in your classroom.

As mentioned in chapter 2, people are like narrators who shape their own life stories. From their individual points of view they select, arrange, and interpret the details of their daily lives. Since all people communicate from their personal perspectives, we need to understand these personal perspectives. In chapter 2, we explored what goes into creating teachers' and students' perspectives: the perception process (selective attention, interpretation, and behavior), self-concept, learning styles, and expectations.

As we learned in chapter 3, nonverbal behavior plays a meaningful role in the classroom, yet it is necessary to emphasize the importance of verbal behavior in forming and reflecting behavior, developing self-concept, and creating and expressing expectations.

- *Words shape perception by naming and giving meaning to what a language community finds important.* Words meet needs, encapsulate values, and express feelings. A culture develops the words it needs. For example, the Inuit have one hundred words for snow but no word for war (Malcolm 1985). Shibui, a Japanese word meaning the kind of beauty that only age can reveal, has no equivalent in English (Reingold 1984). "Far away" is expressed in Zulu by a conglomerate word meaning, "There where someone cries out, 'O Mother, I am lost!'" (Rich 1972). Our experiences with language affect what categogories, concepts, and schemata we form and what meaning they have for us. Our thinking is reflected in our verbal responses when we communicate.

- *Self-concepts are built and evolve through verbal interactions with significant others through their compliments, criticisms, praise, and judgments.* Our self-concept and self-esteem are revealed in what we say about ourselves and in how we interact with others.
- *Students pick up their teachers' expectations for them through verbal interactions.* When teachers expect low achievement from a student, they criticize more, praise less, and do not give feedback to the students' public responses. When teachers expect high achievement from students, they interact with them more frequently, give them prompts, criticize less, and praise more.

Verbal Behavior Is Personal

Who we are and how we communicate are mediated through our verbal behavior—through what we say and how we say it. This is not to downplay our nonverbal behavior, whose significance lies in providing a framework for our verbal behavior and for expressing feelings and attitudes. Verbal behavior allows us to develop our core personal perspective and is the means by which we interact with others. Verbal behavior is the medium through which we communicate our life stories and allows us to reveal who we are. Some authorities think that self-maintenance is the most fundamental need people have when they communicate (Phillips, Butt, and Metzger 1974).

It is important to understand these connections between verbal behavior and identity, so that we remember to treat verbal behavior in the classroom with great care. This connection exists both for us and our students. Verbal behavior is not an abstract, impersonal body of knowledge like mathematics. It is personal, it is lived, and it connects us to the people and things we care about. We grow up speaking the language our families speak and using language the way they use it. We learn the underlying assumptions, attitudes, and expectations of our language community. Our verbal behavior defines us. It is part of who we are. When our verbal behavior is criticized, we tend to take it personally as a criticism of us.

With this caution in mind, let's return to our definition of communication:

> Communication is a dynamic process of interaction between people in which they assign meaning to each other's verbal and nonverbal behavior.

Students and teachers perceive each other's verbal behavior and assign meaning to it. When most people think of verbal behavior in the classroom, they think of words. Certainly, words are important to what goes on in classrooms. Instruction is carried out through words. The content of subjects is made up of words. However, teachers' and students' communication involves more than just words.

The Form and Use of Language

We need a broader definition of verbal behavior, one that includes everything about verbal behavior that teachers and students bring into the classroom. Teachers and students, with their verbally mediated identities and personal histories of language use, enter classrooms poised to talk. In our definition of **verbal behavior**, then, we need to include both the form of the language spoken and how the language is used to communicate.

In order to understand the meanings that are being assigned by you and your students, we need to look at language *linguistically*, how it operates as a system, and *pragmatically*, how it is used. We must also consider the underlying assumptions and attitudes people have about language form and use. These beliefs, which may not be conscious, not only define an individual's verbal behavior but also color his or her expectations and judgments about other people's verbal behavior.

Understanding verbal behavior in the classroom is complicated by several factors. It will require effort on your part to cope with the challenges they pose. Consider the following ideas to keep in mind when focusing on verbal behavior in the classroom.

- *Language is a complex system that takes a long time to learn to use with facility.* Teachers are more sophisticated language users than their students, who are in the process of developing basic verbal skills.
- *Teaching and learning involve knowledgeable people communicating about a subject with novices.* Teachers tend to be people who were good students and went into a subject area because they love it. They probably never experienced having trouble learning it. Also, it is easy to forget what it was like not to know the fundamentals about it.
- *Every language has its own forms and social uses.* Given the immigration patterns to the United States, it is likely that you

will have students for whom English is not a native language. They may have problems speaking or understanding English and lack knowledge about the uses of language in this country. You will likely not know their native language, nor understand communication behaviors from their culture.

- *English within the United States varies linguistically and pragmatically by geographic regions, ethnic groups, and socioeconomic levels.* When such language differences exist in the classroom between you and your students, they may contribute to difficulties with social interactions or to comprehension problems.
- *The greater the differences in linguistic and pragmatic verbal behavior are from a person's own, the greater the possibility that a person will avoid communicating or make negative judgments about the other person.*

Understanding verbal behavior and bringing assumptions and attitudes surrounding it to light are critical for people preparing to teach. When teachers are uninformed about verbal behavior, there is potential for harm. What teachers do not know about verbal behavior can lead to inappropriate teacher expectations, ineffective teaching, poor relationships with students, and negative effects on the students. Talking over students' heads leads to confusion, boredom, and interferes with learning. Not calling on students because it is not clear what they are saying cuts them out of the interaction in the classroom. Criticizing or correcting students' verbal behavior may result in students becoming reticent, angry, or apathetic. Lack of understanding a dialect has resulted in students being recommended for unnecessary speech therapy and placement in special education classes (Wolfram and Christian 1989). Not understanding the meaning of students' pragmatic behaviors can lead to mislabelling the students. Wolfram and Christian (1989) cite an example that occurred with Native American students in the Southwest who did not participate in class. According to their culture, they were behaving respectfully. Their teachers' culture, however, defined talking during class discussions as appropriate pragmatic behavior. As a result of not understanding the differences in meaning for talk and silence between the two cultures, the teachers misjudged the students' intelligence.

This chapter will inform you about verbal behavior and the assumptions and attitudes surrounding it. It will explain what you need to know about linguistics and pragmatics, so you can understand your own verbal behavior and that of your students. The approach is practical: What do you need to know? What do you need to do about it? Its purpose is to enable you to create more meaningful verbal messages for your students and to develop constructive behaviors and support-ive attitudes toward their verbal behavior.

The chapter begins with the characteristics of language that affect verbal behavior. Next the linguistic elements of language and dialect—phonology, semantics, and grammar—and dialects in the schools are examined. The next section explores the pragmatic aspects of lan-guage use and what to do about quiet students. The chapter concludes with advice for creating a talk friendly environment in your classroom.

Characteristics of Language

It is important to begin by examining the fundamental characteristics of language that underlie linguistics and pragmatics. Not understand-ing these basic ideas about language contributes to social, psycholog-ical, phonetic, syntactic, and semantic noise. These misunder-standings can affect self-concept and achievement as well as impair student-teacher relationships.

Words Are Symbolic

Words are labels. They stand in for or point to some referent. They are not the referent that they represent. The word is not the thing. Think of any common words, and you illustrate this point. The word "hot" does not burn, the word "heavy" has no weight, and you cannot sit on "chair." The pairing of a word with a referent is arbitrary as the number of different languages makes obvious. A word stands for what the language community—the speakers of the language—agree it stands for.

The human ability to communicate with verbal symbols gives us the capacity that Korzybski, the founder of General Semantics, referred to as "time-binding" (Korzybski; as cited in Phillips, Butt, and Metzger 1974, p. 119). We are not prisoners in the here and now, limited to what we can communicate in the moment, face to face. The symbolic nature of words permits us to learn from the past, express thoughts and feelings and reach goals in the present, and plan for the future (Phillips, Butt, and Metzger 1974). Words permit us to describe, remember, predict, reflect, argue, and dream.

When we forget that words are symbolic and treat them as if they had a reality of their own, our perception and thinking are affected. Children do this when they believe words have power to make some-thing happen, such as, "I wish you were dead." People who do this act as if words conferred what they named, such as stupid, crazy, or chicken. As teachers, we do this when we treat a concept as if it were a tangible thing in the real world. Concepts are abstractions that stand for a collection of ideas and facilitate talk about complex ideas (Phillips, Kougl, and Kelly 1985) "Intelligence" is a concept. Once we treat it as a thing, we act as if it is something you can measure and do or do not have. In effect, we shut off our thinking about the complexity of ideas that the word represents and may apply the term simplistically in dealing with students.

Meanings Are in People

Words point to or suggest meaning, but meanings are in people. As discussed in chapter 1, meaning is negotiated between the people communicating. Words, which label tangible entities (persons, places, or things) that are apprehensible through the senses, have denotative meanings people can agree on. We may both know the denotative meaning of the words being used, yet have very different connotative meanings. For example, teachers and students know what "homework" is. Teachers see it as positive. To them it is a means to practice or prepare for class work. Students generally view homework as negative. To them it means busy work or punishment.

Designations used to categorize students can have strong connotations that affect the students' and teacher's expectations, perception, and students' self-concept. Think about the words "learning disabled" (LD) and "disabled" from the points of view of the students who carry this label, of the other students, and of the teacher. Some students of mine, who were Special Education majors, suggested new terms with more positive connotations: LD as learning difference, and "other-abled" rather than disabled.

The multiple meanings of words is another reason that meanings do not reside in words. For example, according to the *Oxford English Dictionary*, "communicate" and "communication" both have twelve definitions (1981). It is estimated that the one hundred most frequently used English words have an average of eighty-five dictionary meanings (Bassett and Smythe 1979). You have to respond to how a word is being used in a particular context to figure out what it means. To understand which meaning is meant you have to analyze the context, the topic, and the intention of the speaker.

It is in the nature of language to change. Words come into a language because they serve a need, and meanings change for existing words. According to *The Story of English*, English is the richest of all the world's languages in vocabulary with five hundred thousand words listed in the *Oxford English Dictionary* with a half-million technical and scientific terms uncatalogued (McCrum, Cran, and MacNeil 1986,

p. 19). English is an amalgam of words and meanings gleaned from the languages of conquerors (the Romans, the Anglo-Saxons, the Vikings, and the Normans). English in the United States has been and continues to be enriched by words and meanings from the waves of immigrants, science and technology, popular culture, and current events. Word meanings change. Think of how meanings have changed for words such as gay, liberal, disk, and family.

Lack of sensitivity to the personal element in word meaning results in people using words with their own meanings with no regard for their listeners' meanings. Semantic noise occurs. When teachers speak without considering what the words mean from students' perspectives, the intended message may be missed. I observed an art teacher praising a third grader's class work. She said, "We don't even teach still life to the fifth grade." I asked the boy later if he knew what a still life was, and he said no. We discussed what the teacher meant, and it was clear that he had no idea that his teacher had been complimenting his drawing.

Language Is Learned

Human infants are born to learn language. Babies bring innate cognitive and linguistic abilities to the language acquisition process (Hulit and Howard 1993). This means human brains are genetically ready to learn language. A child raised in a human group and encouraged to speak will learn the group's language through listening, imitating, and through what is encouraged and rewarded or discouraged and punished. Deaf children learn language. Although they do not develop spoken language unless they can be helped to hear it, deaf children can speak through signs and gestures (Naremore and Hopper 1990). In cases of extreme abuse, where a child is isolated and hears and uses little speech, language use is retarded or nonexistent. The social interaction between children and their caregivers and significant others is the key to language learning. The language community's norms and expectations for verbal behavior are reflected in the behavior of the family and neighborhood. Children learn what is available to be learned about verbal behavior. Remember, verbal behavior means both the form of the language used and the content, the meaning conveyed by how the language is used.

Form involves both which language is learned and what variety of the language is spoken. **Dialects** are subcategories of a parent language that use related but not identical rules (Owens 1992). According to sociolinguists Wolfram and Christian (1989, p. 1), dialect is technically, ". . . any given variety of a language shared by a group of speakers." The group may be defined by region, culture, ethnicity, education, or social class or some combination of these factors (Hulit and Howard 1993). Within a regional dialect there may be several social dialects spoken by people grouped by the other factors listed. According to Wolfram and Christian, ". . . if a person speaks the English language, that person necessarily speaks some dialect of the English language" (1989, p. 2).

The dialect children learn depends on the language community in which they grow up. Children growing up in the South will speak a regional Southern dialect, while children growing up in the Midwest will speak a regional Midwestern dialect. The dialect referred to as Black English is a socio-cultural dialect, not a racial one. Many African Americans do not speak Black dialect. It shares many characteristics with the standard and nonstandard dialects of the South (Owens 1992). Some Caucasian children living in areas where the dominant dialect is Black English may use Black English or another vernacular dialect (Adger 1995).

Content involves the pragmatics of language use: who speaks to whom about what, when, where, how, and under what circumstances. Remember, pragmatics also includes learning appropriate nonverbal behavior. Children learn through interaction to fit into the various roles expected of them in the family. This shaping process occurs through observation, overt instruction, and imitation. Role, as discussed in chapter 2, involves appropriately meeting the expectations of a specific situation. Success in performing any role means mastering the communication skills that define the role, *talking and acting right*, as judged by the people in charge (in this case, family and caregivers). The more experimentation with alternatives within a role and the more roles children are encouraged to experiment with, the more variety there will be in their communication skills.

Basil Bernstein, the sociologist, explains different family styles of shaping language use through the concepts of restricted and elaborated codes (Bernstein; as cited in Allen and Brown 1976, chapter 2). Bernstein uses the word "code" to mean how language is brought to bear in a particular context. The two codes represent different ideas of what is appropriate behavior in a given situation. A restricted code is context-bound and assumes shared knowledge. Meanings are implicit. The basis for behavior is one's position. A misbehaving child might be told, "You're old enough to know better," or, "Girls don't behave that way." An elaborated code establishes a shared context through language. It assumes intent and orientation cannot be taken for granted, so meanings are made explicit. A misbehaving child would be given reasons: "You shouldn't have hit Billy. You're older and stronger than he is, and he can't fight back. It's not fair" (Allen and Brown 1976, p. 25).

Children's basic repertoire of role behaviors and communication skills form the basis for their behavior when they move into other communicative settings such as school. The greater the discrepancies between the norms of the school and what the child learned at home, the more likely the child will encounter communication problems in school (Allen and Brown 1976, p. 18).

Discrepancies in the types of social and psychological noise that teachers experience versus what the students experience may occur. Schools are middle-class institutions. Teachers are usually from the middle class. Middle-class people tend to have been reared with, use, and expect others to use an elaborated code. Such teachers may have trouble interpreting the verbal behaviors of students raised with a restricted code. Perceiving such students through their own language assumptions, teachers might label them reticent, uncooperative, not bright, or defiant. If these perceptions become expectations that the teacher acts upon, the students' self-concept, achievement, and relationship with the teacher may be affected. The differences need to be viewed for what they are: differences in what is learned appropriate behavior. ". . . the communication roles that children have learned in their environment must be recognized and taken into account" (Allen and Brown 1976, p. 29). The form and content of students' verbal behavior reveal who they are and where they come from. Devaluing their language is to devalue them, their families, and their language communities.

Language Is Rule Governed

"Languages are structured on several different levels, and each of these can be subjected to dialectal variation" (Wolfram 1991, p. 42). These levels include: **phonology**, the sounds of a language; **semantics,** the meaning of words; grammar, the ways words are put together to make meaningful utterances. These three levels will be explored in the next section of this chapter. Dialects vary on all three levels.

The rules of English and its dialects as spoken in the United States need to be considered from technical and social perspectives. From the technical viewpoint, dialect is a neutral, descriptive word. All dialects are linguistically equal. "Each dialect is a systematic rule system that should be viewed within its social context" (Owens 1992, p. 429). They all work well for communicating among the members of the language community who use them. They all are governed by norms concerning what is acceptable speech. All dialects vary in formality or informality according to the situation, topic, and participants. Speech is grammatically correct when it follows the rules of a particular dialect. Wolfram and Christian (1989, p. 20) give two examples to illustrate this point. "We was here" is grammatical, since it follows the rules of a particular dialect. "I bought a hat yellow" is ungrammatical, since it does not follow the rules of any English dialect.

From the social point of view, people use the term dialect in several ways. According to Wolfram (1991), one use of dialect is: different from the local, speech natives. Dialect is something that other people have. In this sense of the word, people may use "dialect" and "accent" synonymously (Hulit and Howard 1993). If you have ever traveled to another part of the United States, people probably commented on your accent, while you were noticing theirs. Wolfram says a second use of dialect is to refer to varieties of English whose distinctive features have become recognized and commented on by the entire country. "Brooklynese," Southern drawl, and Boston accents are frequently depicted (sometimes caricatured) in the media. A third use that he mentions is dialect as a deficient form of English. An example of this would be when the term "three mile" is considered an imperfect attempt to say the correct "three miles." People applying this last meaning perceive dialect differences as mistakes and view them as signs of carelessness or of lack of intelligence. It is this last meaning for dialect with its negative connotations that many people intend when the term "nonstandard dialect" is used.

But *nonstandard* only means different from *standard*, so we need to look at what the words mean in terms of dialect.

What Is Standard Dialect? The dialect referred to as "Standard English" or, more accurately, "Standard American English," (SAE) *is not a single dialect* but actually, "a number of different varieties that qualify as standard" (Wolfram and Christian 1989, p. 13). Communities develop their own norms of what is socially acceptable language use, so what is considered "standard" varies. This can be understood by looking at how SAE operates on the formal and informal levels.

Formal Standard American English is subject to prescription, more similar to the written language of established writers, codified in grammar texts, and espoused in English curricula. There is strong agreement among authorities about what the rules are. Many people believe this form of the language is *the standard*, what is meant by the term "Standard English." However, few people consistently speak Formal Standard English, even those who insist on its use (Wolfram, 1991). Although its norms are not maintained in everyday spoken language, they are observed in written language and in formal speaking situations, such as speeches, job interviews, and professional settings.

Informal Standard American English is a community's norms for socially accepted language usage. This is the form of the language that people actually speak every day. A community's informal norms evolve over time and are a blend of the language use that is modelled, rewarded, and expected by a community's most influential and/or admired members. Who these people are and what norms evolve vary place to place and result in regional variations in terms of pronunciation, vocabulary, and grammar. On this informal level, Standard English is a "pluralistic notion" which recognizes "regional standards" within it (Wolfram 1991, p. 8). These differences in how the Informal Standard is defined in different parts of the country (South, Midwest, Northeast) means there are a number of different dialects of Standard American English. (This fact explains why "Standard English" is often written as "standard English, to recognize this variability.) Judgment is subjective whether someone is perceived as meeting these informal standards and speaks "Standard English." Wolfram (1991, p. 9) observes that SAE is " . . . determined by what it is *not* more than what it is." Informal Standard American English is defined negatively by the avoidance of grammatical features that are socially stigmatized, such as, "'double negatives' (e.g. They didn't do nothing.), different verb agreement patterns (e.g. They's okay.), and different irregular verb forms (e.g. She done it.)."

Vernacular Dialects.   Dialects that are outside of the Informal Standard American English are usually referred to as "nonstandard." Linguists prefer the term **vernacular** to nonstandard because it lacks the defective-deficit connotations often associated with the latter term. There are many vernacular dialects in English, such as Appalachian English, which the linguists refer to as "AVE," Appalachian Vernacular English. Another is Black English, which the linguists identify as "AAVD," African American Vernacular Dialect.

It is important to realize three points that apply to each of the vernacular dialects of English. (1) Linguists do not necessarily agree on what the essential or core structures are; (2) not all speakers of a vernacular dialect use all of its structures; and (3) lack of knowledge about a vernacular dialect contributes to communication problems with speakers of the dialect.

AAVD or Black English is the most widely known and widespread vernacular dialect in the United States. As has been pointed out, African Americans may or may not use AAVD. However, misunderstandings about the linguistic and pragmatic language behavior of African Americans serve as an example of what can happen to other dialect minorities.

Black English is a viable dialect with its own complex rules. Its origin is traceable to the collision of English with the West African languages spoken by the people brought to the United States as slaves. Linguists have studied its phonological and grammatical similarities to West African languages (Weber 1994). Black English shares more similarities with Standard English than differences. The variations are not errors. Problems occur when the rules of one dialect are applied to the other dialect. What is correct in Black English may be incorrect if Standard English's rules are applied.

The problem is not language form, but people's attitudes about particular forms and their subsequent expectations and treatment of speakers of the forms. Consider what your attitudes and judgments are about speakers of other dialects. Think about your own dialect. Teachers are expected to use Standard English in the classroom. What assumptions and judgments have your teachers made about you based on how you speak? Teachers and students all speak English according to the norms that they learned in their respective language communities. The rules may be different, but all dialects deserve respect.

Language Use Is Goal Driven

People speak or choose to remain silent because there is something they want to accomplish. Language is the means to do it. As discussed in chapter 1, purposes may be simple or complex, singular or multiple, or involve short- or long-term goals. Whether conscious or unconscious, goals are accomplished through language. The dynamic interaction of communication is sparked by people trying to meet their individual purposes. The more each person understands the purposes involved (his or hers and the other people's), the more likely responsible and effective communicative choices will be made. Whether people are clear about their goals or not, they will express themselves through whatever verbal behavior they possess.

This connection between purposes and verbal behavior is complex. When teachers focus exclusively on their own instructional purposes, they may not think about students' purposes. Students' psychological and social development affects how self-reflective they are about their or anyone else's purposes. Also, students are still developing their language skills and the level of their development determines how effectively they can communicate their purposes. Differences in norms for verbal behavior between teachers and students can complicate understanding both students' purposes and how they seek to achieve them. Age, experience, and role differences further separate teachers from understanding their students' purposes. Social noise can result.

Teachers need to be clear about their own purposes and ask themselves, "What are my students' goals?" Teachers need to study their students' verbal behavior to answer this question. Once teachers link their students' verbal behavior to how their students achieve goals, a whole new perspective opens up on what goes on in the classroom.

Looking at your goals and the students' goals for overlap can generate speculation about issues like motivation and classroom management. These connections will be explored in chapter 6, "Communicating Interpersonally."

These characteristics apply to all verbal behavior. Keep them in mind as you read the rest of the chapter. The next section deals with the linguistic aspects of verbal behavior.

Linguistic Dimensions of Verbal Behavior

Let's consider language form from a practical standpoint: what you need to know about it to understand your students' language and to improve your own verbal communication. We will examine each level of language structuring: phonology, semantics, and grammar.

Phonology

Every language is made up of **phonemes**, the smallest units of sound, that are used in various combinations to form words. Each language's sound system is unique. Languages are described by how many sounds and which sounds they contain. English has approximately forty-three sounds, while Spanish has about twenty-four (Naremore and Hopper 1990). Languages may or may not share sounds. English and Spanish both have the sound represented by the letter "p" in English. Spanish does not distinguish between the phonemes "sh" and "ch," although English does (Bassett and Smythe 1979).

Regional and social dialects may have the same number of phonemes but have different rules for using and combining sounds. For example, in Black English, the second of two sounds in some final consonant clusters is deleted (Owens 1992). The word "desk" would be said "des": "test" is "tes"; "bend" is "ben."

Linguistic universals are the ways all languages are the same. Their existence demonstrates humans' biological and cognitive predisposition to learn language. Some linguistic universals are phonological. All languages differentiate between sound contrasts, such as between vowels and consonants, use syllables, and draw from the same set of sounds (Naremore and Hopper 1990). All babies are capable of producing all sounds. They start making the universal contrasts and then specialize in the distinctive features of their native language. For example, voicing is a distinctive feature in English. A sound is voiced if the vocal cords vibrate when the sound is being made. English has more voiced sounds than any other language: b, d, g, v, th (as in these, those), z (as in buzz, ease), zh (as in measure, inclusion), j (as in fudge, gem, just), m, n, ng (words ending in ing), and the glides kw (as in queen, quest), y (as in young, cute, beyond), r, and l (Glenn, Glenn, and Forman 1989). The sounds children do not use drop away and become harder to produce as they get older. By three to five years of age, children can produce most phonemes in their language accurately (Allen and Brown 1976).

As was mentioned in chapter 1, phonological noise happens when there are unexpected differences in articulation and pronunciation. The result is people are not sure what is being said. It is important to understand the difference between these two terms: *articulation* is the formation of sounds in a language; *pronunciation* is the saying of a word in the manner acceptable to the speaker's language community.

Phonological Noise. Differences in articulation, pronunciation, or both, can cause phonological noise. It is important to distinguish whether a phonological difference is due to dialect or language or is a problem needing speech therapy. Let's look at some examples:

1. A friend's young daughter is having trouble making the sounds represented by the letters "r" and "l." English is the language spoken in the home. She is still in the process of learning to articulate English sounds.
2. Students who are native speakers of English lisp. They have not learned to correctly make the sounds represented by the letters s and z. They have an articulation problem.
3. A student pronounces the vowel sounds in "leave" and "live" the same way. The child's native language is Spanish. Spanish does not distinguish between these sounds (Naremore and Hopper 1990). Phonological rules from Spanish are interfering with English rules.
4. "Help" sounds like "hep." "Cold" sounds like "code." The student is from the South. In parts of the South, "l" is omitted before plosive sounds (p,b, k, g, d, or t). The words are being correctly pronounced according to the rules of the dialect.
5. A student of mine gave a speech on deaf education. Every time he said the word "deaf" it sounded like "death." It is a characteristic of Black English to substitute "th" for "f" at the end of a word. He was pronouncing the word correctly according to the rules of Black English. Since he could pronounce "f" when it appeared elsewhere in a word, he did not have an articulation problem.
6. Students drop "g" at the ends of words. Standard and nonstandard dialect rules vary in formality-informality according to the situation. The dropping of endings is characteristic of informal situations for both dialects.

Many people deal with phonological noise, when it involves a heavy accent, by smiling and pretending to understand. Their intentions may be not to embarrass the person, but it is a self-defeating strategy. The other person will realize he or she is not being understood and may stop attempting to communicate or may even avoid the person to prevent uncomfortable situations. It is more constructive to ask for help when you cannot understand. If you are the one with the accent, help your students: repeat words or phrases, slow the rate at which you speak, use visual aids. Students and teachers can become accustomed to accents with time.

Since the public expects teachers to have good articulation and pronunciation, you need to think about your own speech on the phonological level. Is what you do phonologically going to be an asset to your teaching, or a barrier? A sophomore education major in one of my classes could not articulate "r." He was a native speaker of English, but he consistently substituted "w" for "r." Young students might copy his pronunciation. Older students would probably make fun of him. I suggested he change his major or get speech therapy. (He chose the latter.) On the other hand, I had a friend from south Texas who went to teach in Philadelphia. Her elementary students were entranced by her accent and hung on her every word.

Semantics

All languages have their own *lexicon*, and dialects also have some unique words. The process of learning the words of a language community and their adult level meanings is a life-long process. Words come into a person's vocabulary based on functional need. Toddlers and young children pick up words to describe people and things in their immediate physical environment. A word, initially, is the thing it stands for. Words are not used symbolically. With time and experience, word meanings develop horizontally and vertically. Meaning expands horizontally as new semantic dimensions are added making the definition more specific. A definition expands vertically as additional meanings are learned. Hulit and Howard (1993) use the example of "crack." When a child first learns the word, it may name a particular opening. Semantic dimensions are added until crack means a fissure occurring anywhere. Eventually, other meanings are learned, such as hit, lose control, to open, quip, attempt, and cocaine.

The acquisition of new words and the expansion of meanings go on rapidly during the school years. Vocabulary grows and meanings multiply. Most dramatic is the shift from concrete, literal meanings to symbolic, abstract meanings. As this shift occurs, children discover and become intrigued with word play, such as codes, puns, and riddles. Older children understand and use figurative language, such as metaphors, similes, idioms, and proverbs. A word is like a pebble being dropped into a lake. A word enters the vocabulary and each meaning adds another ripple with the ripples expanding outward.

Semantic Noise. The semantics of any particular person depends on his or her language background and experiences. Teachers, as adults, have different meanings from their students. The more diverse the students are, the more variation there will be in their meanings relative to each other. As stated in chapter 1, semantic noise happens when speakers and listeners do not have the same meanings. We, or our students, can create semantic noise by failing to think about words and meanings from our listeners' point of view.

As teachers, we need to be alert to potential sources of semantic noise, so we can avoid generating it, recognize it when it occurs, and rectify it.

Development. Have you ever had a teacher who talked over your head? If so, then you have experienced a teacher using words without thinking of the developmental level of students. "Development" applies in two senses of the word. First, children may not have encountered the word yet or only have literal meanings for it. A student of mine recalled his fifth grade teacher coming up behind him and saying, "I'll break your other arm [one was broken at the time] if you don't stop that." He said he was afraid of his teacher the rest of the year.

Second, teachers use jargon which their students do not understand. **Jargon** is technical or specialized terminology used by a business, profession, or special interest group. The field of education and each subject have specialized language. Teachers are so familiar with the terms that they use them, forgetting to explain them. Jargon can also become a barrier in talking to parents. Imagine what parents might think if a teacher said, "Your child has dyslexia," and did not explain what it meant. It sounds like a disease. Think about some terms specific to your teaching fields that students or their parents may not understand.

Dialect Differences. Dialects develop distinctive vocabularies that reflect the culture of the people who speak them. Each dialect has terms which are unique to it. There may be differences in "content words" (words which carry primary semantic reference, such as pop, tonic, and soda), or the same content words may be used differently. For example, in one dialect you would "carry" someone (as in escort), while in another you would "take." There are also differences in "function words," words that carry grammatical information, such as prepositions and articles. For example, depending on the dialect, someone with a stomach ache would be sick to, at, in, or on the stomach (Wolfram and Christian 1989).

Dialectal differences can affect instruction. Shirley Brice Heath (1983), an anthropologist, did an ethnographic study of the language use in a middle-class town and its two adjacent working class communities, one white (Roadville) and the other black (Tracton). Heath found many differences in communication between the Roadville and Tracton children that reflected their community's use and value of language. The attitudes and communication patterns of the townspeople, who were black and white, had more in common with each other than with either of the two communities. The differences in what "story" and "storytelling" mean illustrate how these language differences manifest themselves in school. For children from Tracton the best stories were "junk," which included exaggeration and imaginative embellishment. Stories were valued for entertainment and verbal display. For children from Roadville, however, a story was "a piece of the truth." Stories were straightforward, factual accounts about self or others, which were told for the purpose of making fun. Think of how each group of children might respond to a teacher's asking them to write or tell a story. One group might view the other as boring, while the other group viewed them as liars.

Slang. Informal words sharing the following characteristics are considered **slang**: identification with a particular group, replaces a conventional term, and meanings have a short life span. The group may be a class, a school, a neighborhood, an age group, or even a generation. Slang facilitates communication within a group, defining the membership and reinforcing identification of members with the group. It also prevents being understood by nonmembers, who do not know the terms. Slang is a verbal short-cut that works like a code. Members can communicate clearly among themselves, yet keep outsiders from knowing what they mean.

As a teacher, you need to think about slang in terms of yourself and your students. There are two reasons why you should not use slang in the classroom. First, the slang you used when you were your students' age will not fit. Even if some of the words are the same, the meanings will be different. Second, teachers' and students' different roles make slang inappropriate for teachers to use. The classroom is a formal speaking situation for teachers, who are there in a professional capacity. Teachers are expected to provide a model of more formal language usage.

However, you should try to understand students' slang because it will help you to understand them better. As you get to know your students, they will likely translate for you or respond to your asking what words mean. Since many slang terms are adopted from the popular culture, you may be able to learn the meanings from viewing your students' favorite television shows, movies, or rock videos.

Verbal Traps. Some uses of language limit possible meanings, creating barriers between communicators. These uses negatively affect perception, listening, expectations, and interpersonal relationships. We need to recognize when others use these language traps and avoid using them ourselves. We also need to help our students identify and avoid them. Here are the most common traps with some suggestions of how to avoid them and how to counter them when others use them:

- *Allness.* This kind of statement uses extreme language implying complete knowledge. Allness statements sound definitive. They are signalled by words like "always" and "never." The antidote is "etc." Ask, "What else can be said about the topic?" Allness statements are punctured by any evidence to the contrary.

- *Bi-polar Thinking.* This kind of statement sets up either or categories, such as good/bad, smart/stupid, and positive/negative. Bi-polar statements divide up reality into two extremes, instead of permitting its infinite variety. This kind of thinking is being used when people label language as good or bad. Language is a system of symbols. Words do not have inherent value. The relevant criterion is appropriateness. Ask, "How appropriate is the language for this situation, topic, purpose, and the people involved?" The antidote for bi-polar thinking is everything that actually exists between the two extreme choices.

- *Static Evaluation.* This occurs when verbal statements made about people and objects remain the same, although the people or objects have changed. The antidote is to "date" statements. Dating means to be specific about when the statement occurred. "Leslie is poor in math" is a static evaluation. "Leslie did poorly in math during the first grading period" is a dated evaluation.

- *Stereotyping.* Words are symbols representing categories that share characteristics. Stereotyping occurs when we apply the meaning for a category to each instance of the category. In other words, generalities are involved, not what is unique about the person, object, or event. Stereotypes may be positive or negative. Teachers are often stereotyped in positive ways. Teachers are educated, smart, poised, and so forth. Minority groups are usually stereotyped in negative ways. The antidote is "indexing." Indexing accounts for individual differences. "Students are lazy" is a stereotyped statement. "Most of my students do not do their homework" is an indexed statement.

Grammar

All languages and dialects have their own grammar. Grammar involves two levels of organization. One level involves how words are formed from their meaningful parts, which are called **morphemes.** The word "girls" has two morphemes: girl and the plural suffix "s." Some morphemes change meaning (derivational suffixes like "er"), while others augment meaning (inflectional suffixes like plural "s"). Some languages rely heavily on inflectional endings on nouns, verbs, and modifiers, such as German, Russian, and Latin. English has a small number. According to Wolfram (1991), they are: plural "s," possessive "s," third person present tense "s," past tense "ed," participle "ed" (have help*ed*), progressive "ing," and comparatives (small*er*, small*est*). The second level of organization is **syntax**, how phrases and clauses are structured. Syntax is made evident through word order in English.

Most of the basic principles of grammar are acquired by the age of four or five (Naremore and Hopper 1990). Meaningful utterances start with one word and grow in the direction of length and complexity. Early development goes through a process of rule induction and differentiation. Children learn a new grammatical rule when they have some new meaning and need to find a way to differentiate and express it (Naremore and Hopper 1990). A rule is induced, such as "ed" for past tense. It is overgeneralized and applied to all verbs such as: I walked, I goed, I jumped, I runned. In response to feedback, differentiation occurs, and new rules are formed. Then "ed" is used appropriately for regular verbs, and irregular past tense forms are acquired. Exceptions to general rules and complex transformations are not mastered until ten or twelve and are believed to be acquired through imitation and modeling (Naremore and Hopper 1990).

Grammatical Noise. When communicators are using different grammatical rules, grammatical noise occurs. The noise may result from interference of rules from another language or dialect. In the case of another language, you accommodate by translating the sense of the sentence, so you understand its meaning. Since dialects of English are only variations of English, the grammatical differences should not interfere with comprehension. You can study the dialect to become familiar with its rules through listening to your students, asking your students questions when you do not understand the meaning of a construction, and reading research on the dialect.

As an example of variations between dialects, let's look at some of the different rules for Standard American English (SAE) and Black English (BE) (Hulit and Howard 1993).

- The two dialects differ on what rules are obligatory. In SAE, plurality must be indicated by adding "s," while in BE you may add "s" or indicate the amount. The result is "I have two dogs" vs. "I have two dog." In SAE, possession must be indicated by adding "'s." In BE, possession is understood if the possessor is identified. The difference would be "This is Chris's dog" vs. "This is Chris dog."

- Some irregular rules in SAE are regular in BE. In SAE, the third person singular form of a verb differs from first and second person (I talk, you talk, he or she talks). In BE, the third person form is regularized, so all three forms are the same (I talk, you talk, she or he talk).

- The rules differ for using "be" to signal habitual or infrequent action. BE makes a distinction between whether an action or event is frequent and presently occurring ("He be talking") or rare but presently occurring ("He talking."). SAE makes the distinction with an adverb ("She is talking" vs. "She is always talking.")

Dialects in the Schools

There is controversy about what schools should do about vernacular dialects. Most people agree that facility with the standard dialect is necessary for students' job access and social acceptability in the mainstream society. The disagreement comes over what to do and when to do it. Some teachers *correct* every instance of nonstandard speech. Since grammatical and phonological rules are acquired at home before students enter school, correcting students according to rules they may not have learned or become proficient with is confusing and ineffective.

Another approach is treating Standard English as a second dialect and teaching students the similarities and differences between the dialects. This approach respects the students' language from home and makes sense from a communicative perspective. Each dialect is accepted as appropriate in certain situations, depending upon the participants, goals, and topics. The significant differences between the rule systems are identified for students, and the standard dialect is learned like a second language. The popular TV program, *60 Minutes* (March 5, 1995), reported on school programs using this approach with Black English in New York, Chicago, and Los Angeles. In a pilot program in the Los Angeles school system, sixteen hundred teachers and paraprofessionals went to workshops and seminars on language and cultural issues to learn about Black English (Schnaiberg 1994). As one fifth grader explained, he uses dialect with his friends because if he used Standard English, "They be thinking like you a nerd" (Schnaiberg 1994, p. 18). He said he wants to learn Standard English, so he can "switch up" like his dad and go to college.

Dialect, no matter what it is, is the vehicle that carries people's meaning. Form gives shape to verbal substance—content, what people do with language. In the next section, we will look at the practical uses of language.

Pragmatic Dimensions of Verbal Behavior

Pragmatics draws together role behavior, communication skills, and the purposive nature of language use. The cycle—role expectations, goals, appropriate communication behaviors—is repeated every time we enter a communicative interaction. Children learn to perform appropriate pragmatic behaviors (who says what to whom, when, how, and under what circumstances) to succeed in the roles expected of them. They learn how to use language to meet goals important to them, such as winning the approval (love, attention) or not precipitating the anger (or apathy) of caregivers. They learn to perform **communication acts**, which are pragmatic units of discourse, within the "web of customs" of their speech community, according to traditions of "how things are done around here" (Naremore and Hopper 1990, p. 109). Which communication acts are learned and how they are performed are defined by the referent group's pragmatics. What children learn forms their personal stockpile of pragmatic rules, their repertoire of possible behaviors. When they move beyond the home into new settings, like school, they communicate with what is in their repertoire.

New settings mean new people, probably new roles, and possibly new, different expectations for appropriate pragmatic behavior. Survival and success in the new situation means figuring out what is expected and effectively performing the appropriate communication acts. This may involve learning variations on old pragmatic rules or learning entirely new rules. The more help people have in understanding what is expected and how to perform effectively, the more likely they will be judged positively. This is true throughout our lives, but has special impact on students in classrooms. Teachers need to be careful of what assumptions they make about their students' communicative behavior. Teachers also need to identify for students the pragmatic norms they expect in their classrooms. Teachers should promote the practice of any necessary communication acts before they judge or evaluate students by how well they perform.

As teachers, you need to consider students' repertoires of pragmatic behaviors for two reasons. First, if you want to communicate more effectively with your students, you need to interpret their verbal behavior from their perspective of appropriateness. You need to understand the pragmatic rules of their language communities. Students who call out may simply be doing what they have learned is appropriate, not being rude or defiant.

Second, you need to think about what kind of communicating you will ask students to do. Learning pragmatics is a life-long process of developing communication competence, that is, how to use language appropriately in all kinds of social contexts. Competence is characterized by four components (Allen and Brown 1976):

- a repertoire of communication skills to accomplish the communication acts required in the social environment;
- selection criteria for choosing strategies from the repertoire (appropriateness is gauged according to the setting, participants, purpose, and topic);
- implementing the strategy;
- evaluating the results.

As competence grows, more informed judgments are made about one's own communication. These judgments influence future strategic choices, implementation, and enlarge the repertoire (Allen and Brown 1976).

Your expectations for the roles students are to play in your classroom define what they will learn about pragmatics. We learn to communicate by communicating. When roles are restricted, communication learning is restricted. For example, if the student role is restricted to listening to the teacher, then success depends on how well they are silent. If roles are elaborated in terms of numbers and flexibility, then communication learning and practice expands. Think of what students would be doing in terms of communicating if their roles included the following expectations: explainer, decision maker, questioner, discussant, team member, storyteller, and problem solver.

The learning of pragmatics is a result of social interaction and begins in infancy, as does language learning. Parents frequently remark that their babies respond differently to the father than they do to the mother. Small children vary how they speak according to whom they are speaking (parent, a sibling, a toy). They also speak differently to the same person under different circumstance (Naremore and Hopper 1990). Between the ages of three and five, children use a variety of strategies to engage adults in conversation (Allen and Brown 1976).

Also, their conversational skills are interactive, spontaneous, and follow conventionalized patterns (Allen and Brown 1976).

A crucial element in becoming an effective communicator develops during the school years: the **dual perspective**. Children become less egocentric and more sociocentric in their thinking and communicating. They are able to behave symbolically toward others. This means they can place themselves in the position or state of mind of other people and take their thoughts, feelings, and responses into account when communicating (Phillips, Butt, and Metzger 1974). A dual perspective simultaneously encompasses your own *and* other people's perspectives. Research reports the emergence of communicative behaviors related to the development of dual perspective. Allen and Brown, (1976, pp. 182–85) report the development by children's ages:

- three to five—adapt their language to listeners, try on roles, engage in dramatic play;
- five to nine—empathize, interact in appropriate interpersonal communication roles, use these roles to reach personal goals, and infer other people's thoughts and feelings;
- nine to twelve—"answer questions from a variety of perspectives" (p. 184), and use a variety of persuasive ploys;
- twelve to eighteen—decide what to say and how to say it to aid understanding, give feedback, adjust message to perceived feedback, respond to listeners' needs, and conceptualize thought (theirs and others').

A dual perspective is not automatic, nor is it always positive. It is a potentiality, not a given. Its development depends on whether a person experiences it. We learn what is available to be learned. What a person does with the perspective depends on personality, goals, and personal ethics. While people operating from this perspective may be more considerate or reasonable, they might also use it to manipulate or to take advantage of others.

Communication Functions

The essence of pragmatics is that language is used functionally—to do something. All the separate little communication acts we perform can be grouped according to five major functions: informing, controlling, expressing feeling, imagining, and ritualizing.[1] These functions apply to you, as teacher, and to your students in and out of the classroom.

Use the functions to analyze communicative behavior, your own and your students': "What is the function of the communication act? How effectively is it being accomplished?" Use them to think about communicative growth in terms of breadth (develop more ways to do a function); and depth (make finer, more appropriate distinctions in choosing and executing strategies to accomplish the functions). "How can I help my students discover more effective ways to accomplish a function? What questions can I ask that will help them be more reflective about their communicative choices?"

In using these functions, keep several points in mind: (1) The functions are both active and receptive. Teachers and students need strategies to do the functions and also to react to someone's else's doing them. (2) Any particular utterance generally simultaneously involves more than one function. For example, a teacher gives a report to the PTA on an upcoming fundraiser (informing), meets the expectations for a speech (ritualizing), and tries to motivate parents to volunteer (controlling). (3) How people execute communication acts varies according to the pragmatic rules they have learned. This has positive and negative consequences. We can all learn to appreciate differences in pragmatic styles and to be more effective by observing others. However, students may be uncomfortable or intimidated when different pragmatic rules affect how communication acts are done or produce new communication acts. Teachers need to be alert to social and psychological noise generated by different pragmatic rules. They need to bridge the gaps, so students understand each other better.

"Call and Response" is an example of different pragmatics leading to different definitions of appropriate listening behavior. The African-American culture views speakers and listeners as co-participants unified by the speaking event. The speaker's "statements ('calls') are punctuated by expressions ('responses') from the listener" (Smitherman 1977, p. 104). Listeners' spontaneous verbal and nonverbal responses indicate agreement and encouragement. Both parties talk and listen, giving each other feedback to gauge effectiveness (Weber 1994). This kind of participatory listening is viewed as necessary, positive, and encouraging. However, for groups whose cultural pragmatic rules define good listening as silence, the continual feedback is perceived as interruptions.

Informing. These are communication acts seeking to give or get information. These acts include behaviors such as stating information, questioning, answering, justifying, naming, pointing out an object, demonstrating, explaining, and acknowledging (Allen and Brown 1976). Much of students' and teachers' communicating in the classroom involves seeking, giving, or sharing information. For example, students working in a small group to research a topic are seeking information and then must determine what it means. When teachers give directions for an assignment, their talk functions to inform. When students ask questions seeking information, teachers need ways to answer simply and directly.

Controlling. These are communication acts attempting to influence the thought or behaviors of others. These acts include behaviors such as commanding, offering, suggesting, permitting, threatening, warning, prohibiting, contracting, refusing, bargaining, rejecting, acknowledging, justifying, persuading, arguing, nagging, convincing (Allen and Brown 1976; Bassett and Smythe 1979).

Some experts view persuasion as central to the teaching-learning process. Teachers reach their educational goals by helping students achieve their goals (Phillips, Butt, and Metzger 1974). Teachers spend time motivating (persuading) students about the relevance of assignments, homework, the subject, and school. Students try to persuade teachers about many things: not to give homework, to change due dates, to modify assignments, to allow work to be turned in late, and to raise grades. Students try to persuade each other that they are socially "with it." Teachers need to be sensitive to what strategies they and their students use to persuade each other.

"Rap" is an African-American communicative act that has spread to the popular culture. The content of a rap may vary: to give information, persuade, introduce oneself to a woman, or entertain through music with a message (Kochman 1981). However, the basic function remains the same for the rapper. Dandy (1990) notes that he or she seeks a position of control and to impress the listener through rhythmic verbal display; rap is highly stylized, accompanied by gestures, movement, vocal effects, and flamboyant language; it follows a call-response pattern; and a good rap elicits an overt response, such as a smile, handshake, applause, or consent. Depending on whether a listener understands the act's function, a rap may be viewed as bragging or appreciated for its artistic merits.

Expressing Feeling. This function includes behaviors such as exclaiming, responding, expressing, taunting, praising, commiserating, tale telling, blaming, disagreeing, and rejecting (Allen and Brown 1976). Sadness, happiness, liking, dislike, excitement, fear and anger need to be included in the spectrum of feelings. People, who can easily see informing and controlling functions to be the business of classrooms, often do not understand how feelings come into play. Some people remember only negative feelings expressed by teachers, such as scolding or expressing disappointment or disapproval. The positive expression and acceptance of feelings are important in the development of self-concept, interpersonal relationships, and the classroom climate.

Children and adolescents need to learn to understand, express, and respond appropriately to their feelings and those of other people. "Psychological noise," which was discussed in chapter 1, may involve feelings generated within the classroom or brought in from other situations. Often students are confused about how to deal with their feelings or appropriately express themselves because of their exposure to violence in society, the decline or absence of clear standards of behavior, and media role models. The news media continually report stories of students who get angry and resort to violence against other students, teachers, or community members. Clearly, these students need help in learning how to express anger appropriately and to resolve problems peaceably. Violent neighborhoods and dysfunctional families produce feelings that students may need help in understanding.

Teachers need to remember how their expression of feelings affects students as individuals and sets the tone of the emotional climate within their classrooms. Teachers need to be professional in their expression of feelings about students. Teachers, like other professionals such as doctors and lawyers, may not like all of the people with whom they must deal, but they are obligated to treat them with respect.

Imagining. These communication acts cast participants in imaginary situations. These acts include such behaviors as role-playing, fantasizing, speculating, dramatizing, theorizing, and storytelling (Allen and Brown 1976). This function occurs whenever an imaginative leap is made from Point A to Point B.

Bassett and Smythe (1979) suggest this function is activated by other functions, since they involve an element of simulation or some imaginary component. Note the following examples. A student answers a factual geography question (informing function), and then the teacher responds with a speculative "what if" question (imaginative function). If Chris were trying to persuade Pat to lend homework (controlling function), Chris would need to imagine reasons that would make sense to Pat. Telling your fellow student teachers how you feel about student teaching (informing function) involves you in storytelling and, perhaps, dramatizing.

Ritualizing. These communication acts serve to facilitate social interaction and to maintain social relationships. These acts include such behaviors as greeting, taking leave, participating in verbal games, reciting, turn-taking in conversation, participating in culturally appropriate speech modes (teasing, praying, punning, playing the dozens), and demonstrating socially appropriate amenities (Wood 1977).

Wood's list refers to social rituals in the broad sense of society, but teachers need to think of the rituals they need to establish in order to facilitate and maintain relationships in their classroom. Classroom rituals are part of classroom management. Right now, make a mental list of the rituals you have experienced in classrooms. Now, think about how you felt about them as a student. Which ones do you think you will keep? Why? What rituals do you want to add? It is important not to assume that students will automatically know what rituals you expect or how to do them. Other teachers may require different rituals in their classrooms. Be clear about what you expect. Explain the whats, the whys, and the hows of the classroom rituals you expect. Give students chances to practice. When your students change classes, allow time daily for them to shift mentally from the rituals expected in their previous classes to those you expect.

These functions represent what people do with language. The next section looks at students who do not do anything with it: the quiet ones, the silent students.

Quiet Students

People who habitually choose silence or avoid communicating are called many things—shy, communication apprehensive, and reticent. Although each term represents a different point of view on the problem of communication avoidance, the terms overlap (Kelly 1982). "Shyness" emphasizes lack of self-confidence and inadequate social skills. "Communication apprehension" (CA) underscores fear or anxiety of either real or anticipated communication. "Reticence" stresses the lack of adequate communication skills.

All quiet students are silent and avoid communicating. It is helpful to ask about each quiet student: "Why is silence being used? Does quietness interfere with his or her life? Does it represent a choice from among the student's communication strategies, or is it the only strategy in a student's repertoire of skills?" In other words, is the student choosing to be silent or does the silence control the student? When silence is a strategic choice, then the student is not reticent or shy or CA. If the student is trapped in a pattern of avoidance and silence, then the student has a problem.

In order to understand your quiet students, think of all the possible reasons they might not talk. In learning verbal behavior, people learn what is available to be learned and what is reinforced. Students raised with the dictum, "Children should be seen and not heard," learn to be quiet. Quiet parents tend to have quiet children. If students' roles are restricted in their home and community, then they lack opportunities to develop their communication skills. For students who were labelled shy, expectations for shyness affected how they defined themselves and how others interacted with them, producing a self-fulfilling prophecy. Restricted roles in the classroom may have thwarted development of communication skills. Previous teachers, who believed "a good student is a quiet student," may have rewarded silence. Disruptive students or classes that were too large may have prevented teachers from soliciting or promoting talk. Students whose communicative efforts have been punished learn they are inept and communicating is painful. Reticent college students with whom I have worked often point to some personally traumatic event which they believe was the starting point of their problem. Often, the scene is in school and in front of a class. The event caused them to avoid communicative situations when they could and choose silence when they could not. In this way, they hindered themselves from developing appropriate communication skills.

There are also social and psychological reasons students may be quiet. Students' cultural background may not value certain communicative strategies that are routine in classrooms, such as speaking out and having everyone's attention focused on you individually. If students feel different or are alienated from their classmates, they may be quiet. Minority students may experience school as threatening to their personal identity. Lujan et al. (1987) reported that Native American students, for whom active participation represented assimilation into non-Native American culture, maintained personal balance by remaining aloof, separate, and silent. Other students may be silent due to feelings of inadequacy about their ability in your subject or apathy toward school. Students may be silent because participation in class is not viewed as "cool" by their peers.

Whatever the reasons for the quietness, it is necessary to gain an understanding of quiet students' pragmatic communication skills: First ask yourself, "Can students use language appropriately to accomplish their goals when they want to?" Then ask yourself, "How do I distinguish between students with adequate communication skills, who choose not to talk, and students with inadequate skills, who cannot handle themselves through talk? Am I dealing with a motivation problem, social or psychological noise, or a pragmatic skill problem?" To get students actively involved in their own learning, teachers need to identify who has which difficulty.

Although there are self-report scales that ask questions about anxious feelings in general situations, the best method to identify why students are quiet is to observe and be sensitive to students' interactions over a period of time. Kelly, Phillips, and McKinney (1982) state the most effective identification method is a combination of the person's self-perception of a communication problem and the confirmation of this problem by observation. Of course, the age of students and their self-awareness will affect whether they realize silence is their habitual response and/or perceive it as a problem. Thus, identification of the problem through self-perception may not always be an option. Yet, teachers have professional training, an adult perspective, and the opportunity to observe students' interactions throughout the school year. Observant teachers can listen, watch, and even discuss with the student the reasons for the silence.

Teacher Observation. Use the following suggestions to guide your observations of quiet students. Remember, the goal is to understand what the pattern of communication avoidance means in the particular case, so you know how to respond appropriately.

1. Observe students' nonverbal behavior when they are confronted with communicative interaction. Do they look comfortable and relaxed?

2. What is the nature of their interaction with peers? Do they initiate and respond to talk with classmates? Do classmates like them and pay attention to them? Do they have friends? Do they actively participate in small group work with peers?

3. What is the nature of their interaction in class? Do they volunteer either questions or comments? If so, when and on what topics? Do they respond when called on? Do they begin and then quit? Are they apologetic about what they have said? Do they talk about how nervous they feel? If so, in what setting (whole class, small group) and with what topics?

4. Do they communicate differently outside the classroom in other settings with other people? Do students demonstrate a variety of communication skills with peers outside the classroom? with other adults, such as coaches, other teachers, or parents?

5. Listen to what the students say about their own communication. Do they make disparaging remarks or negatively label themselves ("I'm shy." "I know what I mean, but it didn't come out right." "That was dumb.")? Do they make excuses for not talking ("I'm a good listener." "They aren't worth talking to." "Everybody talks better.")?

6. Find out about the students' background. What are the pragmatic norms for verbal interaction in their background (social, national origin, religious, ethnic)? Are there conflicts between these norms and the classroom talk tasks? (For example, is it inappropriate to speak out individually when situated in a group vs. each person should have the opportunity to speak out in a group or class setting?)

7. Talk with the parents or caregivers to understand what communication skills they model for the students.

Skills Training. When quietness is related to not being able to handle communicative situations, then skills training is necessary. People, no matter what their age, who cannot accomplish their goals through talk are usually frustrated, undervalued, and isolated. Students may know they are ineffective but not know what to do differently. Consequently, they often have negative attitudes about themselves as communicators and are nervous about communicating. Once they start developing their communication skills, they get more positive responses from others. Success with one goal leads to confidence to try other goals. They start to see the connections among preparation, practice, competence, and confidence. Their attitudes and feelings about communicating become more positive, and their nervousness decreases.

Gerald Phillips (1991) developed a method for skills training that can be adapted to any age student. The method is goal specific and focuses on pragmatic communication behaviors. The student chooses a personally meaningful goal and learns how to do the subprocesses involved in effective communication: set clear goals; understand situational norms and the needs/goals of others; adapt the message to the audience; actually speak; and fairly assess the results. This method of preparation provides strategies for achieving appropriate and effective communication likely to effect a positive response from others and serves as a model for how to accomplish other goals.

The method may be used in a variety of ways in a classroom setting. You might work with one student; you might have a small group of students work on personal goals that are similar, such as those involving social rituals or class participation. It is possible to have several small groups, each of which is composed of people working on similar goals. You might want to work with the whole class on one goal that is problematic for all of the students.

Let's see how the skills training model is applied to a common communication problem for many students, "I don't want people to think I'm dumb when I talk in class."

> **Step I: Write a behavioral goal.** Rewrite this fuzzy wish into a realistic, behavioral goal from the student's viewpoint (Mager 1972). The statement should include where, when, with whom, and the duration of the goal. "I want to ask (or it could be answer) one question in class on Friday." The specific number of questions (in this case, one) should be realistic from the student's perspective. For a reticent student, one may be one more than he or she has ever asked. For another student, the meaningful goal might be two or more.

Step II: State criteria for success. Write a list of criteria that defines for the student what successful achievement of the goal looks like. Include message delivery strategies and behaviors that the student can control. The list should include what to do and what to avoid, such as: ask the question, speak loud enough so the teacher does not ask me to repeat, look at the teacher when speaking, and don't slouch.

Step III: Prepare and practice. List what must be done to prepare for and implement the goal. Preparation is where the situation, topic, and other people are analyzed and taken into account; norms must be understood; expectations and needs must be met. Getting ready usually involves such activities as observation, discussion, preparing questions, modeling, role-playing, and practice. How much effort should be put into each activity is a pedagogical decision based on your circumstances and the student's response. Think of the following activities as a menu of possibilities for your students.

1. Answer the following questions: What is a good question? How do you know when you have asked a good question? Observe classmates asking questions and how the teacher responds. Study the material to be covered in order to have substance for questions.

2. Practice phrasing clear questions.

3. Write out several questions that could be used from which one will be chosen on Friday.

4. Read the planned questions out loud to hear how they sound, revising as necessary for clarity.

5. Use the questions in role-plays with other students (playing the roles of both student and the teacher).

6. Practice asking questions in settings outside the classroom to gain confidence in the role of questioner.

7. Write out a detailed description of what he or she will actually do the day the goal is attempted. (This visualization helps the student feel prepared.)

Step IV: Plan for contingencies. Imagine what is the worst, best, and most likely outcome and plan a response. This step helps the student be more realistic and defuses anxiety. A student might anticipate the worst scenario as the other students laughing. The student's response to this might be to force him- or herself to ignore the laughter and remember that the question was clear and relevant despite the laughter. The best outcome might be applause and the teacher calling the question brilliant.

The student's response would probably be to smile and enjoy it. The most likely response is the teacher will listen to the question and answer it or redirect it to the class. The student's response is relief.

Step V: Attempt the goal and assess the outcome. The student checks what actually occurred in implementing the goal against the criteria from Step II to determine success. The student reflects on the process of doing the goal to determine which strategies can be used for other goals. If not all of the criteria were met, the student analyzes why and plans what to do differently the next time a question needs to be asked. The student might want to continue working on this goal area by increasing the number of questions, changing the setting, adding the goal of answering questions, or some combination of possibilities.

Cognitive Restructuring. As students learn new skills, they often need help in changing their *self-talk*—what they say about themselves, about their communicating, and their attitudes and beliefs about communicating. Making such changes is known as **cognitive restructuring**. Negative self-talk needs to be substituted with supportive, reasonable self-talk. Students need to recognize the verbal traps they spring on themselves, such as statements of allness ("I always mess up.") and static evaluation ("I ask dumb questions."). Then they need to make fair statements about their performance. "My question yesterday was not clear, but today it was."

Mistaken ideas about communication need to be replaced with accurate information. For example, students need to know communication is a transaction between people, and they cannot control the behavior of another person. They may speak well, yet get a negative response. Students need to realize that people are focused on their own goals and how they are being perceived, rather than worried about judging other people. Students also need to develop an appreciation of nervousness as a normal, healthy response to being asked to do something they do not know how to do or think they cannot do well. Learning anything means going from the known, which is comfortable, to the unknown, which is risky and tension inducing. As coaches and directors know, learning performance behaviors is possible no matter what barriers the feelings might be creating. "People learn to respond to their tensions by involvement in practice and rehearsal" (Phillips 1991, p. 229). Even proficient people respond with nerves when something is important to them, as famous entertainers (musicians, actors, speakers) and professional athletes attest.

Skills training and cognitive restructuring are ways to work with reticent students. Friedman suggests the best treatment for reticence is to prevent its occurrence, ". . . to alter the conditions under which this problem is likely to develop" (1980, p. 20). In the next section, we will look at ways to make the classroom a more interactive place.

Tips for a Talk Friendly Environment

Recognize the conditions under which people of all ages feel comfortable to talk: they have something they want to say, someone they are comfortable with who wants to listen, the opportunity to say it, a place conducive to talk, and enough time to say it. You need to think about your classroom's communication comfort zone from the point of view of your students. Think back to your classroom experience. What did your teachers do to make it inviting to talk? Here are some suggestions.

1. Create as many opportunities as possible for students to talk. Meaningful talk aids thinking and learning and develops communication skills and confidence. The more chances each student has to speak, the less it matters if a particular response is wrong or unclear or a student has nothing to say at that moment.

2. Get to know your students. Learn names and use them. Do your homework and learn about their backgrounds. Become informed about linguistic and pragmatic differences, so you can avoid or compensate for linguistic and social noise as much as possible (yours and the students).

3. Set up clear norms for classroom interaction, so students know what is ruled in and out. Everyone should be expected to be an active participant. Each person should be listened to with respect and be expected to show respect to everyone else. Interrupting, ignoring, name-calling, and belittling are unacceptable. Students need the security of knowing they will be protected if they do speak.

4. Work at being a good listener. Concentrate when you listen to your students. Listen to what they are saying verbally and nonverbally. Be a responsive, supportive listener. Give students feedback, so they know if what they are saying makes sense. Listening is discussed in the next chapter.

5. Use small group assignments whenever possible. It is easier to talk in a small group than in a large group. Also, while working together, students will get to know each other better and become more comfortable talking and listening to each other. Developing communication skills and confidence by working in small groups enables students to speak as part of larger groups. They may eventually become at ease speaking out in class.

6. Students should not be asked to perform a verbal activity, such as giving a report or being in a group discussion, without prior training (Phillips 1995). Never assume they learned how somewhere else, no matter what the age of your student. For the students who do know how to do the activity, it will be a useful review. For students who do not know how or do it poorly, the training will enable their success.

7. Avoid judging your students based on their linguistic or pragmatic behavior. If you have students who speak vernacular dialects, examine your assumptions and analyze your purpose when you speak with them. If your purpose is to understand your students' meaning, then the particular form of the language in which it is expressed does not matter. Clarity and relevance do. If your purpose is to make sure they know some Standard English rule, then teach it to them before you require them to use it in class. Keep the purposes distinct when interacting with your students.

8. Encourage your students' interests, needs, and concerns to surface whenever possible. People are more likely to talk about topics that are meaningful and interesting to them. Consider implementing the following activities when creating learning experiences: writing word problems or questions; leading a discussion; planning group work; thinking of and asking students for examples, ideas, or applications; and letting them design projects.

Note

[1] These functions characterize predominant uses of language in spoken and written discourse. The functions are being used as the structural framework for integrative language arts programs (speaking, listening, writing, reading). See *Learning Language through Communication: A Functional Perspective*, by R. R. Allen, K. Brown, and J. Watvin. 1986. Belmont, CA: Wadsworth; *A Guide to Curriculum Planning in English Language Arts*, October, 1991. Wisconsin Department of Public Instruction: Madison.

References

Adger, Carolyn. 1995. Research Associate, Center for Applied Linguistics. Personal communication.

Allen, R. R. and K. Brown, editors. 1976. *Developing Communication Competence in Children. A Report of the Speech Communication Association's National Project on Speech Communication Competencies.* Skokie, IL: National Textbook Company.

Bassett, R. and M.J. Smythe. 1979. *Communication and Instruction.* New York: Harper & Row.

Civikly, J. 1992. *Classroom Communication: Principles and Practices*. New York: Wm. C. Brown Publishers.

Dandy, E. March, 1990. "Sensitizing Teachers to Cultural Differences: An African-American Perspective." ERIC: ED 323 479.

Friedman, P. 1980. *Shyness and Reticence in Students*. Washington, DC: National Educational Association.

Glenn, E., P. Glenn, and S. Forman. 1989. *Your Voice and Articulation*. Englewood Cliffs, NJ: Prentice Hall.

Heath, Shirley Brice. 1983. *Ways with Words: Language, Life, and Work in Communities and Classrooms*. Cambridge, England: Cambridge University Press.

Hulit, L. and M. Howard. 1993 *Born to Talk: An Introduction to Speech and Language Development*. New York: Merrill.

Kelly, L. 1982. "A Rose by Any Other Name Is Still A Rose: A Comparative Analysis of Reticence, Communication Apprehension, Unwillingness to Communicate, and Shyness." *Human Communication Research* 8(2): 99–113.

Kelly, L., G. Phillips, and B. McKinney. 1982."Reprise: Farewell Reticence, Good-Bye Apprehension! Building a Practical Nosology of Speech Communication Problems." *Communication Education* 31:211–19.

Kochman, T. 1981. *Black and White Styles in Conflict*. Chicago: University of Chicago Press. Cited in E. Dandy, "Sensitizing Teachers to Cultural Differences: An African-American Perspective" (March, 1990. ERIC: ED 323 479).

Lujan, P., L. Hill, W. Kennan, and L. Long. 1987. "Communication Reticence of Native Americans in the Classroom: A Reconceptualization and Approach." *Journal of Thought* 22(4): 62–71.

Mager, R. 1972. *Goal Analysis*. Belmont, CA: Fearon Publishers.

Malcolm, M. 1985. *The Canadians*. New York: Random House.

McCrum, R., W. Cran, and R. MacNeil. 1986. *The Story of English*. New York: Viking.

Naremore, R. and R. Hopper. 1990. *Children Learning Language*, 3rd edition. New York: Harper & Row.

Owens, R. 1992. *Language Development: An Introduction*. New York: Merrill.

Oxford English Dictionary. 1981. Oxford: Oxford University Press.

Phillips, G. 1991. *Communication Incompetencies: A Theory of Training Oral Performance Behavior*. Carbondale: Southern Illinois University Press.

———. April 18, 1995. Personal communication.

Phillips, G., D. Butt, and N. Metzger. 1974. *Communication in Education: A Rhetoric of Schooling*. New York: Holt, Rinehart and Winston.

Phillips, G., K. Kougl, and L. Kelly. 1985. *Speaking in Public and Private*. Indianapolis: Bobbs-Merrill Publishing.

Reingold, H. 1984. *They Have a Word for It*. New York: L. A. Tarcher.

Rich, Adrienne. April 22, 1972. Interview in *Saturday Review*.

Schnaiberg, L. October, 1994. "Talking the Talk." *Teacher Magazine* 6(2): 16–18.

Smitherman, G. 1977. *Talking and Testfyin. The Language of Black America*. Boston: Houghton Mifflin.

60 Minutes. March 5, 1995. "The Language Factor."

Weber, S. 1994. "The Need to Be: The Socio-Cultural Significance of Black Language." In L. Samovar and R. Porter, *Intercultural Communication: A Reader*. Belmont, CA: Wadsworth.

Williams, W. and W. Wolfram, 1977. *Social Dialects: Difference versus Disorder*. Rockville, MD: American Speech-Language-Hearing Association. Cited in L. Hulit and M. Howard, *Born To Talk* (New York: Merrill, 1993).

Wolfram, W. 1991. *Dialects and American English*. Publication of the Center for Applied Linguistics. Englewood Cliffs, NJ: Prentice Hall.

Wolfram, W. and D. Christian. 1989. *Dialects and Education: Issues and Answers*. Publication of the Center for Applied Linguistics. Englewood Cliffs, NJ: Prentice Hall Regents.

Wood, Barbara. 1977. *Development of Functional Communication Competencies Pre-K–Grade 6*. Falls Church, VA: TRIP Series- SCA.

Suggested Reading

Genie: An Abused Child's Flight From Silence, Russ Rymer. 1993. New York: HarperCollins.

An account of an abused child's life after being locked away from her family for thirteen years by her father. It recounts her journey toward language and a life with the researchers who worked with and studied her.

Language Variation in the School and Community, W. Wolfram, D. Christian, and C. Adger. Anticipated publication 1997.

This is an updated, revised, and expanded version of *Dialects and Education: Issues and Answers*. Its question and answer format makes it very readable. It explains clearly how to study your students' dialect. See chapters on language variation and the language arts, reading, and language disorders. Appendices: selective inventory of vernacular structures, sample lessons from a language awareness unit.

Speaking with Skill and Confidence, Lynne Kelly and Arden Watson. 1986. Latham, New York: University Press of America.

This text explains how to develop communication skills through skill training techniques, attitude change, and relaxation techniques. It focuses on three areas: interpersonal interaction, small groups, and public speaking. Although written for adults, its ideas and exercises can be adapted for younger people. See chapters on assessing yourself as a communicator, setting goals, assessing situations and listeners, and specialized settings (social, group, and public).

Voices of the Self: A Study of Language Competence, Keith Gilyard. 1991. Detroit: Wayne State University Press.

A personal report of how it feels to speak a dialect. The author, who describes himself as a "native Black English speaker" and is now an English professor, recounts how he acquired Standard English going through an urban public school system. He blends autobiographical narrative (even numbered chapters) with sociolinguistic analysis (odd-numbered chapters).

1994 Summer Institute Proceedings—National Center for Research on Cultural Diversity and Second Language Learning. The Center is operated by the University of California, Santa Cruz, through the University of California's statewide Linguistic Minority Research Project, in collaboration with other institutions nationwide. Proceedings include reports on: elementary teaching strategies, effective programs for language minority students, teaching academic language in content areas, and organizing classroom for diversity.

Speaking and Listening Competencies, Speech Communication Association. 1994. Annandale, VA: SCA.

Competencies for K–12 intended to assist schools in developing and evaluating oral communication programs by identifying essential skills to be achieved. Skills for elementary students focus on applications to home, school, and community; while high school skills focus on occupational, civic, and daily applications.

Teaching Linguistically and Culturally Diverse Learners: Effective Programs and Practices, edited by C. Montrose. 1994. Santa Cruz: University of California.

Chapter 5

Listening
Behavior

Ideas to Remember

* Listening has an enormous impact on life in the classroom: the content of what gets communicated, the feelings and attitudes that develop, and how learning is evaluated.

* Listening is the most used and the least taught of the language skills.

* Listening is defined by the following characteristics. Listening:

     is more than hearing,

     requires effort,

     is learned,

     is purposive, and

     is responsive.

* The many causes of poor listening operate in- and outside the classroom. Understanding these causes will help us better understand our and our students' listening behavior. The causes are:

     unwillingness to listen,

     uncontrolled bias,

     poor listening skills,

     speech-thought rate disparity,

     noises.

* Improving the listening that goes on your classroom starts with your practicing specific listening and speaking behaviors that will promote the development of your students' listening abilities.

> * Suggestions for these specific behaviors are grouped accord-
> ing to teachers' communicative roles: as role model, planner,
> speaker, and listener.

Up to this point, we have focused on what you need to know about verbal and nonverbal behavior in order for you and your students to become effective communicators in the classroom. Now, we turn to how to "listen" to verbal and nonverbal behavior.

As noted in the previous chapter, two of the necessary conditions for talking are having something to say and someone who wants to listen. Speaking assumes a listener; listening is the counterpart of speaking. Speech communication cannot happen unless someone listens. When we communicate, the roles of speaker and listener are not fixed. As our definition of communication reminds us, communication is a dynamic process in which the participants continuously, simultaneously talk and listen as they try to understand each other. The participants are you (the teacher) and your students.

How you listen to each other is crucial to what gets communicated between you both in terms of subject content and your relationship. What you do to aid or hinder your students' listening affects what they learn. How you listen to them affects their feelings and attitudes about themselves, you, and the subject. When students feel listened to, they tend to have a more positive attitude toward their teacher and feel more comfortable in class. Effective listening promotes task related talk and is important in developing a positive atmosphere in the classroom.

The Skill of Listening

Studies of the amount of time adults spend using the various forms of communication (speaking, listening, reading, writing) indicate listening is used the most (Purdy 1991). This has been true since the first comparisons were made in the 1920s. Purdy states that, depending upon the occupation, 42–60 percent (or more) of communication time is spent listening. One study reports college students spend 52.5 percent of their time listening (Barker et al. 1980). Gilbert (1988) states that students in grades K–12 spend 65–90 percent of their time listening. If students spend that much time listening, then we need to be concerned about what kind of listening skills they have.

Listening is the most used of the communication forms, but it is also the least taught. In fact, the amount of time spent in teaching the forms of communication is the reverse order of the amount of time we spend using them (Steil 1980). The order of use is listening, speaking, reading, and writing. The amount of instructional time is: writing, reading, speaking, and listening.

It is interesting to note that the order of use is also the same sequence in which we acquire the forms, which probably accounts for the reasoning behind the instructional order: since students enter school already speaking and listening, no further instruction is needed. Such a conclusion is built on a faulty understanding of what is involved in the complex process of speaking-listening. It rests on the incorrect assumption that listening is the same thing as effective listening. It is not. If it were, then students and teachers would never have trouble listening to each other.

This paradox—students have to listen, but schools do not teach listening—violates the spirit of chapter 4's tips for creating a talk friendly environment. Do not ask students to perform a skill or activity unless they have had prior training. Evaluation should not be based on skills that have not been taught, yet schools routinely do this with listening. Students are not helped to develop their listening skills, but they are continually assessed academically and personally by how well they listen. Under such circumstances, the students, who come to school able to meet the school's expectations for listening, are more likely to succeed. If the other students do not receive help in developing their listening behavior, they likely will receive lower evaluations whenever listening is involved. This paradox leads to a second paradox involving teachers.

It is likely that most teachers have never been taught about listening and thus may not understand what is involved in listening or may have poorly developed listening skills themselves. Nevertheless, they will use speaking and listening as their primary modes of instruction and will evaluate what students have learned based on how well they listen. Teachers in this position are unable to understand what causes ineffective listening and to help their students listen more effectively. For example, they may mislabel indicators of listening problems—not following directions, continually asking for something to be repeated, daydreaming—as something else, such as lack of ability or intelligence. Once expectations form (even if they are the result of incorrect conclusions), the potential exists for self-fulfilling prophecies to develop. As discussed in chapter 2, when teachers treat students differently because of low expectations, students may absorb the teacher's belief about their poor academic ability. When this occurs, students may *live down* to the low expectations. In such a scenario, teachers have missed the students' original listening problem and compounded it with another problem, negative feelings about themselves as learners.

You need to examine what you know about listening and develop your own skills in order to avoid both paradoxes in your classroom. Think about what you know about listening. Since instruction in listening is rare, people's listening behavior is frequently based on misinformation and myths. For example, many people believe listening is easy and that it is a passive activity. Think back to your own teachers, particularly the ones who taught the subject and grade you plan to teach. What were their listening skills like? What did they teach you about listening, either directly or indirectly? How do you rate your own listening skills now?

This chapter begins with an examination of the basic characteristics of listening. Next, it looks at some of the common causes of poor listening. Finally, it ends with suggestions for improving listening in the classroom—yours and your students'.

Characteristics of Listening Behavior

The characteristics of listening are what define listening. Lack of awareness of these basic ideas leads to ineffective listening behavior, which we will explore in the next section. As we go through the characteristics, consider them in light of your own experiences and beliefs.

Listening Is More than Hearing

Although people use "hearing" and "listening" interchangeably, the words refer to two different behaviors. **Hearing** means auditing sound. Sound waves strike the eardrum which vibrates. These vibrations move as electrical energy or neural impulses along the auditory nerve to the brain. **Listening** is the interpretation of these impulses. The brain assigns meaning to them. First, you must hear; then, you can listen. Think of listening as a conversion process. Sounds are converted into meaning in the mind (Lundsteen 1971).

The distinction becomes clearer if you recall from chapter 2 that the perception process is always selective. Hearing involves selecting sound for attention. Which sounds people choose to attend to at any given moment depend on their needs, motivation, the novelty or intensity of the sound, their feelings, and all the other possible filtering stimuli. Listening begins at step two of the perception process, the interpretation step.

Listening Requires Effort

Although it looks easy and does not take long, listening takes effort. The mainstream norm for polite listening only requires silence until it is the listener's turn to speak. In an intense conversation or a fast paced argument, there may only be seconds between the end of one person's words and the listener's response; indeed, sometimes they overlap. What goes on in the listener's silence while someone else speaks is the creation of meaning.

Remember from chapter 1 that messages may be intentional or unintentional and composed of verbal and nonverbal dimensions. The meaning of messages is in the participants. Listening is when we actively search our memory banks in an attempt to understand the messages we receive. People usually think of listening as referring only to sound. However, the inevitability of nonverbal behavior means we must listen with our ears and eyes.

Listening is like a juggling act. It takes effort and concentration to keep all the balls in the air. Listeners must interpret all the separate bits of verbal (linguistic and pragmatic) and nonverbal behavior and coordinate them into a meaningful whole. Listeners must sustain their attention and concentrate while doing all of this.

Many people do not work at listening, either because they do not know they are supposed to or they do not know how. They listen passively, acting like bystanders or spectators. Lapses of attention may occur as listening priorities change. The mind wanders. For example, you explain an assignment to your class. When you collect the assignment, you find a dozen different versions of what you said to do.

Listening Is Learned

We are born hearing, and we develop the ability to listen. The middle and inner ears reach their adult size at twenty weeks of fetal development, so they function at birth (Owens 1992). However, immaturity of the auditory cortex and fluid in the middle ear make it difficult to integrate sounds. Yet newborns can distinguish loudness and duration of sound (Hirschman and Katkin 1974), discriminate between different sounds (Morse 1979), and prefer the sound of the human voice. Infants by two months can discriminate speech sounds and by three months vocalize in response to speech. True linguistic perception develops with brain maturation. In order to develop spoken language, children must be able to store sounds, to use this information for later comparison and identification, and to develop sound-meaning relationships (Owens 1992). Children develop their ability to respond to and produce sounds from seven to twelve months. Experts define the first meaningful word as one produced in the presence of its referent, that is, the word is associated with its meaning (Owens 1992). This occurs around the first birthday.

Once the ability to listen develops, what listening skills are acquired depends on children's experiences. Recall that learning pragmatics involves learning to enact expected roles. Success in meeting the verbal and nonverbal expectations for each role requires mastering the necessary communication skills. How listening fits into each role— what listening tasks are required, what norms for listening behavior are insisted on—determines what listening skills children develop. Children imitate the listening skills modeled by their caregivers and significant others. As with verbal and nonverbal behavior, children learn what is available to be learned.

For many students the listening tasks required outside school are limited. For example, time spent speaking and listening within the family is often brief and focused on practical, family maintenance topics. One study reported the average family with teenagers spends fourteen and a half minutes a day engaging in parent-child communication (Fornaciari as cited in Barbour 1981). Twelve and a half minutes were devoted to discipline, directives, and informational exchanges. The remaining two minutes dealt with feelings and personal issues.

Most of children's listening time is spent watching television. Before children enter the first grade, they will already have spent as much time watching television as they will later spend in class during four years of college (Public Broadcasting System 1992). A 1990 Neilsen Report on TV states that the average six to eleven year old watches twenty-six hours of television a week. By the time students graduate from high school, they will have spent eleven thousand hours in school and fifteen thousand hours watching television (Public Broadcasting System 1992).

The problem with so much television viewing is that listening to it is passive, easy, and entertaining. Television is a visual medium that tells stories through dramatic images and music. Neil Postman says television has three commandments that are observable in all programming and are in direct opposition to school expectations (1985, p. 147–48): (1) "thou shalt have no prerequisites" (no previous knowledge required); (2) "thou shalt induce no perplexity" (nothing to be remembered, studied, applied, or endured); (3) "thou shalt avoid exposition" (avoid hypotheses, discussions, reasoned discourse). School builds on continuity, requires perplexity, and thrives on exposition. In other words, listening for academic purposes is active and requires effort and thinking.

Students, who have developed the listening skills needed for television, may be unprepared to do the kind of listening expected in the classroom. Television produces listeners who like immediacy, want immediate gratification, have short attention spans, and want to be entertained (Postman 1982). No matter what their ages, students will probably need to develop their listening skills for academic tasks.

Most of what any of us do when we listen is a hodgepodge of habits that we have picked up catch-as-catch-can through our communication experience with family, friends, and school. For the most part, we learned how to listen through informal observation. The point to remember is this. Since we learned our present, often inefficient listening habits, *we can also learn new, more effective listening behaviors.*

Listening Is Purposive

Just as we speak for different reasons, so we listen for different purposes. Understanding why you are listening is prerequisite to figuring out how to listen. If you have a clear listening goal, then you have a criteria for selecting the appropriate listening skills to help you accomplish it.

Keep several points in mind: (1) Most people (including teachers and students) are unaware of why they are listening, consequently they do not think about choosing appropriate listening strategies. (2) Teachers and students have purposes for listening. They may or may not be the same purpose for the same event. For example, a teacher might want students to listen for comprehension, but some students may be listening for appreciation. As teachers, we need to realize there may be a need to identify and coordinate purposes. (3) Any listener may have several purposes during the course of any communicative event (conversation, discussion, lesson). For example, students listening to you lecture may listen for comprehension, appreciation, and evaluation. (4) Listening purposes need to be chosen with the speakers' purposes in mind. Review the five functions for speaking that we examined in the preceding chapter: informing, controlling, expressing feeling, imagining, and ritualizing. If you perceive someone is speaking to express feelings, then you need to listen therapeutically. If your students are listening to a debate, then they need to realize that they need to listen critically.

According to Wolvin and Coakley (1985), there are five listening purposes: discriminative, comprehensive, critical, therapeutic, and appreciative.

- *Discriminative.* This type of listening involves distinguishing the verbal and nonverbal features of a message, so we can understand the full meaning. Discriminative listening is the basis for the other four listening purposes. In other words, lis-

teners must identify, interpret, and concentrate on the auditory and visual cues as part of any listening task (Wolvin and
Coakley 1993).

- *Comprehensive*. Comprehensive listening seeks to understand
  the message and to retain its information for future use. Much
  of the educational process is based on this type of listening.
  Students are expected frequently to listen for comprehension.
  Teachers listen for comprehension at faculty meetings, conferences with parents, and workshops. To be effective requires
  note-taking skills, concentration, listening strategies, and
  memory skills.
- *Critical* (evaluative). We listen critically whenever we make
  judgments about a message in order to accept or reject it. Critical listening assumes that discriminative and comprehensive
  listening have already occurred, and the message is understood. When listening critically, listeners must evaluate the
  speaker's credibility (trustworthiness, believability), reasoning, evidence, and emotional appeals. Critical listeners must
  recognize the verbal traps and distinguish facts from inferences. We need to listen critically to persuasive and informational messages whether they occur in- or outside the
  classroom. Commercials on television, politicians speaking
  about policy, and friends asking us to make choices are all
  examples of messages that blend information and persuasion.
  We and our students need to listen critically to each other during discussions.
- *Therapeutic* (empathic). When we listen nonjudgmentally to
  help another person feel better, we are engaging in this type of
  listening. The listener acts as a sounding board, so the speaker
  can express feelings or talk through a problem. Therapeutic
  listening builds on discriminative and comprehensive listening. It requires a dual perspective, the ability to identify with
  someone's thoughts and feelings from his or her point of view.
  When listening therapeutically, it is important to be supportive, nondirective, and nonjudgmental.

     Teachers need to listen therapeutically when students come
  to them with a problem. Teachers need others (teachers,
  friends, families) to listen therapeutically when they have had
  a bad day. Students need to listen therapeutically to their
  friends. Secondary schools throughout the country are exper-
  imenting with peer counseling, training selected students to listen therapeutically to other students who feel the need to
  discuss a problem (Leslie et al. 1988).
- *Appreciative*. This is listening for "enjoyment or sensory stim-

ulation." It results from a person's individualized response, which is created from his or her sensitivities, tastes, knowledge, and standards. We may all have the same listening experience but enjoy it differently. For example, you may take your students to see *Romeo and Juliet*. The boys may enjoy the fight scenes, while the girls prefer the love story, and you appreciate the acting.

Listening Is Responsive

Listening looks passive, but its responsiveness is critical to communication. Speaking and listening are responsive to each other in the creation of meaning. The feedback between speakers and listeners affects both the process (what is communicated and the meaning that is assigned) and the relationship that develops between participants. Not to give feedback or to give it poorly affects the communication in negative ways. As already mentioned, students may listen to teachers the same way they listen to television. In terms of feedback, this means they would probably not give it. They may continue doing other things as if the teacher could not see or hear them, just as the actors on television cannot see or hear them.

Listeners' responses enable the person speaking at the moment to evaluate how his or her message is being understood, which affects the speaker's behavior. Listeners' responses also affect what they say when it is their turn to speak. When we listen as part of our participation in any communicative event (conversation, discussion, lecture, argument), we respond in two ways: internally and externally.

The internal response is what we think as we listen to the person speaking. It is the **silent dialogue** we have with the person speaking as we try to interpret what is meant. The interpretation step of perception is at work as we compare what we are listening to against what we know. We may be quiet, but we are definitely active as we mentally agree-disagree and understand-get confused. This internal dialogue produces our external responses.

Our external responses provide **feedback** for the speaker. They occur on two levels: the unconscious and the conscious. The unconscious responses are reflections of what is going on in the silent dialogue. These reactions occur as we listen and are usually nonverbal. Most people are unaware of what their bodies are doing as they listen, what meaning they might be communicating. Nonverbal behavior, particularly kinesics and proxemics, can provide clues as to what listeners are thinking and feeling.

As teachers, we need to recognize the potential for the good and the harm in these unconscious reactions. When we speak, students' nonverbal listening cues can help us decide whether they are listening and understanding what we are saying. However, we should be careful not to jump to conclusions when we perceive negative reactions. As the chapter on nonverbal behavior explained, any nonverbal behavior has multiple possible meanings. When we listen, we need to become aware of and monitor what we may be communicating nonverbally. Our listening demeanor will be *listened to* by our students and will affect their participation.

Conscious external responses are a result of the meaning we assign to what we have listened to. At some point, turn-taking occurs and then we must respond in a coherent, appropriate manner. This external response to listening corresponds to the final step in perception, behavior. The conscious response is verbal, which necessarily includes its accompanying nonverbal behavior. Questions, comments, and statements and how they are delivered (tone of voice, rate, facial expression, gestures, posture, etc.) provide feedback to speakers. As the speakers listen to this feedback, it affects their responses. The dynamic cycle continues.

As teachers, we need to recognize the importance of constructive feedback for ourselves and for our students. Whether we respond and how we respond communicates our attitudes and our expectations for students. Realize, too, you may need to teach your students what feedback is, why it is important, and how to give it.

Lack of awareness and understanding of these characteristics frequently lead to listening problems. With these defining characteristics in mind, let's look at some of the common causes of poor listening.

Causes of Poor Listening

The causes of poor listening are the same in and out of the classroom. They democratically can affect anyone's listening behavior, regardless of age, gender, educational level, or national origin. Teachers, students, administrators, and parents can all be guilty of poor listening due to these reasons. As you read through these causes, think about them from the points of view of you, as listener, and your students, as listeners. Think about times when you have listened poorly and see if you can decide which causes were at work.

Unwillingness to Listen

Listening requires involvement and effort. Some people refuse to get involved or to make any effort. Such people may have listening skill, but they do not choose to use it.

Lack of motivation to listen can result from several causes (Weaver 1972). One reason is preoccupation with private thoughts, a preference for daydreaming. Another reason is a belief that other people's opinions are not worth listening to. This belief might center around a specific topic or a specific relationship. A teacher with low expectations for certain students may not listen to them. An administrator may solicit ideas from experienced teachers but not listen when the rookies speak. Students may listen to you, but not listen when other students talk. A final reason is laziness. People listen to easy or familiar topics when not much effort is necessary. Students may stop listening as soon as complex material comes up. Whatever the cause, unwilling listeners often are good at faking attention. They may look attentive but do not know what the speaker said. In effect, they have "closed their earlids" (Wolvin and Coakley 1985, p. 1).

Sometimes students start out motivated to listen but lose interest as the listening task drags on. Think back to the figures for the amount of time students K–12 are expected to listen. Having to listen for long periods of time produces fatigue, and students lose heart. This also puts too much emphasis on one modality of learning for students who do not learn best by listening (Dunn and Dunn 1987).

Uncontrolled Bias

Every category or concept we form has an emotional dimension to it. Weaver (1972, p. 65) calls this dimension **bias**. This means we have a positive, negative, or neutral reaction to everything. In general, teachers might be biased in favor of bright students and small classes, biased against hall duty, meetings after school, and the new superintendent, and neutral on the senior prom theme and whether the Department of Education should be abolished. The point is each person has feelings of like, dislike, and apathy for everything. You do, and so will each of your students, their caregivers, and administrators.

Once formed, however, biases become part of the filtering process and affect concentration. We listen through our personal biases. Biases can affect anything involved in a communicative event: speakers, words, phrases, topics, situations, activities. We listen easily and sustain attention to things that agree with our biases, but we listen inefficiently or block out what disagrees with them (Weaver 1972). It is as if people's listening goes on automatic pilot in the presence of positive biases, and tunes out when they are negative or neutral.

Poor Listening Skills

Many people have undeveloped listening strategies (Nichols and Stevens 1957). They do not distinguish among possible listening purposes and lack different listening strategies for working with the speaker to create meaning. They often listen passively to everything in the same way. In other words, they treat every word as having equal importance. They act like an empty bucket into which speakers pour what they have to say.

Listening this way is like taking verbatim notes of a lecture (Kougl 1988). If you have ever done this, then you will appreciate why treating every word as crucial does not work. The problem with writing down every word is you cannot keep up. You miss a lot of what is said and get further and further behind. When you study your notes, they do not make sense. Nothing stands out as more important, so you cannot identify main ideas. Listeners who lack listening strategies often run into the same problems. They are confused about the purpose of the message or what the main ideas are. Although they try to remember everything, they forget a lot and often remember only novel or unimportant details that strike their fancy.

Speech-Thought Rate Disparity

This is the difference between how fast the average speaker talks and how fast people can think. In general, people think faster than the average person speaks. While figures are not available for children, adults speak at 125–150 words per minute and can comprehend up to 500 words a minute (Brownell 1991). However, there are many factors that affect an individual's listening rate for any particular message.

How fast a specific person assigns meaning depends on his or her categories, what is in the categories, the complexity of the message, and the speaker's rate. All of these elements can vary throughout a message. The potential always exists for concentration to flag. If a person is listening fast, then there is left-over thinking time for the mind to wander. The silent dialogue gets off the track. Wandering minds may take small productive departures from the topic, go off on tangents, engage in private argument with the speaker, or make complete detours away from the subject (Lundsteen 1993). When a person listens slowly, then he or she may be left behind while the speaker continues talking.

Noises

In chapter 1 we examined noises, anything that interferes, distorts, or complicates the creation of meaning. Noises distract us from concentrating when we listen. They are barriers that can get in the way at any point in the listening process: attending-interpreting-responding. Since noises thwart listening, they affect both the content of what gets communicated and the feelings that develop between the communicators. Noises, then, act like static on the radio. Both prevent you from receiving the whole message and garble the meaning.

Noises represent possibilities. They may or may not occur in some combination for each person involved in any communicative interaction. Teachers tend to think of noises as causing poor student listening, but they need to be aware that noise can wreak havoc on their own listening, too.

Noises affecting teachers' listening can be generated from students or themselves. Teachers have trouble hearing when there is physical noise. When teachers are ill or tired, the physiological noise prevents them from putting in the effort that listening takes. Psychological noise, such as not liking certain students, can affect how teachers listen to those students. Social noise, such as different pragmatic rules, can interfere with how teachers relate to students and sidetrack their listening. In the preceding chapter, we saw how phonological, semantic, and grammatical noise can make it harder to understand messages.

Now that we have reviewed the common causes of poor listening, let's look at suggestions for improving listening in the classroom—yours and that of your students.

Improving Listening

If you want to improve listening in your future classroom, then you need to consider listening from the points of view of yourself and your students. The path to more effective listening is the same for all of you. Becoming a better listener requires motivation, knowledge about listening, and practice. Right now, you may be motivated to become a better listener, have information about listening from this chapter, and be ready to embark on conscientious practice. Your students are likely to need persuading that they need to work on their listening skills. Whether or not you are successful in motivating them, you can inform them, provide opportunities, and supply guidance.

The following suggestions for improving teacher-student listening are discussed in terms of teacher input about listening: teacher as role model, planner, speaker, and listener.

Teacher as Role Model

There is consensus that the listening behavior teachers model has an enormous impact on classroom listening. According to Wolvin and Coakley (1991, p. 161), teachers who demonstrate effective listening behavior, "elicit effective listening behavior from others." The loudest lessons about listening are how teachers listen. When students see teachers lead by example and convey that listening is a valued skill, they are more likely to *listen back*. Having someone listen carefully to what we have to say is gratifying for all of us. For students, having an adult actively listen to them may be a new experience. This alone may help motivate them to work on their listening.

A first step in becoming an effective listening model is eliminating listening problems that you have now. In the preceding section, I asked you to identify what causes your poor listening. Think about how these causes could interfere with your listening to students. Set goals to overcome these listening problems.

- If you discovered circumstances in which you were unwilling to listen, then shape up your attitude. Analyze what it was about those situations that depressed your listening effort. Replay those occasions in your mind from the perspective of the people to whom you were not listening. Did they know? What difference did it make in terms of what happened? Remind yourself of the important role listeners play in the communication process. What might make you unwilling to listen to students? Try to remember when your teachers demonstrated unwillingness to listen.

- Recognize your biases and monitor them. In particular, analyze your extreme positive and negative biases. Understanding why something causes an automatic listening response, whether positive or negative, gives you the power to choose to respond in other ways.

- If you do not distinguish listening purposes, then start doing so as you listen. Be flexible in adjusting your purpose as you listen to people. Recognize the connection between listening purpose and choosing appropriate listening strategies. Evaluate what listening skills you have in your repertoire of communication skills. If you do not have many skills, then you need to develop your own as you promote those of your students. The suggestions throughout the rest of the chapter will help you do both. As you read, select skills that you need to work on and practice them.

- If you are not handling the speech-thought rate disparity well, find ways to do so. For instance, you could summarize what the speaker says, formulate questions, and look for connections to what you know. Developing your listening skills will supply the means to help you manage your left-over thinking time better.

- Become a noise detector. Always keep the possibilities in mind for yourself and your students. Prevent them when you can, such as closing the door to the noisy hallway before you start class. Control them as you can. For example, park your anger (at your spouse, principal, the previous class) outside the classroom door and do not take it out on your students. Cope with noises as they occur. Mediate between students when semantic or social noises get in the way of their listening to each other.

Teacher as Planner

When planning a lesson, consider how listening fits into it. Look at your objectives and activities in terms of the listening tasks you are setting up for students. Think carefully about the listening purposes in terms of your students. Plan how you can help students listen well.

As you plan, keep in mind some basic principles drawn from research about what influences listening. Activities involving verbal response and interaction enhance listening comprehension (Pearson and Fielding 1982). Attention and memory are sustained when information is meaningful, interesting, useful, novel, organized, and visual (Lafrancois 1979). Students pay more attention and achieve more when teachers clearly discuss goals, structure the lesson, and give directions (Fisher et al. 1980). Also, remembering is aided when new information is associated with previously learned, familiar information (Hunter 1967). Lastly, students have trouble concentrating for long periods of time (Wolvin and Coakley 1985).

These principles can be applied to planning through the following suggestions:

1. Organize lessons in a logical sequence that is easy for students to follow (Wolvin and Coakley 1985).
2. Keep chapter 4's "Tips for a Talk Friendly Environment" firmly in mind as you plan.
3. Avoid input at inappropriate levels of difficulty (Lundsteen 1971).
4. Consider the length of students' attention spans when structuring the lesson (Wolvin and Coakley 1991).
5. Avoid too much input without students having opportunities to respond (Lundsteen 1971). Build in time for students to react and to interact—ask questions and share thoughts.
6. Decide on the lesson's general listening purposes, specific listening goals, and what listening strategies will be helpful.
7. Prepare introductions that focus students' attention on what is to occur in the lesson (see previous suggestion), and why they

should listen. Any subpart of a lesson needs an introduction, too. (Introductions to lectures, discussions, and group work will be discussed in later chapters.)

8. Plan explanations and directions that are clear, precise, and concise (Wolvin and Coakley 1991).

9. Establish classroom listening expectations with students. Be clear about responsibilities for speakers and listeners for each activity and for types of interactions (Wolvin and Coakley 1991).

10. Think about how you can make the environment conducive to good listening. Set up the spatial and physical arrangements to encourage the kind of listening you are asking students to do. Eliminate physical distractions.

11. Over time, vary the listening purposes, activities, situations, and stimuli.

Teacher as Speaker

No matter what the talk format (interpersonal, discussion, lecture, small groups), what you say and how you say it affects students' listening. Everything covered in part II of this text needs to be applied. Ask yourself what you can do to improve your **listenability**—that is, make yourself easy to listen to. Think of your role as a "listening enabler," finding ways to enable students to listen effectively.

Try these suggestions to prevent listening problems and strengthen listening skills:

1. Gain attention before you speak.

2. Monitor your verbal behavior to prevent semantic and grammatical noise.

3. Speak in short, direct sentences. Long complex sentences may be good written form, but they are poor oral form. Listeners need short, easy-to-follow sentences to keep up with what you are saying. It is easier to get meaning from a series of short, simple sentences than long, rambling ones with strings of dependent clauses.

4. Avoid information overload. Do not give too much or too complex information too fast.

5. Monitor your nonverbal behavior, so it is appropriate and varied, enhances your verbal meaning, and does not distract from your intended message. Review chapter 3 on nonverbal behavior for specific suggestions.

6. Monitor students' unconscious nonverbal reactions for feedback about what you are saying.

7. Give "speaker signals" whenever possible. **Feedforward** is information which contains speaker signals that set the stage before you start your main message (Richards 1951). Feedforward can preview the contents, importance, or style. It can provide disclaimers ("This is the state policy on smoking on school premises."). Sometimes it **altercasts**, tells listeners what role to play, how to respond ("Listen to this as if you were the county commissioners having to make a ruling."). Speaker signals help listeners stay focused and keep track of how statements fit together. Signals are appropriate when they follow through on whatever focus you give in your opening comments, whether in a lesson, a lecture, an activity, or conversation. For example, if you tell students that you are going to tell a story, then you need to give cues that signal sequence, such as first, then, next, and finally.

8. Practice the "once-only" rule for giving directions and making important announcements (Wolvin and Coakley 1991). When implementing this rule, Wolvin and Coakley (1991) suggest explaining it the first day of class and then having it go into effect after a trial period. Then, only clarifications would be made in response to specific questions.

   "Say it again, Sam" offers a variation (Garber 1984). Ask volunteer students, in turn, to repeat the directions accurately until someone successfully does so.

9. Suggest specific listening strategies that aid in fulfilling different listening purposes. These strategies help focus and organize listening, understanding, and remembering.
   - The acronym, ARC, stands for one listening strategy (Bentley 1989). "A" stands for *attention*; "R" is *rephrasing*, putting the message into the listener's own words; "C" is for *connecting* the message in some meaningful way or organizing it into a pattern.
   - Search for speaker signals and use them to follow what the speaker is saying.
   - Self-questioning is another strategy. In their silent dialogue, listeners listen and answer relevant questions. Bozik (1989) suggests a series of self-questions that students can use when listening to lectures. If students cannot answer any of the questions, they should ask the teacher. She suggests helping students learn how to use these questions by periodically stopping during a lecture to ask and discuss the answers to questions from the following list (Bozik 1989, p. 2).
     1) What is the topic?
     2) What is the main idea?

3) What ideas or details has the teacher said two or three times? Repetition is used to emphasize important concepts and information.

4) When does the teacher stop and ask if there are any questions? Asking for questions usually means the teacher is particularly concerned that students understand what was just presented.

5) What is an example of the idea the teacher is talking about? Write down the teacher's examples. If the teacher does not give examples and you cannot think of one, ask for one.

6) How does what the teacher is talking about relate to yesterday's topic? If you cannot see a relationship, ask the teacher what it is.

7) How does this topic relate to the course subject? Remind yourself of the connection between the small idea of today's class and the big idea of the course.

8) What did I learn today? Review in your mind what was new to you.

9) If I were the teacher, what would I ask on a test? Write a few test questions at the end of your notes.

10. Always provide a conclusion to the lesson. Conclusions provide closure and help organize and reinforce the elements of your message. The information and activities covered during a lesson need to be tied together into a meaningful whole (Shostak 1990). Subparts of lessons need to be concluded, too, before moving onto other parts. (Conclusions for lectures, discussions, and small groups will be discussed in later chapters.)

Teacher as Listener

An important part of creating a positive listening environment depends on how you listen. What kind of verbal and nonverbal response you make when students speak affects how they feel about participating. It is helpful to remember your teachers who were good listeners and think about what they did. Think about how you like to be listened to, and what listener behaviors invite you to speak.

Here are some suggestions for listening effectively as a teacher:

1. Establish quality listening time during class and before and after school (Wolvin and Coakley 1991).

2. Listen to all students.

3. As you listen, identify what your listening purpose is and decide which listening skills are appropriate.

4. Concentrate actively on what the student is saying.

5. Monitor your nonverbal behavior so it demonstrates interest, understanding, and supports the person speaking. Wolvin and Coakley (1991) list such *attending behaviors* as direct eye contact, responsive facial expression that matches the speaker's concern, and comfortable interaction distance. DeVito (1995, p. 72) calls these listener nonverbal responses **back-channeling cues**. They provide information to the speaker about attention (sincere head-nodding and vocalizations like "mm-hm," and "uh-huh"), interest (attentive posture, focused eye contact, leaning forward), and need for clarification (a puzzled expression).

6. When waiting for a response, consider silence as thinking time. ("Wait time" will be discussed further in the chapter on discussion.)

7. Do not interrupt students who are speaking. Let them complete what they have to say.

8. Encourage students to continue when they hesitate.

9. Check your understanding when you are not sure what is meant by paraphrasing what you think was meant or asking specific questions about what is unclear (Wolvin and Coakley 1991). Paraphrasing encourages speakers to confirm your interpretation, elaborate on their original statement, or clarify what they meant.

10. Avoid judgmental responses. Recognize the distinction between critical listening and being judgmental. Critical listening involves evaluating the substance of what is said in order to decide what you think about it. Critical listeners respond by pointing to evidence and reasoning. Constructive comments that are critical, in this sense, can aid thinking. For example, "What are your reasons for your position?" is a critical listening response. Judgments are pronouncements that come from the emotions and bypass analysis. Judgmental responses sound like personal attacks and make people feel defensive. For example, "That's a stupid idea" is a judgmental response.

11. Ask for feedback from students about your speaking ("What questions do you have about the directions?").

12. Keep emotions under control while listening (Wolvin and Coakley 1991).

13. When listening therapeutically, respond reflectively. This means that you reflect back to the speaker what you think his or her thoughts and feelings are.

Are You Really Listening?

Listening is the counterpart of speaking. How we speak and listen to our students affects how our students listen and speak to us. Use the causes of poor listening to examine your own listening habits now. Practice the constructive behaviors listed for improving listening—modelling, planning, speaking, and listening—see what difference these behaviors make in how people listen to you. Improving your listening skills now will serve you well when you have a class full of students to listen to.

References

Barker, L., R. Edwards, C. Gaines, K. Gladney, and F. Holley. 1980. "An Investigation of Proportional Time Spent in Various Communication Activities by College Students." *Journal of Applied Communication Research* 8:101–10. Cited in D. Borisoff and M. Purdy, editors, *Listening in Everyday Life: A Personal and Professional Approach* (Latham, NY: University Press of America, 1991).

Bentley, S. 1989. "Building Memory Power." International Listening Association Conference, Atlanta. Cited in Michael Purdy "Intrapersonal/Interpersonal Listening." In D. Borisoff and M. Purdy, editors, *Listening in Everyday Life: A Personal and Professional Approach* (Latham, NY: University Press of America, 1991).

Borisoff, D. and M. Purdy. 1991. *Listening in Everyday Life: A Personal and Professional Approach*. Latham, NY: University Press of America.

Bozik, M. 1989. "Teaching Students to Listen to Teacher Talk." *Teacher Talk* 7(2): 2.

Brownell, J. 1991. "Listening Environment: A Perspective." In D. Borisoff and M. Purdy, editors, *Listening in Everyday Life: A Personal and Professional Approach*. Latham, NY: University Press of America.

DeVito, J. 1995. *The Interpersonal Communication Book*, 7th edition. New York: HaperCollins.

Dunn, K. and R. Dunn. 1987. "Dispelling Outmoded Beliefs About Student Learning." *Educational Leadership* 45:55–62. Cited in H. Funk and G. Funk, "Guidelines for Developing Listening Skills." *The Reading Teacher* (May, 1989): 660–63.

Fisher, C., D. Berliner, N. Filby, R. Marliave, L. Cahen, M. Dishaw. 1980. "Teaching Behaviors, Academic Learning Time and Student Achievement: An Overview." In Denham and Lieberman, editors, *Time To Learn*. Washington, DC: U.S. Department of Education. Cited in D. Berliner, "The Half-Full Glass: A Review of Research on Teaching." *Using What We Know About Teaching* (Alexandria, VA: Association for Supervision & Curriculum, 1984).

Fornaciari, S. n.d. "How to Talk to Kids About Drugs." Cited in John Barbour, "Lines of Communication," *The Evening Sun*, 18 March 1981, p. B-1. Cited in A. Wolvin and C. Coakley, *Listening* (Dubuque, IA; W. L. Brown, 1985).

Garber, G. 1984. "Motivational Strategies for Listening and Following Directions." *The Reading Teacher*, 37(January): 442–43.

Gilbert, M. 1988. "Listening in School: I Know You Can Hear Me—But Are You Listening?" *Journal of International Listening Association* 2:121–32. Cited in M. Purdy, "What is Listening?" In D. Borisoff and M. Purdy, editors, *Listening in Everyday Life: A Personal and Professional Approach* (Latham, NY: University Press of America, 1991).

Hirschman, R. and E. Katkin. 1974. "Psychophysiological Functioning, Arousal, Attention, and Learning During the First Year of Life." In H. Reese, editor, *Advances in Child Development and Behavior*. New York: Academic Press. Cited in R. Owens, *Language Development: An Introduction* (New York: Merrill, 1992).

Hunter, M. 1967. *Retention*. El Segundo, CA: TIP Publications. Cited in A. Wolvin and C. Coakley, *Perspectives in Listening*. Norwood, NJ: Ablex, 1993.

Kougl, K. *Primer for Public Speaking*. 1988. New York: Harper & Row.

Lafrancois, G. 1979. *Psychology for Teaching*, 3rd edition. Belmont, CA: Wadsworth. Cited in A. Wolvin and C. Coakley, *Perspectives in Listening* (Norwood, NJ: Ablex, 1993).

Leslie, C. and D. Gonzalez, N. Abbott, S. Hutchinson, and T. Namuth. 1988. "Listening, Feeling, and Helping." *Newsweek*: October 31.

Lundsteen, S. 1993. "Metacognitive Listening." In A. Wolvin and C. Coakley, editors, *Perspectives in Listening*. Norwood, NJ: Ablex.

———. 1971. *Listening—Its Impact on Reading and the Other Language Arts*. Urbana, IL: NCTE/ERIC Studies in the Teaching of English.

Morse, P. 1979. "The Infancy of Infant Speech Perception: The First Decade of Research." *Brain, Behavior, and Evolution* 16:351–73. Cited in R. Owens, *Language Development: An Introduction* (New York: Merrill, 1992).

Nichols, R. and L. Stevens. 1957. *Are You Listening?* New York: McGraw-Hill.

Owens, R. 1992. *Language Development: An Introduction*. New York: Merrill.

Pearson, P. and L. Fielding. 1982. "Listening Comprehension." *Language Arts* 59(6): 617–29.

Postman, N. 1985. *Amusing Ourselves to Death*. New York: Penguin Books.

———. 1982. *The Disappearance of Childhood*. New York: Delacorte Press.

Public Broadcasting System. September, 1992. *Television and Our Children*.

Purdy, M. 1991. "What Is Listening?" In D. Borisoff and M. Purdy, editors, *Listening in Everyday Life: A Personal and Professional Approach*. Latham, NY: University Press of America.

Richards, I. 1951. "Communication Between Men: The Meaning of Language." In H. Von Foerster, editor, *Cybernetics, Transactions of the 8th Conference*. Cited in J. DeVito, *The Interpersonal Communication Book*, 7th edition (New York: HarperCollins, 1995).

Shostak, R. 1990. "Lesson Presentation Skills." In J. Cooper, *Classroom Teaching Skills*. Lexington MA: DC Heath.

Steil, L. 1980 *Your Personal Listening Profile*. Minneapolis, MN: Sperry Corporation. Cited in P. Cooper, *Speech Communication for the Classroom Teacher* (Scottsdale, AZ: Gorsuch Scarisbrick, 1991).

Weaver, C. 1972. *Human Listening—Processes and Behavior*. Indianapolis: Bobbs-Merrill.

Wolvin, A. and C. Coakley. 1993. "A Listening Taxonomy." In their *Perspectives in Listening*. Norwood, NJ: Ablex.

———. 1991. "Listening in the Educational Environment." In D. Borisoff and M. Purdy, editors, *Listening in Everyday Life: A Personal and Professional Approach*. Latham, NY: University Press of America.

———. 1985. *Listening*, 2nd edition. Dubuque, IA: W.C. Brown.

Suggested Reading

How to Talk So Kids Will Listen and Listen So Kids Will Talk, by Adele Faber and Elaine Mazlish. 1982. New York: Avon Books.

A how-to book on communication skills for parents based on the work of psychologist Hiam Ginott and the authors' workshops around the country. Many examples enliven chapters dealing with feelings, cooperation, alternatives to punishment, autonomy, praise, and playing roles.

How to Talk So Kids Can Learn at Home and at School, by A. Faber and E. Mazlish. 1995. New York: Rawson Associates.

The authors apply their communication strategies to the specific concerns of the classroom in order to motivate students to succeed.

Listening, 3rd edition, by A. Wolvin and C. Coakley. 1988. Dubuque, Iowa: W. C. Brown.

A thorough exploration of the process of listening. Looks in detail at the five listening purposes—what is involved and how to develop skills.

Part III

Shaping Oral Communication Interactions in the Classroom

In part I, we stressed the importance of effective oral communication in the classroom and the need to develop a communicative perspective. We examined the elements in the process of communication. We looked at how self-concept, perceptual processes, learning style, and teachers' expectations affect the communicative behavior of students and teachers.

In part II, we explored the basic forms of communication that we use whenever we communicate. We examined each of these building blocks from the practical point of view of how to make more effective communicative choices in the classroom. We looked at distinguishing characteristics and types of nonverbal behavior, as well of the functions it serves for teachers. For verbal behavior, we focused on the characteristics of language and the linguistic and pragmatic elements of language. We discussed dialect in the schools, quiet students, and how to create a talk friendly environment. We reviewed the basic characteristics of listening and the causes of poor listening, concluding with suggestions for improving student and teacher listening.

Part III is about applying this information. Everything that we have dealt with so far comes to bear in part III, which examines the fundamental ways teachers structure communicative interactions in the classroom. The next four chapters deal with the basic ways of shaping communicating: communicating interpersonally (all interpersonal exchanges), shared speaking (discussion), working together (small groups), and lecturing (giving information). The chapters focus on promoting effective communication when you engage in each type of interaction.

The strategy (or strategies) appropriate for any given lesson must be based on your analysis of the classroom situation, your students, your goals and objectives, and the subject or topic. All aspects of communication considered in parts I and II are part of this communicative analysis. Your analysis enables you to decide how best to structure the classroom interactions to facilitate your students' learning.

As we examine teaching-learning strategies in the next four chapters, keep in mind how learning styles (see chapter 2) can affect what learning takes place with any of them. All four strategies are equally good, but no one is universally good for all students all the time. Each one organizes talk and listening differently for different purposes and with different outcomes. They may be used alone or in combination. Any one may supply the structure for an entire lesson, or several may be used as parts of a lesson. For example, an entire lesson may be devoted to students working in small groups. Another lesson may begin with a brief lecture, which leads into a discussion, and then puts students in small groups to work together on an application exercise. However, total reliance on any single strategy makes learning more difficult for some students. Varying strategies and using them in combination are more likely to appeal to different learning styles. It is critical when planning and implementing any of the strategies that you make it as accessible as possible for all students to ensure successful learning experiences.

Chapter 6

Communicating Interpersonally

Ideas to Remember

* Interpersonal communication is defined by the following characteristics:

    The impersonal/personal dimension

    The nature of talk

    Interpersonal needs

    The stages of relationships

* The distinct role differences between teachers and students affect the nature of their interpersonal communication. Three topics exemplify these role differences:

    Purpose (goals)

    Status (power/control)

    Evaluation

* Since teachers are always trying to influence their students to change in some way and students seek to influence their teachers, it is important to view change from a communicative perspective.

* There are factors involved in influence and persuasion that operate as options in interpersonal communication:

    Mutual goal achievement

    Credibility

    Intrinsic motivation

    Extrinsic motivation

Classroom management
Modeling
* Conflict is normal, pervasive, and inevitable. How it is handled may result in three possible outcomes:
  Destructive consequences
  Dysfunctional consequences
  Constructive consequences
* Conflict management needs to be viewed from a communicative perspective. Suggestions for managing conflict:
  Stop, look, and listen
  Use "I" language
  Perception checking
  Molehill minders
  Problem solving

We begin with interpersonal communication because it forms the basis for all communication both in and out of the classroom. "Inter" means between or among, while "personal" refers to persons. Broadly defined, **interpersonal communication** is communication that takes place between persons who are connected in some way (DeVito 1995). This one-to-one communication is called *dyadic communication* ("*dyad*" meaning two). Dyadic forms of communication in classrooms are one-on-one conferences (with a student or a parent), two persons in conversation (i.e. student-student or student-teacher), and the supervision of individual seat work. In chapter 2 we examined how each person communicates from an "I," (a personal, unique) perspective. When two "I"s communicate, then interpersonal communication happens.

As we saw in earlier chapters, one-to-one communication is fundamental. Child to parent is the earliest form of communication. It is through our many relationships—child-parent; sibling-sibling; teacher-student; friend-friend—that roles and expectations for behavior are transmitted and learned. We develop an identity, learn language and how to use it, learn how the world works and how to navigate through it. Interpersonal communication is the process through which we initiate, develop, maintain, and end our relationships. It is our day-to-day interpersonal communicating that continually defines and refines us as people and connects us to others in a complex network of social relationships.

As we learned in chapter 1, all communication involves a content and a relationship. The *content* is the topic or subject of the communicative event. The *relationship* is the connection that happens between people as they communicate about the content. No matter what the nature of the connection initially, it can change as they communicate. Feelings, attitudes, and reactions about the other person are generated, which, in turn, affect the communication process and further define the relationship. When our perceptions are positive, we communicate more and regard the relationship in a positive way.

All communication, then, simultaneously generates these content (task-related) and relational (social-personal) meanings. If the process of communication were a coin, then these two types of meanings would be the two sides. We communicate with others through our prism of "self" with its store of needs, goals, and expectations. We receive feedback and process it, which affects what we "learn" from the situation. We always perceive both kinds of meaning. We are always trying to figure out what something means from our own point of view. We are continually, although often subconsciously, asking ourselves, "What does this mean?" "How am I doing?" "What do I think of this person?" "What do they think of me?"

The Interpersonal Communication Environment

This is what makes dyadic communication the fundamental unit of communication. No matter how many people are involved, what the situation or topic, we take it personally. We listen and speak for ourselves. We assign meaning personally, not generally. As we continually try to figure out content meanings, our personal radar is always sensing relational meanings between us and each person present. We are aware of being part of a group, but we experience it dyadically. For example, when people listen to a lecture, they experience it personally. They may demonstrate appropriate audience behavior, but they listen and react to the content for themselves. They react to the ideas and form personal impressions. They form a dyadic connection to the speaker. It is as if the speaker were speaking only to them.

We think and act in dyadic ways when we communicate even when members of a group. Think of it as always being "half" a dyad with each person in the group as the other "half." The more people involved in a communicative event, the more possible dyadic connections there are. For example, if there are four of us in a conversation, then each of us experiences three dyads. We may be in a group, but we do not perceive the other three people as a group. Each of us perceives the others personally, forming both content and relational meanings with each one. If there are twenty-five students in a class, then each one experiences the other twenty-four personally and dyadically.

This personal dyadic basis of communication has special significance for you as a teacher. It presents you with a paradox. You look at a class and see a sea of faces. The paradox is that each student looks at you and sees one person. The communicative interaction from the students' perspective is dyadic. The meaning of your communication will be interpreted dyadically from each student's point of view for content and personal-social cues. No matter how many students you have, each one will form an interpersonal relationship with you. Large classes and many classes may make it difficult to think in terms of dyadic links with individual students, but that is how each student experiences you. In essence, teachers have to be aware of the class simultaneously at the interpersonal relationship level and at the group level, balancing the needs and demands of both.

The nature of the communication and of the relationships that develop in a classroom are reflected in the **climate**. Climate is the social-emotional atmosphere that develops as a result of the dynamic interplay of interactions among students and teachers. People describe a class's tone or atmosphere from a sense of how the participants feel about each other and about being together. It is the group's characteristic flavor or ambience. Climate is the result of the mix of all the communicative dyadic connections among a group of people over a period of time. The dynamics of the group result from the interpersonal communication and the relationships that develop. This is why the climate can be so different from one class to the next, even when the teacher, the subject, and the age of the students are the same. The people, their communication, and how they relate to each other are different.

Interpersonal communication skills, interpersonal relationships, and climate affect each other. Effective interpersonal communication leads to constructive interpersonal relationships and a positive, supportive climate. Supportive climates nourish positive feelings about the self and others, encourage learning and achievement, and promote communication. Conversely, ineffective interpersonal communication leads to weak relationships and defensive or apathetic climates. If ineffective communication persists, negative or neutral attitudes are fostered about the self and learning.

This chapter focuses on what you need to consider to promote productive interpersonal communication and relationships and a positive classroom climate that is supportive of learning. The chapter begins with the general characteristics of interpersonal communication that apply in and out of the classroom. It then examines what is different about interpersonal communication between teachers and students.

Next, it looks at the content of teachers' talk that is designed to change student behavior. The chapter ends with a look at conflict and how to deal with it.

Characteristics of Interpersonal Communication

What attitudes and skills each of us brings to an interpersonal interaction depends on our own self-concept, goals, expectations, pragmatic behavior, and past experiences. However, there are general characteristics that comprise the interpersonal playing field for everyone, regardless of their individual differences. In this section, we will examine these four elements: the impersonal/personal dimension, the nature of talk, interpersonal needs, and stages of relationships.

The Impersonal/Personal Dimension

Generally, interpersonal communication takes place (for all of us) on many levels and in many contexts. Although interpersonal communication is characterized by dyadic connection, clearly all interpersonal interchanges are not the same. Communicating with a store clerk is not the same as communicating with a friend or a parent. The developmental nature of interpersonal communication helps explain the differences.

Interpersonal communication exists on a continuum ranging from impersonal at one end to personal in the middle to intimate at the other end (DeVito 1995).

Impersonal	Personal	Intimate

When two people meet initially, their communication is impersonal. They communicate within the bounds of public norms and the social roles that bring them together. For example, teacher-student relationships are initially impersonal. Students respond to a specific teacher as they would to any teacher. Teachers respond to students as they would to any students. People's relationships may continue at this impersonal level each time they communicate, or they may become more personal. The connection between two people does not necessarily move in a personal direction. It is only a potentiality. For example, relationships centered around services tend to remain impersonal and formal, such as those with store clerks, bank tellers, and doctors. Some teachers choose to maintain an impersonal level with students.

If people get to know each other better, their communication becomes more personal. They begin to interact as unique individuals rather than on the basis of impersonal roles. They take a personal interest in each other and are able to understand and to predict behavior based on personal information that has been shared. Public norms are replaced gradually by mutually meaningful private norms. For example, people make allowances for people whom they know well that they would not make for strangers or acquaintances.

If people get to know each other very well, then their communication is intimate. Beware of semantic noise. Intimacy, in this sense, refers to psychological closeness, which is achieved only in people's closest relationships.

This developmental dimension is affected by the teaching strategies a teacher uses (Berliner 1984). For example, lecturing distances teachers from students and limits opportunities for personal contact. Small groups involve the teacher as monitor, coach, and resource person, so there are more chances for personal interaction.

The Nature of Talk

The movement from impersonal to personal communication changes how people talk and what they talk about. The nature of the talk evolves as the interpersonal relationship develops. In effect, the better you get to know someone, the easier it becomes to talk with him or her. According to Knapp (1992, pp. 12–18), as a relationship develops, talk changes in eight ways. It becomes:

1. Broader—more topics are talked about in more depth
2. More Unique—more adapted to the individual
3. More Efficient—increased accuracy and speed in sending and interpreting verbal and nonverbal messages
4. More Flexible—greater number of ways any given message can be communicated
5. Smoother—easier to synchronize communicating with the other person
6. More Personal—reveals more personal information about the self
7. More Spontaneous—more informality and comfort about what to bring up and how to react
8. Overt Judgments Given—more giving and getting of positive and negative feedback (more praise and criticism)

Keep in mind this list applies to how your talk and that of your students changes as you get to know each other. Notice most of the items have to do with the *how* of communicating. Numbers 1 and 6 relate to the *what*. Knowing more about each other can help you and your students feel at ease, build trust, and develop greater understanding. Knowing more about your students may help you work more effectively with them (diagnose, remediate, and teach). However, self-disclosure needs to be handled with care.

Self-disclosure is the voluntary revelation of information about yourself that would otherwise be unavailable. According to DeVito (1995), people are more likely to self-disclose in a small group than a large group, but dyadic relationships are the most common setting. Children self-disclose more than adolescents or adults (Stewart et al. 1990).

Keep in mind that people may not be aware they are self-disclosing or the reason for it. When it occurs in school, M. Booth-Butterfield (1992, pp. 95–97) says self-disclosure serves five functions:

- *Expressive.* The expressive function occurs when someone shares intense feelings or important events. For example, a student might disclose something which has occurred at home (an argument, street violence, a new pet).
- *Clarification.* The clarification function is when people discuss something so it becomes clearer to themselves. It is similar to thinking out loud.
- *Information.* The third function involves giving personal information that a person believes the other person needs. For example, a teacher might explain a physical disability to reduce a student's discomfort with it.
- *Relationship Building.* This involves self-disclosures to deepen or strengthen the relationship.
- *Impression Management.* This function occurs when we selectively share information to create or maintain a specific image.

It is important to be alert to possible problems that can arise from self-disclosure. Information may be disclosed that a person later regrets revealing or the other person cannot handle. Instead of greater closeness or understanding in the relationship, embarrassment or avoidance could result. Also, self-disclosure invites reciprocal self-disclosure, that is the other person feels he or she must also self-disclose. Your self-disclosure, as a teacher, might make a student feel pressured to self-disclose also. Finally, students sometimes self-disclose personal problems. Anytime a student begins a conversation with, "You have to promise you won't tell anyone," consider your answer carefully. You could put yourself in the position of not being able to get the student to the kind of expert needed to deal with the problem or withholding important information from the parents or caregivers.

Effective self-disclosure is appropriate and occurs incrementally in the context of a developing relationship. This means a little at a time, incidentally as it seems to fit to make a point. Pamela Cooper (1991) suggests the following guidelines for deciding whether a particular disclosure (yours or someone else's) is appropriate: timing, motives, the other person's capacity to respond, relevancy, feelings (of discloser and the other person), and short-term effects.

Interpersonal Needs

Meeting our basic interpersonal needs is as important to our psychological-social health as meeting our physiological needs (food, water, air) is to our physical life. Our "self" must meet these interpersonal needs in order to thrive. We continually strive to meet these needs through our interpersonal relationships. We may not be consciously aware of having these needs or of how we try to meet them, yet they affect how we communicate. These needs are part of who we are—teachers and students—when we enter classrooms. Understanding what these needs are gives us another way to interpret the interpersonal behavior of other people, as well as our own. Asking the question, "What interpersonal need does this meet?" may make sense out of otherwise inexplicable behavior.

As teachers, we need to question how interpersonal needs affect classroom communication, relationships, and climate: ours with our students' and students' with each other's. We can ask these questions about individual relationships or about relationships collectively. "How am I attempting to meet my needs in my interpersonal relationships with my students?" "How do students meet these needs in class (with me/each other)?" "Do I let how students are meeting their needs in other relationships (for example, joining a gang) affect my relationship with them?" "How can I help students meet their interpersonal needs in class?" "How can meeting these needs help foster a supportive climate?"

According to Schutz (1966), there are three basic interpersonal needs: inclusion, control, and affection. Each need has two dimensions: the degree to which a person needs to give it and the degree to which he or she needs to receive it from others. Think about your personal needs to give and to get.

1. *Inclusion.* This is the need to be included and socialize with others. It is the need to fit in and feel that you belong. Meeting this need makes people feel recognized as individuals. People with

high inclusion needs may "hang out" and prefer having a lot of social activities. When the need is not met, loneliness and alienation may result (Civikly 1992). People with low inclusion needs prefer solitary activities.

2. *Control.* This need involves matters of responsibility, decision making, achievement, and influence. When we feel in control, we feel competent and empowered. If people have high control needs, they want to make their own choices and decisions. People with low control needs prefer to follow someone else's lead. M. Booth-Butterfield (1992) points out that teachers' perceptions of students' behavior may actually be a reflection of control needs. What a teacher labels as "stubbornness" may result from a high need for control, while "lack of initiative" may be due to a low need for control.

3. *Affection.* This involves the need to feel emotionally close to others and to feel liked. Recall from the nonverbal behavior chapter how people demonstrate liking (or dislike) nonverbally through proxemics, kinesics, touch, and paralanguage. Younger children are more direct in their attempts to satisfy affection needs than adolescents and adults (M. Booth-Butterfield 1992). Students with high affection needs may ask others to tell them that they like them.

The Stages of Relationships

Researchers have developed models of the stages that interpersonal relationships go through from inception to termination.[1] These models refer to adult interpersonal relationships and differ in their terminology and number of stages. However, this concept of stages can be applied to understanding the nature of relationship development between teachers and students. Knowing what to expect at different stages in the process can help you understand the communicating that occurs. How long any stage lasts depends on the situation and the participants.

1. *Initiating.* Teacher and students experience first-day apprehension and anticipation. They meet as strangers armed with their past experiences and expectations. First impressions form.

2. *Exploration.* Teachers and students start to get to know each other and explore the possibilities in the situation. Teachers set parameters by establishing rules, explaining procedures, and developing routines. They diagnose, review, and discover what students respond to. Students test the boundaries.

3. *Intensifying*. Teachers and students know each other better. The behavior of each is more predictable to the other, which makes for a more comfortable communication environment. Communication may become more personal. The tone or climate of the class is apparent. Classes with warm, positive climates may develop their own slang and personalized norms or routines.

4. *Navigating*. The relationships that have been established continue. Whether the climate is positive (supportive) or negative (nonsupportive), people know what they need to do to get by in the situation. The norms, roles, and routines keep everyone on a more or less even keel.

5. *Differentiation*. The end of the relationship is signalled by the calendar and the end of the instructional unit. This stage is defined by the nature of the relationships established and the level of the students. When positive relationships have developed, both teacher and students may regret their ending. If relationships are impersonal or negative, there may be either apathy or glee.

6. *Termination*. Teachers know on the first day of class that their relationship with their students will officially end on the last day of class. Students, whether they like their teachers or not, still prefer summer vacation to attending school. Some students, usually few in number, drop back for a visit, or keep in touch, at least, for a while.

The impersonal/personal dimension, the nature of talk, interpersonal needs, and stages of relationship operate in all interpersonal communication. However, because the teacher-student relationship is institutionalized, it is unlike other interpersonal relationships. Government provides the means, regulates the training of teachers and the operation of the schools, and specifies outcomes; society defines role expectations for teachers and students.

Role Differences between Teachers and Students

Teachers and students have distinct roles which are bestowed with rights and obligations. Students have feelings, attitudes, and perceptions about their own and their teachers' roles as do teachers. Appreciating the differences between the roles of teachers and students is fundamental to understanding interpersonal communication and relationships in the classroom. Three topics exemplify the kinds of differences that exist: purpose, status, and evaluation.

Purpose (Goals)

Teachers and students come to the classroom with different purposes. Teachers choose to be there because they like working with young people. They choose a subject to teach because they enjoy it. Definitions of teaching and learning vary, but they all share a common purpose, that the student will be different after the experience in some positive, useful, or productive way. Teachers are in the business of changing students as knowers and thinkers. Sprague (1993) refers to teaching as a "transforming" experience, in which people and consciousness are transformed. Teachers' focus is on students accomplishing specific, task-related learning goals.

Although students have goals in their personal lives, school is not usually integral to that life. They come to class without any clearly defined academic purpose. Many students come out of habit, because it is the thing to do, or their parents make them. Society expects children to attend school, and the law demands it until the age of sixteen. If pressed to explain their purpose in school, many students may cite social reasons (to be with their friends), practical reasons (a safe place to be), or reasons related to an activity (sports, band). For some students, the reasons may be to get a job or to get into college. But for most students, purposes for being in school are personal, vague, and non-academic.

Status (Power/Control)

A relationship based on differences between individuals in status, experience, and authority is called **complementary.** This means the behavior of one person serves as a stimulus for the other's complementary behavior. The person in the superior position in the relationship has power and control and is expected to demonstrate leadership. Teachers and students are unequal in status. Teachers have the greater status and are defined as "in charge" in the relationship. Examples of other complementary relationships are doctor-patient and employer-employee.

Traditionally, people believe teachers have power and students do not. Actually, they both do, although students have a different type of power. The power of each affects the other. The exercise of teachers' and students' power is part of the dynamic process of interpersonal communication. According to French and Raven (1968), there are five types of power.

1. *Expert power* is based on knowledge.
2. *Legitimate power* is the perceived right to influence.

3. *Reward power* is based on the control of awards.
4. *Referent power* is identification with a person as leader.
5. *Coercive power* involves inflicting punishment.

The state officially grants teachers the right to use four of these five types of power. Teachers' status assumes they have the greater knowledge, the right to influence, and the license to dispense rewards and punishments. The fifth type, referent power, rests on the students' perception of the teacher and depends on the relationships that develop between the teacher and the students. **Referent power** is power students "give" teachers when they identify with them as people. S. Booth-Butterfield (1992) points out a connection between student-teacher relationships and discipline. When students like their teachers, they are more involved in class work and interferences are reduced because "students seldom hassle people they like" (p. 93).

Students' power lies in their response to whatever teachers initiate, including teachers' displays of power. The menu of possible student responses includes: accept, comply, become involved with/excited about, withdraw, or protest. "Power to control approval" and "unwillingness to suspend disinterest" are how students balance the classroom power equation in their favor (Brenders 1987, p. 55). Students' other source of power is the power or control that teachers give them in terms of decision making and responsibility.

Student power is effective because getting students' responses—the click of understanding, the "aha" moment—are powerful reasons why teachers teach. Teachers need responses that let them know that their energy and effort are worth it. They need feedback that affirms them in their role of teacher. Sprague (1993, p. 360) says teachers who keep going despite the lack of even a "returned gaze" should be honored for their patience and long-term vision, but they are not realistic models for the rest of us. Teachers who have high needs to be liked by all their students may blur the lines of distinction between themselves and their students. Brenders (1987) says such teachers may change their behavior in order to make students like them, such as reducing standards or requiring less work.

J. Cooper (1990) explains how different philosophical approaches to controlling student behavior leads to differing student responses. *Authoritarian* teachers dominate, using force, competition, and punishment (or its threat). *Laissez-faire* teachers abdicate leadership. Their permissiveness allows students to do whatever they like. *Democratic* teachers guide, treating students as responsible and capable of decision making and problem solving. Cooper states the first two approaches lead to student frustration, hostility, withdrawal, and a lack of productivity. Democratic classrooms foster trust between teachers and students and are more productive.

The state government may confer the right to use certain kinds of power, but it cannot guarantee or predict students' responses to their use. It is up to you to decide which source(s) of power to use under what circumstances with which students. How your students respond will vary with their age, experiences, backgrounds, needs, goals, and their perceptions of you.

Evaluation

Evaluation is something teachers do to students, and students have done to them. Students do not have the opportunity to formally evaluate their teachers. Teachers are expected to evaluate their students' performance and are continually diagnosing, measuring achievement, and trying to determine if learning has occurred. In addition, most states require students to take periodic proficiency or competency tests that measure students' cumulative learning and usually rank their scores against those of other students. Recall from the listening chapter, no one likes to be judged. According to psychologist Jack Gibbs (1960), when people feel judged in a personal way, they often react defensively.

To Sum Up

What the differences between teachers and students mean depends on your point of view. Some students may feel the deck is stacked against them. The school's driving purpose is to change them; they have inferior status; and they are continually being evaluated. Teachers may feel their task is all uphill, since differences often set teachers and students in opposition to each other.

Think of differences in terms of what they imply about students meeting their interpersonal needs (inclusion, control, and affection). The sheer amount of time students are in school makes it imperative to consider their position and the degree to which their needs are recognized, dealt with, or ignored. Whether or not students meet their interpersonal needs depends on how teachers define, shape, and evaluate what goes on.

What the differences between teachers and students mean in your particular classroom depend on the communicative choices you make as you discover who you are in your new role of teacher. Recall the dimensions of the teacher's role: self-presentation, rules and regulations, instruction, feedback, and affect. How you communicate all these aspects of teaching affects your students' perception of you and your interpersonal communication with them. As the teacher, your communication behavior starts the process in motion. You set the tone, respond to students, and model the behaviors you expect.

So far in the text, we have examined elements of effective communication that lead to constructive interpersonal relationships and supportive climates in classrooms. We have examined the importance of positive self-concept, dual perspective (empathy), high expectations, immediacy in nonverbal communication, the importance of respect, flexibility and appropriateness in using language (linguistics and pragmatics), feedback, and effective listening. All of these play an important part in sending positive, supportive relational messages.

In the next section, we turn our attention to the content of teachers' talk, specifically to the options available for influencing students.

Teacher Influence

Since the purpose of teaching is to change students as knowers and thinkers, the content of teacher-talk is related to the task of change. The next three chapters deal with different types of teaching strategies for changing students in some way: provoking thought (discussion), enabling cooperative group effort (small groups), and giving information (lectures). This section looks at the nature of teacher influence in effecting change in students' behavior.

Teachers are always trying to influence students about something, persuading them to change in some way. The "about something" may be the class, the lesson, other students, self, learning, goals, and the list goes on. The sought-after changes may be large (come to school regularly) or small (do additional problems), internal (a more positive attitude toward school) or external (turn in work on time). Sometimes internal changes lead to some kind of observable, external behavior. For example, a more positive attitude might reveal itself through class participation. Hamachek (1971) says good teachers are distinguished by their ability to influence both student feeling and achievement in positive ways. Being able to encourage student cooperation may make the difference between an effective and an ineffective teacher (Kearney 1987).

A frequent goal of teacher influence is motivating students to: be ready for an activity, try, learn, and persevere. Discipline reflects teachers' persuasive powers for it indicates the degree to which students behave appropriately and are involved in classroom activities (Emmer 1987). For most people, discipline has negative connotations of punishment. However, what is important is appropriate behavior for the good of individual students and the class as a whole. **Discipline** defines the boundaries of appropriateness with norms that are necessary and useful to facilitate learning. Teachers influence students to be disciplined in this sense and for this reason—to stay in bounds so everyone has more of a chance to learn.

A Communicative Perspective on Change

It is important when thinking about influencing students to remember several points about change. To help view change from the students' perspective, let's think in personal terms: (1) When someone insists we change, it implies we are wrong, defective, or inadequate. Even when the setting is school and the content appears neutral (do math this way), there are still relational meanings. If the content is personal, for instance attitudes and beliefs are involved, students may feel their referent groups (family, neighborhood, culture) are being criticized, which will likely produce resistance. (2) Change is risky business because it pushes us out of our comfort zone (the habitual, the familiar) into the new and unknown. Our sense of self is at risk. Although it is popularly believed that only Eastern cultures are concerned about loss of face, this is not the case. We all fear looking incompetent or stupid in front of other people, especially people whose opinion we value. For students, the significant others may be peers or perhaps the teacher. (3) Students are also continually trying to influence and persuade teachers. Think of how and about what you have tried to influence your teachers. The possible goals are as numerous as students: to like you; to leave you alone; to give you good grades; to show you respect; to confirm your self-image, your liking for them, your indifference to them; and so forth.

Think from a communicative perspective when trying to influence or persuade student(s). Analyze the context, your goals, the student(s), and their goals before choosing how to proceed. There is no one set of answers or magic formula that works all the time. What works with one student or class may not work with another (or even with the same student or class on another day). You must consider the possibilities within the framework of your immediate situation.

The following factors are involved in influence and persuasion. Think of them as available options. It is up to you to decide if and how to use them: mutual goal achievement, credibility, intrinsic motivation, extrinsic motivators, classroom management, and modeling.

Mutual Goal Achievement

The dynamic, mutual influencing and persuading going on between teachers and students is fundamental to classroom communication

(Phillips, Butt, and Metzger 1974). Mutual goal achievement involves teachers reaching their own educational goals by helping students reach their goals.

Persuading Students. Phillips, Butt, and Metzger believe teachers need to persuade students in terms of students' own goals rather than influencing them through rewards, threats, and punishments. Teachers must search for compatibilities among their goals, those of the school, and those of the students and then make the connections clear to students. This involves getting to know students well, accepting and respecting them for who they are and encouraging their *real lives* to enter the classroom in every possible way.

When trying to persuade students, teachers should "beam their appeals" to students' needs and remember Aristotle's dictum, "The fool tells me his reasons, the wise man persuades me with my own" (Phillips, Butt, and Metzger 1974, p. 16). The success of persuasive efforts depends upon the people receiving them. Do the reasons for change make sense from the students' point of view? Are the reasons supported by others, such as parents or care givers?

Parental Influence. Research indicates the attitude of parents about education and school have an enormous impact on what and how their children do in school. Wlodkowski and Jaynes (1990) say parents are the primary influence on a child's motivation to learn, and their attitude impacts on every stage of development through high school and beyond. *Strong Families, Strong Schools*, a 1994 U.S. Department of Education Report, cites the following outcomes when parents are involved in positive ways: higher grades and test scores, better attendance, more positive attitudes and behavior demonstrated, more homework completed, and greater enrollment in higher education (Henderson and Berla 1994; Becher 1984).

You need to tap into this reservoir of influence and solicit parents' help in achieving the goal that you have in common: promoting their children's learning. Although any caring parent or caregiver embraces such a goal, many do not become involved in their children's school. Their potential influence on their children's motivation and achievement in school is lost. Lack of involvement may be interpreted by their children as meaning that school does not matter. The question is, "Why don't they get involved?"

Why Parents Do Not Get Involved. Try to think from the parents' point of view in answering this question. If you can discover what the obstacles are, then you can find ways to overcome them. Consider possible psychological or social noise and present circumstances. Parents may be embarrassed, intimidated, or dismissive due to bad personal school experiences, never finishing school, or doing poorly. Different cultural or language backgrounds might make parents self-conscious about their English or lack of English or inability to read notes and invitations sent home. They may not know that it is O.K. to be involved. Depending on their background, they might assume teachers will contact them if there is a problem. Other parents might assume contact from the school means their child has done something wrong and has brought shame on the family. With single-parent families and with families that need two incomes, parent-teacher conferences scheduled once a term may be impossible to attend due to a conflicting work schedule or lack of money for a baby-sitter.

Enlisting Parent(s). For many parents, the role of team member working with the teacher is a new one. Recall from our examination of pragmatics, we learn new roles when we understand what the expectations are and have a chance to practice them. You need to discuss your expectations with parents and find ways to work together. There are many ways to improve parent-teacher communication and coordination of efforts. What works for you will depend on you, your students, and their parents. Consider literacy levels and the language spoken at home. To prime your creative thinking consider the following ideas that have worked well. (Some of these ideas were suggested by my former students.)

1. The teacher sent a note home to all the parents at the beginning of the year with her phone number. She reassured parents that it was normal for students to have problems and questions and to please call her at home when they did. Soon after, my student's son, who was in the second grade, was confused about an assignment, so he called the teacher. The teacher talked to him for half an hour. When he hung up, he said he would not need to call her any more. "I can just talk to her in class from now on."

2. The following is from a secondary teacher who supervised one of my student teachers: In the fall the teacher called every parent, introduced herself, explained what the class would be doing, and asked them to call if there were any problems. She followed up when she needed help with projects, discipline problems, and to invite parents to special class functions.

3. Ask for involvement that fits parents' schedules and comfort levels. At the beginning of the year send home a check-list of the kinds of help you need with an "other" category included. The student who shared this idea had received a checklist from her child's elementary teacher with the categories: trips, tutoring, reading, parties, and other.

4. Let parents know what is going on. Send home copies of rules, procedures, and policies. Some teachers send home a monthly calendar page with tests, special events, deadlines, etc. Other teachers use periodic newsletters to inform parents and share achievements of the class. (These could be put together by different groups of students.)

5. Send home notes for positive reasons, such as effort and improvement, not just for negative behavior.

6. Many parents would help their children with schoolwork if they knew what to do. Give parents specific suggestions and explain how it aids their children's learning: listening to them read, checking problems, discussing issues (current events), discussing what is going on in school, helping with projects, or simply being with them while they do their homework.

7. Try to meet and talk with parents as often as possible, however you can arrange it. Try to build the expectation that frequent communication is most helpful for their children. Set up periodic parent-teacher conferences at the parents' convenience. Consider the advantages of inviting the parents and their children to conferences. If school policies allow, invite parents to drop in and observe. To meet parents, set up dates and times to meet parents that work out with their schedules.

8. When you meet with or talk to parents, be positive about your expectations for their child and appreciative of their time (in talking to you, working at home with their child). Be specific in comments about effort and improvement, be nonjudgmental, ask for feedback, and ask for questions. If there is a problem with the child's behavior or work, problem-solve together to arrive at a workable, mutually satisfying goal for you, the parents, and the child.

Credibility

What students think of you is called credibility. Since it is based on an individual's perceptions, students vary in whether they think you are credible or not. These perceptions may change as they get to know you better. Credibility involves belief, not facts, so accuracy or even agreement with reality is irrelevant. According to Bassett and Smythe (1979), would-be persuaders must be perceived in positive ways in order to be able to persuade. In other words, if your students find you credible, then you will have more influence with them.

Contributing Factors. According to McCroskey (1982), credibility has five dimensions. How a student perceives you in terms of these qualities determines the degree of credibility you have in the mind of that student. As you read each item, think about what behaviors might cause a student to decide a teacher had the quality. What did your teachers do that demonstrated each dimension?

1. *Expertise*. Is the teacher knowledgeable about the topics taught? Is the teacher a well-informed, intelligent person?
2. *Trustworthiness*. Does the teacher come across as a decent person? Is the teacher fair to everyone, consistent, honest, and ethical?
3. *Composure*. Does the teacher seem to be in control of what is going on and comfortable in the situation?
4. *Dynamism*. Is the teacher active, energetic, and attentive?
5. *Sociability*. Is the teacher outgoing, accessible, available, and friendly?

Types of Credibility. There are two types of credibility which differ in terms of timing. **Initial credibility** is the credibility you have before students interact with you. It is based partly on the reputation of the school, which is reflected on you when you are hired. It can also be based on the reputation you earn when you teach in a school. The school and community grapevines spread word about you. Students, who have never met you, enter class *knowing* what you are like. **Derived credibility** results from actual, first-hand experience with you. It evolves on a continual basis from what you say and do in your daily interactions with students. Teachers need to achieve and then try to maintain high derived credibility with their students (Bassett and Smythe 1979).

Intrinsic Motivation

When an individual likes or enjoys an activity for its own sake, **intrinsic motivation** usually occurs. It is not the same as motivation to learn, which is finding academic activities meaningful and trying to derive the intended academic benefits from them (Brophy 1987b). However, teachers can capitalize on students' intrinsic motivation by planning academic activities that they will take part in because they are interested in the content or enjoy the task. Using intrinsic motivation may influence students to take part in class activities and lead to learning.

Brophy (1987a, pp. 44–46) suggests the following ways to allow for individual differences in what students find intrinsically motivating. As you read the list, reflect on their compatibility with ideas already discussed. Many of these intrinsic motivators are inherent in the strategies that we will examine in the remaining chapters.

1. *Adapt tasks to student interests.* When using examples, applications, and activities, choose content the students can relate to.

2. *Include novelty/variety elements.* Something about each activity should be new or different, whether in form, content, media involved, or nature of response.

3. *Allow choices.* As possible, offer students alternative ways to meet requirements and make autonomous decisions about how to organize their time and effort. If students need to learn how to make effective decisions, give them a menu of choices or require them to get their choice approved.

4. *Provide opportunities for students to respond actively.* Most students prefer active involvement to passive listening and reading. Provide opportunities to do: projects, experiments, role-play activities, drama, simulations, educational games, and creative applications of what is being studied.

5. *Allow students to create finished projects.* Students experience a sense of accomplishment when they complete projects that have meaning or integrity in their own right and can be used or displayed, such as maps, models, or essays.

6. *Incorporate game-like features into exercises when possible.* This includes test-yourself challenges, elements of suspense, puzzles, and brain-teasers.

7. *Provide opportunities to interact with peers.* Schedule discussion, debate, role-play or simulation. Plan follow-up activities that permit students to work together in pairs or small groups to tutor one another, discuss issues, or work on group projects or problems.

Extrinsic Motivation

Teachers use **extrinsic motivation** (outside or external to students) to persuade students to behave in ways the teachers want. The premise of extrinsic reinforcement is that consequences influence behavior. According to Piper (1974), there are four basic categories of consequences: positive reinforcement (a reward is introduced), extinction or time out (a reward is removed), punishment, and negative reinforcement (a punishment is removed).

Kohn does not believe rewards should be given for things that students should do for their own sake, like reading, writing, and acting responsibly ("The Case Against . . . ," 1994). He suggests giving students a chance to find material intrinsically interesting instead of promising rewards for compliance. Chance and Kohn (as cited in Miller 1994, p. 2) advise:

1. Avoid using rewards as incentives.
2. Avoid competition between students.
3. Set high standards for performance.
4. Help students find their own inner reasons for wanting to learn.

Brophy (1987a) recommends rewards be given for good or improved performance in a way that emphasizes the knowledge and skills being developed. He thinks there is a place for competition for rewards as an individual or as a team member. He points out that rewards and competition are more effective for stimulating intensity of effort than for affecting thoughtfulness or quality of performance. He recommends rewards be used with practice tasks designed to produce mastery of specific skills and with tasks where speed or quantity matters. Brophy organizes rewards into five categories:

1. Material objects—prizes, consumables
2. Activity rewards and special privileges—games, self-selected activities
3. Symbolic rewards—grades, displays of good work
4. Praise and social rewards—teacher or peer attention
5. Teacher rewards—opportunities to do things with the teacher

In traditional behavior modification, the timing and frequency of rewards and punishments are important in achieving the desired effect. "Timing" means the consequence must follow the behavior immediately. Behavior that is not reinforced at once is weakened, while behavior that is not punished immediately is strengthened (J. Cooper 1990). "Frequency" refers to how often a behavior is reinforced. Consistent reinforcement of a behavior results in its being learned more quickly.

Reward and Punishment Issues. There are several issues about rewards and punishments that we need to consider:

- *Rewards and punishments must be defined by the individual student.* One student's reward may be another student's punishment. The classic example involves students who keep repeating the same behavior, which gets them sent to the office. Getting thrown out of class is meant as a punishment, yet it is experienced as a reward. Any of the listed rewards could be a punishment for an individual student.

    As pointed out earlier in the chapter, it takes time to get to know students and to figure out what they respond to. Observation helps. You could find out what students think are rewards or punishments by asking them individually, discussing the topic with the whole class, or putting students into small groups to generate answers. The groups' ideas could then be shared with the class and further discussed.

- *There may be more meaningful sources of reinforcement than the teacher's rewards or punishments* (M. Booth-Butterfield 1992). For example, the peer group or the neighborhood may be the significant reinforcers. Former students of mine have reported that corporal punishment in their high schools was not taken seriously. Being "whacked" resulted in prestige with peers, who viewed it as a sort of thumbing your nose at the system.

- *Rewards and punishments are not opposites but two sides of the same coin, both are forms of external control* ("The Case Against . . . ," 1994).

- *The desired behavior may be produced only in the face of the reward; the student has not internalized the desired behavior.* M. Booth-Butterfield (1992, p. 75) says the teacher must then continue providing the correct consequences in order to get the desired behaviors. He raises the question, "Who is being trained, the teacher or the student?" The nationwide pizzas for reading campaign illustrates this idea. John Nichols says the program has produced the predictable result of "a lot of fat kids who don't like to read (Cited in "The Case Against . . . ," 1994, p. 6).

- *Extrinsic rewards may undermine students' intrinsic motivation.* Studies since the 1970s indicate that the greater the incentive, the larger the negative effect on intrinsic motivation (Miller 1994). Extrinsic rewards are most likely to hurt motivation when students' initial level of interest is very high and the rewards are held out in advance as incentives (Chance 1992).

- *The more students and behaviors that are involved, the harder it is to maintain good timing and frequency.*

- *Punishment produces negative consequences.* Punished students may respond by avoidance of the situation physically (cut class) or psychologically (not listen) (Dembo 1991). Good and Brophy (1994) say punishment communicates a lack of confidence in the students, a belief the misbehavior is deliberate, and a feeling the student is not trying to improve. They say even when these perceptions are accurate, communicating them can harm students' self-concepts and further reduce their willingness to cooperate.

- *Praise* is one type of reward which is used in the belief that it is effective as a reinforcer. Much teacher praise is *not* a deliberate reinforcement attempt but is a spontaneous reaction to student behavior. Students elicit and reinforce teacher praise through the quality of their performance, requests for praise, or personalities (extroverted or sociable) (Brophy 1979).

Praise. Let's examine more closely what praise does. Praise provides information to all students who observe the student receiving the praise (Brophy and Good 1986). This information involves: knowledge about answers, desired behaviors, and teacher expectations for performance. According to (Brophy 1979) commonly observed meanings and functions of praise are:

- *Balance for criticism or vindication of expectations*—Praise given for improved work with the connotation, "See, I told you that you could do better."
- *Vicarious reinforcement*—Praise for a particular student's behavior with the purpose of letting the other students know what they should be doing. The student who is the focus may feel embarrassed or punished.
- *Positive guidance or avoidance of criticism*—Praise given in positive language instead of nagging or criticizing. "I like the way . . ." Often used as part of developing a friendly, cooperative atmosphere.
- *Transition ritual*—Praise given to acknowledge a student has finished one activity and is ready to begin another.
- *Consolation prize or encouragement*—Praise given to provide general encouragement and reaffirmation of the student-teacher relationship.

The meaning students assign to praise depends on its verbal and nonverbal content, the situation (where, when, who else hears it), their own needs and expectations, and their relationship with you. What works for one student may be perceived as manipulation, condescension, or ridicule by another. Praise of a high-ability student for success on an easy task may lead to a lower self-concept of ability (Wittrock 1986). Teachers need to monitor their students' reactions to their praise efforts and respond accordingly.

Praise is likely to be encouraging if it is *contingent* (upon performance of the behavior to be reinforced), *specific* (about the particulars of the behavior, the criteria for praise), and *sincere or credible* (content varies according to the situation and the student's effort) (Brophy 1979). Brophy says that infrequent praise meeting these criteria is more encouraging than frequent but trivial or inappropriate praise.

Others also emphasize descriptive feedback but place more emphasis on the students' responses:

1. Talk to students about what they have done and why they have done it. This opens a conversation in which students reflect on their work and feel supported by their teacher ("The Case Against . . ," 1994).
2. Give information about the quality of the performance. Chance (1992) says such *informational rewards* maintain or enhance intrinsic motivation.
3. Provide a specific description, rather than a global evaluation. For example, instead of "great job," describe the job, "you finished all the practice problems." This allows students to praise themselves (Farber and Mazlish 1995).

Classroom Management

Teachers encourage learning activities in their classrooms using **classroom management.** When teachers can influence their students to become and to stay involved, there are fewer interruptions, more time is spent in learning activities, and more student achievement (Berliner 1984). Greater and more student involvement and achievement could increase motivation for learning and contribute to students having more positive perceptions of themselves as learners. Effective classroom management might also contribute to students' positive perceptions of your credibility, particularly the dimensions of composure, dynamism, and sociability.

Management techniques focus on running the classroom efficiently and preventing inattention and boredom, which lead to discipline problems. Regulating the flow and pace of activities is viewed as essential. According to Kounin (1970, ch. 5), effective management is characterized by "smoothness" (absence of teacher behaviors that slow the pace) and "momentum" (building and maintaining momentum). The focus is on preventing problems that would interfere with learning tasks and, if disruptions occur, dealing with them quickly. Suggestions contributing to efficient classroom management include:

1. Establish clear rules and consequences for violations at the beginning of the year. Rules should be posted. Some teachers have parents and students sign a copy of the rules, so everyone knows what is expected. Since the focus is preventative, the number of rules should be limited to the essential (S. Booth-Butterfield 1992). The more rules to break and enforce, the more interruptions and downtime, when learning activities are not occurring. Consequences should be logically related to the rules

and nonjudgmental. Rationales should be given.

Gordon (1974) suggests establishing rules and consequences through class discussion. There are three steps to developing a set of rules: description, rationale, and consequences. Agreed-upon rules are posted. Student participation in the decision-making process has four positive benefits: (1) It contributes to a sense of group identity and a more positive climate. (2) Students are more motivated to follow rules they helped create. (3) Less enforcement by the teacher is needed. The group is responsible for enforcing the rules. (4) The rules will be more relevant and usually of a higher quality than those set by the teacher alone.

2. It is a good idea to monitor continually what is going on all over the room in order to nip problems in the bud, whether they are academic, social, or inappropriate behavior (S. Booth-Butterfield 1992). Kounin (1970, p. 79) calls this "with-it-ness." When teachers are observant and scan their students' nonverbal behavior for meaning, they are demonstrating this quality.

3. Kounin (1970, p. 85) uses the term "overlapping" when teachers handle more than one thing at a time to prevent problems. For example, two students begin talking while the teacher is giving directions. The teacher would continue with the directions and deal with the talking before it becomes disruptive using nonverbal cues: proxemics (moving towards the students), paralanguage (speaking louder, slower, pausing), or kinesics (frowning or making eye contact with the students until they stop).

4. Plan lessons that are cohesive and give clear signals to avoid downtime. Clear signals let students know what they are to attend to and move them smoothly from one activity to another (Dembo 1991). We discussed these kinds of signals in the previous chapter on listening. Downtime occurs whenever there is discontinuity in a lesson. Possible causes of lesson discontinuity are: inadequate teacher preparation for the lesson, inappropriate level of difficulty, breaks to handle misbehavior, or stopping to do something that could be handled at another time.

Modeling

Throughout our lives we learn through observing and imitating other people. What we do and say in the classroom serves as a model for our students. **Modeling** means demonstrating the behaviors that we want students to adopt. The more credible we are and the better they get to know us, the more likely our students will be influenced by our example. Brophy (1987a, p. 46–48) suggests that teachers model the following behaviors because they influence a student's motivation to learn:

1. *Demonstrating an interest in learning and a motivation to learn.* Show your students that you value learning as a satisfying activity. Brophy suggests sharing your interest in books, articles, television programs, or movies on the subject you teach. Make connections between your subject, students' lives, and local and current events.

2. *Communicating high expectations about your students' motivation to learn.* Let them know that you expect them to want to learn and to apply what they are learning.

3. *Projecting intensity.* Use nonverbal behavior to emphasize that the material deserves attention. Brophy feels that being dramatic is especially important when introducing new content, demonstrating skills, and giving assignments.

4. *Projecting enthusiasm.* Let students know what you find interesting about various topics and assignments.

5. *Verbalizing and demonstrating task-related thinking and problem-solving strategies.* Cognitive strategies are invisible to students unless teachers make them overt by showing students what to do and thinking out loud as they demonstrate (p. 48).

No matter how effective you are in persuading your students or how positive the climate is, conflict is inevitable in your classroom. In the next and final section, we look at the nature of conflict and how to deal with it.

Conflict

Are you dismayed by the inevitability of conflict in your class? If so, then you, like most people, have negative connotations for conflict. Many cultures and religions view conflict as wrong, especially in interpersonal communication. Conflict is seen as a failure of sense, faith, or effort that must be avoided and suppressed or, at least, not admitted.

However, conflict is a normal, pervasive, and inevitable part of all communication. Conflict is expressed, experienced, and managed through communication (Hocker and Wilmot 1985). **Conflict** occurs when people *perceive*:

incompatible goals,

differences (in interests, needs, or values),

scarcity of some resource (money, time, space, attention), inter-ference in achieving personal goals. [2]

If the differing perceptions are about something that is meaningful to the people involved, then a conflict exists. Conflict involves a personal dimension and sometimes an emotional element. Since each of us communicates from a unique perspective to meet personal needs and goals, conflict is a potential whenever two or more people are gathered together. This is true in interpersonal communication and groups of all sizes—teams, families, classes, neighborhoods, businesses and organizations, and nations. In this chapter, we have examined many factors that lead to conflict in the classroom: differences between teachers and students about general purpose and specific goals, power, evaluation, and interpersonal needs.

Benefits of Conflict

Conflict happens. The important issue is our attitude toward conflict, which determines how we respond to it. We need to change our negative outlook to a more positive one. We need to try to interpret conflict as the Chinese do. The Chinese character for conflict is also the character for opportunity. To see conflict as opportunity you need to think about the possible benefits of conflict:

- Provides feedback about students that helps you understand them as individuals (Bassett and Smythe 1979).
- Reduces ambiguity and provides clarification about boundaries, assignments, behavior, and expectations.
- Unleashes creativity. The resolution to a conflict often produces better, more effective, workable, and creative ideas or procedures.
- Improves interpersonal relationships. Dealing effectively with feelings and problems as they occur in relationships helps develop confidence, trust, and security.
- Helps develop and maintain a healthy social climate through reducing tensions, allowing students to air their feelings and problems, and preventing stagnation (Bassett and Smythe 1979).
- Reveals strengths and weaknesses, prevents inequitable power plays, promotes new social networks, and "a vital check-and-balance system" (Bassett and Smythe 1979, p. 263).
- Helps groups make better decisions. This benefit applies to groups of all sizes, small groups as well as classroom groups.

Working through conflict can also bind groups closer together, define their structure, and promote helpful coalitions (Hocker and Wilmot 1985). Groups without conflict can fall into "groupthink," which is decision making with insufficient exploration of issues and alternatives.

Possible Outcomes

Whether conflict proves to be an opportunity or results in disaster depends on how it is handled. There are three typical outcomes to conflict (Bassett and Smythe 1979).

1. *Destructive Consequences*. Conflicts are **destructive** when there is no resolution to the issue. The conflict spirals upward until someone drops out. They are characterized by overt power manipulation, threats, coercion, and deception (Deutsch 1973). There are no winners. The outcomes may be dissatisfaction, distorted self-images, misperceptions of the other people involved, and resentment (Bassett and Smythe 1979). Hocker and Wilmot (1985) feel the best index of a destructive conflict is when some or all of the participants have a strong desire to get even or damage the other(s).

2. *Dysfunctional Consequences*. Conflicts are **dysfunctional** when they seem to have been resolved, but residual negative feelings remain. Winners and losers have been declared, but tension remains. Either teachers or students may be winners or losers, depending upon how the conflict is resolved. For example, teachers may lose because they give in to intimidation by student(s). Students may lose when teachers "pull rank," and they feel the decision is unfair. Classroom life goes on, but there are side effects. Communication becomes strained, and tasks are less easily accomplished. The level of personal-social satisfaction in the class is reduced. Dysfunctional consequences reoccur. A win-lose orientation leaves unexpressed, underlying conflict that evolves into overt conflict (Bassett and Smythe 1979).

3. *Constructive Consequences*. Conflicts are **constructive** when participants receive some measure of satisfaction from the resolution and feel that their efforts were productive (Deutsch 1969). In other words, participants feel heard; they have a chance to express themselves and have their point of view taken into account in the creation of a resolution. This is a win-win situation for everyone involved. Conflicts resolved constructively tend to produce benefits.

In sum, of these three possibilities, constructive outcomes are the most likely to contribute to improved interpersonal communication and a positive, supportive climate. As with any communication, there is no single, surefire answer as to what to do when a conflict occurs. You must think from a communicative perspective in deciding how to manage specific conflicts.

The Communicative Perspective and Conflict

When we think of conflict in the classroom, we may assume it is student initiated and directed at the teacher. However, you will witness a lot of conflict between and among students and may be expected to intervene. Also, keep in mind that you will have conflicts with students, individually and collectively (small groups, the whole class).

Start using your communicative perspective before you are actually in a conflict. Many classroom conflicts are spontaneous, overt in nature, and easily resolved. For example, conflict stemming from a student refusing to do an assignment may be resolved by clarification of the directions.

Think about what your usual problem-solving strategies are. Do you avoid, suppress, erupt, or rationally try to resolve the problem? Whatever your usual strategies are, ask yourself how appropriate they would be in the classroom as a model for students. As a new teacher, it is easy to feel insecure and to experience every conflict as a personal attack. Try not to be defensive. Instead, view conflict as a flag to differing perceptions that need attention. Remember that conflict, like interpersonal communication, becomes more predictable and easier to handle the more you know someone.

Consider your students' backgrounds, age, needs, and goals in relation to how they handle conflict and what issues are likely to be conflict points for them.

- Do they get along with the other students? (need for inclusion)
- Can they clearly state and explain perceived conflicts or do they need help in learning to do so? (chapter 4—"Expressive and Informative Functions")
- Do they react defensively to conflict? (blaming, sarcasm, attacking verbally or physically, suppressing, avoiding, rationalizing)
- Do they have age appropriate ways to resolve conflict or do they need help in learning how? (chapter 4—"Controlling Function")
- What do you know about them academically that may produce conflict due to frustration, boredom, or inattention?

(reading level, learning style, motivation to learn, past measured achievement in the subject area)

Realize how situational factors affect both the expression and the playing out of a conflict. Consider the *where* and the *who* of a conflict. Discussing a major conflict between you and one student in your room after school is different from handling it during class with the class serving as an audience. It could be the difference between a productive conversation and escalation of the conflict. In the latter setting, you would no longer be talking just to each other but both of you would be responding to the class's reactions (the student to look good in front of peers; you to show you are in control). Separate arguing students before a crowd gathers and they start grandstanding for the onlookers, who will egg them on. Of course, if the conflict involves the whole class, then the entire class needs to discuss it.

You also need to analyze the effect of another situational factor: *when*. The best time to deal with the small, easy-to-resolve conflicts is as soon as possible, in a way that does not interfere with the rest of the class or embarrass the student. For the large, intense, complicated conflicts, there needs to be a rescheduling. When intense emotions are involved, whether yours or a student's, time is needed to regain composure, so the conflict can be addressed more objectively.

The following suggestions are applicable whether you are bringing up the conflict, are on the receiving end of a conflict, or are looking for conflict strategies to teach to students. Which ones are appropriate depend on your communicative analysis of the situation, who is involved, the goals, and the meanings that are generated. Remember, whatever you do will serve as a model for your students of how to handle conflict. What you do will affect their conflict style in your classroom.

Conflict Management

Conflicts may appear like slow-gathering thunderstorms that give lots of advance warning or like the proverbial sudden bolt from the blue. You may simply sense unease that needs to be addressed. Conflicts may be phrased as accusations, questions, or requests. However conflicts make their existence known, the recipient is often surprised. The surprise may produce shock, a feeling of being personally attacked, and defensive responses. Immediate, knee-jerk reactions rarely are productive in resolving the conflict.

Stop, Look, and Listen

- When you are the surprised one, suppress your first impulse and work on getting the information needed to get and keep the communication flowing.
- If something you said produces the surprise, slow down and ask yourself why the student is surprised: Is it content (judgmental language)? Is it delivery (tone of voice, sarcasm)? Is it the timing? Is it the setting? When the look of surprise is between students, prepare to make helpful suggestions, so they can deal with the conflict appropriately and objectively.
- Many of the listening guidelines (see chapter 4) have special significance when dealing with conflict, such as nonverbal support, paraphrasing, asking informational questions, avoiding judgmental responses, keeping emotions under control, and reflecting back what you think the thoughts and feelings are. Recognize the value of your attentive silence. Do not interrupt. Realize your initial listening purposes are both discriminative and therapeutic. Once the nature of the conflict is clear and a resolution is being sought then evaluating, solution-oriented talk is appropriate.

Use "I" Language. Avoid *You-messages* and send *I-messages* (Gordon 1974). You-messages place the responsibility for the problem in the other person. You-messages confront in an accusatory, judgmental, guilt-producing way and tend to have negative effects on student-teacher relations and students' self-concepts. These kinds of statements editorialize, but do not give facts about the nature of the conflict in any helpful way. According to Gordon (1974, p. 131–36), you-messages fall into three general categories:

1. *Solution*—ordering ("Sit down."), warning ("One more time and you'll be sorry."), moralizing ("You should know better."), using logic ("If you work now, you won't have any homework."), advising ("Talking instead of working is not a good idea.")
2. *Putdown*—ridiculing or name-calling ("You are acting like spoiled brats."), criticizing or blaming ("You are always starting trouble."), diagnosing ("You're doing that to make me mad."), positive evaluations ("When you try, you do such good work."), interrogating ("Just why are you passing notes?")
3. *Indirect*—digressing, teasing, using sarcasm ("When did they make you principal?")

I-messages are "responsibility-taking messages" because they keep responsibility for the statement inside the person making it and leave the responsibility for the other person's behavior within that person (Gordon 1974). I-messages do not confront but do deal with specific behaviors and feelings. Once the initial I-statement is made, then the teacher and student discuss what is at issue. I-messages need to be used with listening skills, particularly paraphrasing and reflection of thought and feelings. There are three parts to I-statements (Gordon 1974, pp. 142–45):

1. *Behavior*—Nonjudgmental description of problem behavior in factual terms that begins with "When"
2. *Effect*—Concrete effect of behaviors in #1 (above)
3. *Feelings*—Feelings generated because of #2 (above)

Gordon says that this sequence impresses on students that the feelings are caused by the possible effect and not their behavior. Seeing the problem from the teacher's point of view, they are less defensive and more likely to work on a solution. For these reasons, I-messages contribute to better interpersonal communication.

The difference between the two kinds of statements can be illustrated by these examples. "You'll be late for your own funeral" vs. "When you are late, I have to stop what I'm doing, and I feel frustrated."

Perception Checking. As we discussed in chapter 2, perception is idiosyncratic in its operation. Given the same event, what each of us perceives and what it means varies. Perception checking deals with perception's possible contribution to conflict. It checks personal perceptual interpretations against the perceptions of the other person(s) involved. Using perception checking may clarify the nature of the conflict or resolve it altogether. There are three parts to a perception-check:

1. a description of the behaviors perceived;
2. the interpretation or conclusion drawn; and
3. a request for clarification about how to interpret the behavior.

A student teacher appeared in my office in tears, saying she was quitting student teaching. The students in her drama class, normally cooperative, that day had talked among themselves and refused to pay any attention. I suggested that she discuss what happened with the class or she would always wonder. She went through the perception-checking steps. The students were genuinely surprised to hear that she had been upset. They had been preoccupied with their reactions to what they considered an unjust action of their principal, which had been announced immediately preceding her class. He had taken away all of their class's privileges (prom, etc.) because of vandalism to the school by a few students. They felt cheated and had been angry with the principal. They assured her that they liked her and the class.

Molehill Minders. Deal with the conflict molehills to prevent conflict mountains. Good and Brophy (1994, pp. 169–70) suggest the following ideas to eliminate minor conflicts before they escalate.

1. *Eye Contact.* Establishing eye contact is usually enough to compel attention. This is an especially effective for "with-it" teachers who continually scan the room. Students will look up to see if the teacher is watching and make eye contact with the teacher.
2. *Physical Proximity.* Moving around the room, whether lecturing, monitoring group work, or checking seatwork, can prevent or catch problems.
3. *Asking for Responses.* Ask questions or call for a response that an inattentive student could answer even without listening to the previous remark. "Chris, Pat says the title is misleading. What do you think?"
4. *Namedropping.* Insert the name of an inattentive student into an instructional comment, such as, "The next step, Leslie, is to check the previous work."
5. *Reminders.* When rules and consequences have been established, then briefly remind students what the appropriate behavior is in the situation.

Problem Solving. Treating conflict as a problem to be solved introduces a systematic, objective way to resolve conflict. Participants to the conflict collaborate to craft solutions that they can all live with. Power differentials are equalized. Issues of fault and blame are irrelevant. Creativity is encouraged. Participants feel ownership of the solution, which means it is more likely to work than a solution that is given to or demanded of them. Resolving conflicts this way can produce more positive feelings for the others involved and the possibility that the approach will be used for future conflicts. Advocates of the group process approach recommend regular problem-solving discussions led by the teacher to facilitate a more democratic classroom (J. Cooper 1990).

This approach can be used with simple or complex problems with any number of people. The participants may be teacher-student(s) or student(s)-student(s). It may be used by parties to the conflict among themselves or led by an objective person, who is outside the conflict. For example, teachers might use this approach in managing conflicts they have with the entire class or to help two students resolve a conflict between themselves. After students become familiar with this method of conflict resolution through teacher modeling, they can use it on their own.

Many schools throughout the country have adopted the problem-solving approach in peer mediation programs, which train student mediators to work with their peers. One such program was implemented at Brooklyn Technical High School, where rumors were the source of conflict. Before the program, students would resort to violence when they felt they were not being respected or heard. When mediators became role models to their peers, helping students learn how to talk problems out and discover the power of listening with respect, the number of suspensions was reduced (National Public Radio 1995).

The following steps for solving a conflict are adapted from the five phases of reflective thought identified by the philosopher John Dewey (1910). Dewey's ideas were originally intended as a description of how individuals solve problems. His ideas have been applied to group problem-solving discussion and are widely known in the form of the Standard Agenda for Problem-Solving, which will be discussed in chapter 8. Whether his ideas are applied to solving group tasks, improving classroom climate, or resolving conflict, as here, they focus participants on collaborating to accomplish a common goal. All points of view must be represented, expressed in clear, specific, and non-judgmental language, and effectively listened to. The five steps applied to resolving conflict are:

1. *Define the conflict.* What is the nature of the conflict from each person's point of view?
2. *Analyze the conflict.* What are the causes, reasons, effects of the conflict? What problems is it creating?
3. *Generate and evaluate alternative solutions.* Generate possible solutions and discuss how each one addresses #1 and #2 above.
4. *Select and implement the preferred solution.* Choose the most workable solution. When no one solution works, try combining aspects of the different solutions to come up with one that resolves the conflict. Agree how and when to apply the solution.
5. *Obtain feedback and assess how well the solution is working.* Decide how and when you will evaluate whether the solution is working. If the solution is not working, then that becomes the new problem to be solved. Repeat the steps.

Interpersonal Communication: The Heart of It All

All classroom communication is essentially dyadic, simultaneously generating content and relationship meanings between each student and the teacher continuously. Interpersonal communication is occurring no matter what kind of interaction is going on or how many students are involved. It is how you and your students experience the moment-to-moment, day-to-day life in the classroom.

The choices you make about how to influence your students as you seek to achieve your goals have profound effects on your students. How you communicate interpersonally and the interpersonal atmosphere that you shape will affect their attitudes and expectations about themselves, other people, and learning. B.F. Skinner said, "Education is what survives when what has been learnt has been forgotten" (Skinner 1964, p. 484). Although students may forget many of the details that they learn in your class, they will remember how you communicated with them. It will become part of them.

Notes

[1] For stages of interpersonal relationship development, see:

DeVito, J. 1995. *The Interpersonal Communication Book*, 7th edition. New York: HaperCollins.

Knapp, M. and A. Vangelisti. 1992. *Interpersonal Communication and Human Relationships*, 2nd edition. Boston: Allyn and Bacon.

Phillips, G. and J. Wood. 1993. *The Study of Interpersonal Communication*. New York: Macmillan.

[2] This definition is based on definitions from:

Deutsch, M. 1969. "Conflicts: Productive and Destructive." *The Journal of Social Issues* 25:7–41. Cited in R. Bassett, and M. Smythe, *Communication and Instruction* (New York: Harper & Row, 1979).

Hocker, J. and W. Wilmot. 1991. *Interpersonal Conflict*, 3rd edition. Dubuque, IA: Wm. C. Brown.

References

Bassett, R. and Smythe, M. 1979. *Communication and Instruction*. New York: Harper & Row.

Becher, R. 1984. *Parental Involvement: A Review of Research and Principles of Successful Practice*. Washington, DC: National Institute of Education. Cited in U.S. Department of Education, *Strong Families, Strong Schools: Building Community Partnerships for Learning* (U.S. Department of Education: September, 1994).

Berliner, D. 1984. "The Half-Full Glass: A Review of Research on Teaching." In P. Hansford, editor, *Using What We Know About Teaching*. Alexandria, VA: Association for Supervision and Curriculum Development.

Booth-Butterfield, M. 1992. *Interpersonal Communication in Instructional Settings*. Edina, MN: Burgess.

Booth-Butterfield, S. 1992. *Influence and Control in the Classroom*. Edina, MN: Burgess.

Brenders, D. 1987. "Some Perplexities of Power in the Classroom: A Pragmatic Perspective on Instructional Relationships." *Journal of Thought* 22(4): 51–56.

Brophy, J. 1979. "Teacher Praise: A Functional Analysis." Occasional Paper #28. East Lansing, MI: Michigan State University.

———. 1987a. "Synthesis of Research on Strategies for Motivating Students to Learn." *Educational Leadership* 45:40–48.

———. 1987b. "On Motivating Students." In D. Berliner and B. Rosenshine, editors, *Talks to Teachers*. New York: Random House.

Brophy, G. and T. Good. 1986. "Teacher Behavior and Student Achievement." In M. Wittrock, editor, *Handbook of Research in Teaching*, 3rd edition, pp. 328–75. New York: Macmillan.

"The Case Against Rewards and Praise: A Conversation with Alfie Kohn." 1994. *The Harvard Education Letter* X(2): 5–6.

Chance, P. 1992. "The Rewards of Learning." *Phi Delta Kappan* 74(3): 200–207. Cited in E. Miller, "Letting Talent Flow: How Schools Can Promote Learning for the Sheer Love of It." *The Harvard Education Letter* X(2) (1994): 1–3, 8.

Civikly, J. 1992. *Classroom Communication: Principles and Practices*. Dubuque, IA: Wm. C. Brown.

Cooper, J., editor. 1990. *Classroom Teaching Skills*, 4th edition. Lexington, MA: DC Heath.

Cooper, P. 1991. *Speech Communication for the Classroom Teacher*, 4th edition. Scottsdale, AZ: Gorsuch.

Dembo, M. 1991. *Applying Educational Psychology in the Classroom*, 4th edition. New York: Longman.

Deutsch, M. 1969. "Conflicts: Productive and Destructive." *The Journal of Social Issues*. 25:7–41. Cited in R. Bassett and M. Smythe, *Communication and Instruction* (New York: Harper & Row, 1979).

———. 1973. *The Resolution of Conflict; Constructive and Destructive Processes*, New Haven: Yale.

DeVito, J. 1995. *The Interpersonal Communication Book*, 7th edition. New York: HarperCollins.

Dewey, John. 1910. *How We Think*. Boston: DC Heath.

Emmer, E. 1987. "Classroom Management and Discipline." In V. Richardson-Koehler, editor, *Educators Handbook: A Research Perspective*. White Plains, NY: Longman. Cited in M. Dembo, *Applying Educational Psychology in the Classroom*, 4th edition (New York: Longman, 1991).

Farber, A. and E. Mazlish. 1995. *How To Talk So Kids Can Learn at Home and In School*. New York: Rawson.

French, J. and B. Raven. 1968, "The Bases of Social Power." In D. Cartwright and A. Zander, editors, *Group Dynamics: Research and Theory*. New York: Harper & Row. Cited in J. DeVito, *The Interpersonal Communication Book*, 7th edition (New York: HarperCollins, 1995.)

Gibbs, J. 1960. "Defensive Communication." *Journal of Communication*. 11:141–48.

Good, T. and J. Brophy. 1994. *Looking in Classrooms*, 6th edition. New York: HarperCollins.

Gordon, T. with N. Burch. 1974. *T.E.T. Teacher Effectiveness Training*. New York: Peter H. Wyden, Publisher.

Hamachek, D. 1971. "Characteristics of Good Teachers and Implications for Teacher Education." In H. Funk and R. Olberg, editors, *Learning to Teach in Elementary School*. New York: Dodd, Mead, & Co.

Henderson, A. and N. Berla. 1994. *A New Generation of Evidence: The Family is Crucial to Student Achievement*. Washington, DC: National Committee for Citizens in Education. Cited in U.S. Department of Education, *Strong Families, Strong Schools: Building Community Partnerships for Learning* (U.S. Department of Education: September, 1994).

Hocker, J. and W. Wilmot. 1985. *Interpersonal Conflict*. Dubuque, IA: Wm. C. Brown.

Kearney, P. 1987. "Power in the Classroom." *Journal of Thought*, 22(4): 45–50.

Knapp, M. 1992. *Interpersonal Communication and Human Relationships*, 2nd edition. Boston: Allyn and Bacon.

Kounin, J. 1970. *Discipline and Group Management in Classrooms*. New York: Holt, Rinehart, and Winston.

McCroskey, J. 1982. *In Introduction to Rhetorical Communication*, 4th edition. Englewood Cliffs, NJ: Prentice-Hall.

Messick, S. and Associates. 1976. *Individuality in Learning*. San Francisco: Jossey-Bass. Cited in J. Keefe, *Learning Style: Theory & Practice* (Reston, VA: NASSP, 1987).

Miller, E. 1994. "Letting Talent Flow: How Schools Can Promote Learning for the Sheer Love of It." *The Harvard Education Letter* X(2): 1–3, 8.

National Public Radio. June 25, 1995. Reported on "Saturday Morning Edition."

Phillips, G., D. Butt, and N. Metzger. 1974. *Communication in Education: A Rhetoric of Schooling and Learning*. New York: Holt, Rinehart, and Winston.

Piper, T. 1974. *Classroom Management and Behavioral Objectives: Applications of Behavioral Modification*. Belmont, CA: Lear Siegler-Fearon Publishers. Cited in J. Cooper, editor, *Classroom Teaching Skills* 4th edition (Lexington, MA: DC Heath & Co., 1990).

Schutz, W. 1966. *The Interpersonal Underworld*. Palo Alto, CA: Science and Behavior Books. Cited in M. Booth-Butterfield, *Interpersonal Communication in Instructional Settings*. (Edina, MN: Burgess, 1992).

Skinner, B. F. 1964. "New Scientist." *Education in 1984*, May 21, p. 484.

Sprague, J. 1993. "Why Teaching Works: The Transformative Power of Pedagogical Communication." *Communication Education* 42 (October): 349–76.

Stewart, L., A. Stewart, P. Cooper, and S. Friedley. 1990. *Communication Between the Sexes*, 2nd edition. Scottsdale, AZ: Gorsuch. Cited in P. Cooper, *Speech Communication for the Classroom Teacher*, 4th edition (Scottsdale, AZ: Gorsuch, 1991).

Wittrock, M., editor. 1986. *Handbook of Research in Teaching*, 3rd edition. New York: Macmillan.

Wlodkowski, R. and J. Jaynes (1990). *Eager to Learn—Helping Children Become Motivated and Love Learning.* San Francisco: Jossey-Bass Publishers.

Suggested Reading

Among Schoolchildren by Tracy Kidder. Boston: Houghton Mifflin, 1989.

Life in Mrs. Zajac's fifth grade class in Holyoke, Massachusetts, is reported by Tracy Kidder, who spent a year observing the class. What emerges is a sensitive portrait of "Mrs. Z," a caring and committed teacher, and her students with their many problems as they get to know each other and struggle with learning. Their lives together illustrate what the process of classroom interpersonal communication and relationships look like from the inside.

Instruction in Conflict Resolution by Fred Jandt and Mark Hare. Falls Church, VA: Speech Communication Association, 1976.

Part of the "Theory into Practice" series, this pamphlet begins with a short section on major concepts and research findings on communication in conflict resolution. The larger practice section suggests role-plays, games, and simulations to develop students' conflict resolution skills. The practical classroom activities are suitable for speech, English, social studies, or guidance.

Punished by Rewards—The Trouble With Gold Stars, Incentive Plans, A's, Praise, and Other Bribes by Alfie Kohn. New York: Houghton Mifflin Co.

The first half of this book critiques rewards, including praise: why they do not promote lasting behavior change or enhance performance, and often make matters worse. The second half of the book examines the effects of rewards and alternatives to rewards (intrinsic motivation and the Three Cs: collaboration, content, and choice). Chapters 7 and 10 focus on educational issues. Chapters 9 and 12 focus on children's behavior and values.

Small Victories—The Real World of a Teacher, Her Students, and Their High School by Samuel Freedman New York: Harper & Row, 1990.

An observational study of a dedicated Manhattan High School English teacher, Jessica Segal, and her students, who come from poor, violent, and drug-ridden neighborhoods. Their story gives a dramatic sense of the dynamic reality of their separate and collective lives. The texture and complexities of their interpersonal communication and relationships are moving and compelling.

Chapter 7

Discussion

Ideas to Remember

* Discussion is a dialogic form of communication involving two or more participants exchanging ideas or opinions.
* The fundamental connection between language and thought forms necessary background for understanding discussion. The theories of Piaget and Vygotsky explain this connection and have influenced educational practice.
* The current thinking about the strong bonds between language and thought has implications for learning and teaching.
* Discussion plays an important role in "knowing."
* In practice, most teachers hold recitations, instead of engaging students in discussions.
* Having a worthwhile discussion involves the following steps:
  1. Analyze: Set the stage for discussion.
  2. Identify objectives for the discussion.
  3. Plan appropriate questions.
  4. Facilitate participation.
  5. Evaluate the discussion.

Discussion is a dialogic form of communication involving two or more participants exchanging ideas or opinions. According to *Webster's Dictionary*, discussion implies a sifting of possible opinions or ideas, an informal investigation of a subject or topic by reasoning. The word's Latin roots shed light on its meaning: *dis*—apart, and *quatere*—to shake. Discussions are conversation-like interactions in which people explore—*shake apart*—ideas together. Discussions vary in length, complexity, and number of participants, but they all share this same focus. Through the process of discussing, people develop understanding and engage in sense making, that is they create meaning. Discussion is a way we come to know.

To fully appreciate how discussion contributes to our knowing we first need to look at the underlying connection between language and thought. Next we need to examine what this connection implies about learning and teaching, so that we can understand the role discussion plays in the process of knowing. We are then ready to see how discussions can be employed in the classroom. We will explore what is involved in each step of the process of shaping a worthwhile discussion.

Language and Thought

Educational practice has been greatly influenced by the insights of two theorists, Jean Piaget and Lev Vygotsky, who have explored the relationship of language and thought.

Piaget, a genetic epistemologist, was interested in the invariant characteristics of mental development shared by all children. Cognitive development was produced by biological maturation through interaction with the environment. In his view, cognition and language were related, but cognition came first. Language was only one of many symbolic processes that children developed as they interacted with their environment and, as such, was an underlying symptom of cognitive development (Owens 1992). However, in the later stages of cognitive development, language helped to shape thought (Hulit and Howard 1993).

According to Owens (1992), Piaget considered language to be relatively independent of its social-interactive context. Children develop egocentric speech (speak from their own perspective) to label their environment. As children develop cognitively—*decentering* and becoming more logical—then ego-centered speech disappears. Speech becomes sociocentric (adapted, reasoned discourse). In other words, children develop a dual perspective.

Vygotsky, a developmental psychologist, took a very different view. Cognitive development emerged from the context of a child's social experience. In his view, language, which facilitates social interaction, is the catalyst for higher-order thought. Initially, language and thought are separate functions: thought involves basic mental processes (organizing perceptions and regularizing experience), and speech enables communication with members of the speech community. As a result of this social interaction, speech and thought blend into egocentric speech (thought becomes verbal and vocalized) and produce new intellectual possibilities. Egocentric speech eventually withdraws inward and becomes internalized as silent inner-speech (thinking mediated through language) (Wertsch 1985). In other words, what is learned through external, social speech interactions becomes transformed into internal self-talk, psychological structures for thinking.

Vygotsky believed cognitive and communicative skills appear twice: first on the social plane and then on the psychological plane. What takes place in the interpersonal exchanges between child and caregiver are "the precursors of cognitive and communicative functions that will someday be self-regulated by the child" (Tharp and Gallimore 1988, p. 28). Social-communicative interactions socialize and acculturate children. Children learn to think through hearing others speak.

For both theorists, language and thought are intertwined. Each affects the other. For Piaget, language first reveals cognitive development and later shapes it. For Vygotsky, language enables social interaction through which higher mental processes develop. For Vygotsy, speaking is fundamental to thought.

What do these strong bonds between language and thought imply about learning and teaching?

Implications for Learning and Teaching

Piaget, Vygotsky, and the cognitive researchers whom they have influenced define learning as **constructivist**. Students learn through a process of actively constructing connections between existing networks of present knowledge and new information (Good and Brophy 1994). In order to make knowledge usable for thinking, interpretation, reasoning, and solving problems, students must question what they are told, examine it in relation to what they already know, and build new knowledge structures (Resnick and Klopfer 1989). To learn something, then, is to make information your own in a personal way and to construct meaning actively, rather than passively accepting it.

The Role of Learners. According to Bransford and Vye (1989), the emphasis on the active construction of knowledge by learners does not mean that information provided by teachers and text is unimportant. It does mean that when such information is supplied, students must have opportunities to actively use it themselves and to experience its effects on their own performance. In the absence of such opportunities, students will learn facts in context, which remain "inert" (Whitehead 1929) even when they are relevant in new situations. Andersen (1982, 1987) theorizes that learning involves a transition from factual-declarative knowledge (knowledge supplied by a text or a teacher's instruction) to procedural-user-oriented knowledge, which is *conditionalized* (knowing when to apply principles, concepts, and strategies). It is the difference between knowing *what* and knowing *how* and *when.* There is agreement on learners doing their own learning, forging ahead cognitively by constructing and reconstructing what they know. However, interpretations differ in how learners go about it and what teachers should be doing.

In Piagetian terms, adaptation is the essence of intellectual functioning. It consists of two continual, complementary processes: *assimilation* and *accommodation.* Assimilation occurs when an existing structure or behavior pattern is used to deal with a problem in the environment. When a problem in the environment necessitates some change or rearrangement of existing mental structures, then accommodation occurs. Mental equilibrium is achieved when these two processes are in balance. However, learning occurs when they are out of balance. When something cannot be assimilated, disequilibrium occurs. Either accommodation must alter present structures or new structures must emerge. "Intellectual growth is a continual process of equilibrium-disequilibrium states" (Dembo 1991, p. 49). This process of "equilibration" is one of the factors that contributes to individuals moving from one cognitive stage to another. The other factors are: maturation, physical experience (aids the emergence of more complex thinking), and social transmission (influence of language, formal instruction, and social interaction with peers and adults) (Piaget 1964).

The focus is on the individual child who learns through exploration, discovery, and reflection on everyday-life experiences. Teaching involves creating situations that permit students to invent and discover: trying things out to see what happens, manipulating objects and symbols, posing questions and seeking personal answers, reconciling what is found on one occasion with what is found on another, and comparing findings with those of other students.

The Role of Teachers. The teacher's role in creating learning opportunities is to modulate the balance between assimilation and accommodation. The difference between the students' known and unknown must be navigable for them. If the stretch is too great, then students may be frustrated or defeated, but if there is no challenge, then new thinking will not occur.

In Vygotskian terms, the active construction of meaning takes place in a social context. In their natural setting, children learn through interaction with a "someone" who provides responsive assistance. At first, children do not understand what they are learning as the "someone" does. Children do not see causes, effects, or other kinds of connections, but with assistance they can perform the behavior. "For skills and functions to develop into internalized, self-regulated capacity, all that is needed is performance, through assisting interaction" (Tharp and Gallimore 1988, p. 30).

For Vygotsky, the difference between assisted and unassisted performance is where development and learning meet. He called this idea **Zone of Proximal Development (ZPD)**. This zone lies between a child's actual developmental level (as defined by individual problem solving) and the child's potential level of development (as defined by problem solving under adult supervision or in collaboration with more capable peers) (Vygotsky 1978, p. 86)—in other words, what the child is capable of alone and what the child can do with assistance. What lies within the ZPD are developing skills and abilities. Once these skills and abilities mature, they become part of the child's practical intelligence.

The focus of instruction is leading students toward development. The teacher's role is like that of the "someone" (parent, knowledgeable peer, significant other) in a natural setting: to interact with learners, offering responsive assistance and teaching in the ZPD. The amount and kind of assistance vary according to the needs of the learners as they learn. More guidance and structure may be necessary initially, but less assistance is needed as proficiency and independence develop. Think of it as coaching. Coaching is responsive to the ebb and flow of the players' needs at a given point in time. A good coach finds the appropriate words, questions, or activities to nudge performance in a positive direction.

There are many ways teachers may provide nudging or responsive assistance. One way is through **scaffolding**—task assistance and simplification strategies that operate like construction scaffolds, which provide temporary, needed support, and are withdrawn when they are no longer needed. There are many ways teachers can provide scaffolds (Good and Brophy 1994, p. 421):

> *Cognitive Modeling.* Verbalize thinking strategies while demonstrating a task.
>
> *Prompting.* Give cues when students are stuck.
>
> *Questioning.* Ask questions that lead to diagnosis of errors and more effective strategies.

Tharp and Gallimore (1988, ch. 3) suggest the following means for providing responsive assistance:

- modeling;
- contingency management (especially praise of good perfor-mance) (see critical comments on extrinsic motivation in chap-ter 6);
- giving feedback about the correctness of the responses;
- instructing (telling students what to do when necessary);
- cognitive structuring (stating principles that pull things together);
- questioning that stimulates students to think and communi-cate about the task.

Cognitive researchers, who support active learning through prob-lem solving, suggest guidelines for constructive teacher assistance. They warn against the popular activity of solitary practice (students work on problems alone), because students, who do not understand the component strategies or how to coordinate them, are wasting their time. Instead, researchers suggest using "coached practice" (Lesgold 1988). According to Bransford and Vye (1989, pp. 196–99), the fol-lowing characteristics of coached practice help students develop the expertise they need to function effectively. Coaches need to:

1. Monitor and regulate students' attempts at problem solving so they do not go too far in the wrong direction, while suppressing the urge to jump in too quickly. Students need to experience the complexity involved in problem solving.
2. Help students reflect on the processes they use as they solve prob-lems. This may involve thinking out loud, contrasting what they are doing with the work of others, and observing the teacher solve problems.
3. Use problem-solving exercises for assessing students' knowledge.
4. Use problem-solving exercises to create *teachable moments.* This means generating opportunities for students to contrast their initial ideas and strategies with other possibilities.
5. Choose meaningful problem-solving experiences that help stu-dents develop component skills in the context of the overall goal.
6. Create a climate that supports students working cooperatively in groups on reflective problem solving.

The teacher acts as an intellectual coach promoting individual thought (relating new input to prior knowledge) through social inter-actions that are cooperative (working in pairs, small groups, and as a whole class). The social context can include several ways to promote thinking: methods of attacking problems or doing a task are demon-strated, students scaffold complicated performances for each other (peer teaching), students create collaborative solutions that they could not produce alone, and criticism during shared work refines students' knowledge or skill (Resnick and Klopfer 1989). Special emphasis is placed on discussion because it helps to develop cognitive structures. According to Good and Brophy (1994), input from discussions can make students: aware of things they did not know, rethink their ideas, and develop new ideas.

From the perspectives of Piaget, Vygotsky, and other cognitive researchers, learning means active, dynamic interaction between what is presently known and the unknown. Teaching involves shaping, leading, and encouraging students into their own thinking.

The Role of Discussion in Knowing

Discussion is fundamental to thinking because it engages students in expressing and questioning ideas and opinions—theirs and everyone else's. Very often we are unsure of what we mean until we try to talk about it. The act of trying to express ourselves to someone else helps us unravel the knots and fill in the gaps. This improvisational, creative nature of talk produces thought. Britton calls this phenomenon "shaping at the point of utterance" (1982, p. 139). As we talk, we flesh out our thinking—revising, pruning, patching, discovering, and adding— as we go along.

Discussions are crucibles for thought that are fueled by questions. They put us together to raise questions and sort through responses. Questions are spawned in the intersect between the known and the unknown, the understood and the obscure. Questions incite thinking, which is by definition, a creative act. To know anything we must question it, roll it around in our minds, and see how it fits with our present store of knowledge. Dewey defines thinking as questioning, "investigation, turning over, probing or delving into . . . to find something new or to see what is known in a new light" (1933, p. 265). Hunkins (1989) defines good thinkers as good questioners, who use questions to go beneath the surface to deeper meanings. Glatthorn and Baron (1985) place student inquiry and discussion at the center of classrooms conducive to and supportive of good thinking.

Teachers, through the questions they raise, can help students think reflectively, critically, and creatively. According to John Dewey, **reflective thought** is the "active, persistent, and careful consideration of any belief or supposed form of knowledge in the light of the grounds that support it and the further conclusions to which it tends . . ." (1933, p. 9). He says thinking begins when we are faced with doubt or perplexity. Dewey likens it to coming to a fork in an unknown road. We are faced with alternatives and must resolve the dilemma of which way to go. For Dewey, questioning guides learning. He sees the role of the teacher's questions to guide students' thinking and, ". . . to form in them the independent habit of inquiry in both of its directions; namely, inquiry in observation and recollection for the subject matter that is pertinent, and inquiry through reasoning into the meaning of the material that is present" (Dewey 1933, p. 266).

Lippman (1988, p. 39) defines critical thinking as "skillful, responsible thinking that facilitates good judgment" because of three characteristics: (1) Critical thinking relies on criteria, which supply a sort of "cognitive accountability;" (2) critical thinking is self-correcting—it aims to discover and rectify its own weaknesses; (3) critical thinking is sensitive to the specific context and takes into account irregular circumstances, situational meanings, constraints, and the nature of evidence.

Paul (1984, p. 9) points out that something more than technical reasoning procedures are needed for real-life problems, which are not logically neat but instead involve the "criss-crossing of categories, values, points of view, and beliefs and blend intellectual, affective, and moral considerations. Real-life problems generate conflicting reasoning and answers, which need to be addressed through thinking critically about opposing points of view." He emphasizes the need for dialogic discussion to penetrate and assess differing viewpoints.

Hunkins (1989) agrees that discussions nurture critical and creative thinking because they are dialectic in nature—arguments in the best sense of the word. They engage students in contemplating differing, perhaps contradictory, ideas, opinions, and thoughts and encourage students to formulate new conceptualizations, raise new questions, and engage in novel thinking.

When teachers encourage questioning—theirs and their students'—thinking is promoted. These authors see the development of reflective, skillful thought as both necessary and liberating. Dewey (1933) says genuine freedom is intellectual and rests in the power of trained thought, the ability to look at matters deliberately. Lippman says critical thinking is empowering for students because, "it increases the quality and quantity of meaning that students derive from what they read and perceive and that they express it in what they write and say" (1988, p. 43). Paul (1984) sees learning to think critically as fundamental to education for a free society. Hunkins (1989) sees the Information Age with its own overwhelming abundance of data, as placing ever greater demands on individuals to think well.

Discussions are potentially stimulating and enlightening because of the presence of the other participants with their unknown, yet-to-unfold responses. All participants bring their own perspectives, experiences, and thoughts to bear on what gets said. Comments may be inspected like crystals held up to the light. It is important to keep in mind that discussion is not a competition as is debate, where the best speaker wins. *Discussion is a cooperative enterprise with participants trying to be understood and to understand what is being discussed.*

Discussions are opportunities to think out loud together. They engage students at the point of their own experience in meaningful talk that promotes thinking. Each individual's thinking is strengthened first by the expression of personal thoughts and second by hearing the responses and thoughts of all the other participants. What results on any given occasion stems from the dynamic interplay of the topic, participants, questions, and what is said. The potential always exists that someone will think differently, better, or more deeply, or perhaps think about something new for the first time.

With this introduction of how discussion relates to thinking and learning, the rest of the chapter examines what contributes to constructive discussions. So far, we have looked at discussions on an abstract level. Next, we look at the state of the art in actual classrooms. Then, we consider step-by-step from a communicative perspective what goes into the planning and execution of a discussion.

Discussion in Practice

Research suggests that there is very little discussion in most classrooms (Dillon 1984). In an observational study involving 1,000 classrooms of K through 12, only 4–8 percent of classroom time was spent in discussion, regardless of subject matter (Goodlad 1984).

What teachers call discussion reveals a wide variety of behaviors that are more appropriately labeled as something else. Based on their study of classroom transcripts, Swift, Gooding, and Swift find that most discussions turn into a "lecture, drill, or an inquisition" dominated by the teacher (1988, p. 184). They find recitations to be the most used form of interaction. A **recitation** is a series of teacher questions, each eliciting a student response and sometimes a teacher reaction to that response (Gall 1984). These types of questions ask students to recite (repeat or explain) what they already know or are coming to know—usually textbook content or material previously presented by the teacher. Research has shown that up to 80 percent of the questions asked by teachers require recall of knowledge, while 20–30 percent ask for higher mental processes (Klinzing and Klinzing-Eurich 1988). According to these researchers, this has been documented for half a century in the United States, Australia, New Zealand, and West Germany. Roby (1988, p. 164) characterized recitations as "Quiz Shows," in which teachers have the right answers and students win by giving the correct responses.

It is important to distinguish between recitation and discussions. Recitation involves teacher-student interaction and recall of curriculum content, while discussion involves student-student interactions and complex thinking processes and attitude change (Gall and Gall 1976). Stodolsky, Ferguson, and Wimpelberg (1981) emphasize that discussion involves longer exchanges, exchanges among students as well as between teacher and students, and questions that solicit the students' opinions and thoughts.

Dillon (1988) explains the differences between recitations and discussions in terms of turn-taking (who speaks, when) and student and teacher roles. In recitation, teachers know *the* answer, ask low-level questions, and evaluate the correctness of the response. The turns and roles are predictable: teacher question, student answer, teacher evaluation plus next question. Students speak in brief answers, only to the teacher. The pace of questioning is typically fast. In discussion, the turns and roles are flexible and dynamic. Teachers or students at any point may ask a question, give an answer or not, or comment on a previous remark. Teachers do not speak at every turn, although they retain the right to do so. Students make longer responses and refer to each other's contributions.

It is important to point out that recitations are effective in determining the students' level of information, although they are not designed to facilitate student questioning or reflection. Gall (1984) suggests four possibilities of why recitations work for review of text material: (1) Recitations occur soon after exposure to information, so they provide practice through recall and immediate feedback on accuracy. (2) They cue students about what is important to remember. (3) The format of recitations gives practice in performing on traditional objective tests (short answer, multiple choice). (4) Elementary students prefer recitations to seat work because the involvement with the teacher is more motivating.

Often, teachers believe they are having discussions when they are actually holding recitations. Recitations are criticized for the dominance of low cognitive level questions because recall becomes an end in itself rather than serving to stimulate higher-level thinking (Wilen 1987). Discussions, as they commonly exist, feature the teacher talking with few opportunities for students to expand their thinking. The problem is how to construct genuine discussions that involve students in meaningful ways, yet not get in the way of their thinking.

In the rest of the chapter, we consider how to solve this problem by examining what is involved in each step of the discussion process. As we look at the necessities and possibilities in each step, think about how your teachers handled discussions and how you felt about it.

Step I: Analyze—Set the Stage for Discussion

Getting ready for discussion starts with you analyzing yourself, the context, and your students. The attitudes, expectations, and past experiences which teachers and students bring with them to a discussion affect what happens, at least initially. After they begin discussing together, they will develop their own norms and modify their attitudes and expectations based on their experiences.

Yourself

Attitude is everything. What do you believe about discussion? Who do you see doing what to whom? What do you see as its goal? Your answers to these questions will affect everything from here on out about discussion in your classroom: the planning, doing, and evaluation of what occurs. Your students will pick up on your attitude about discussing, and it will affect their attitudes and participation.

If at this point you have negative attitudes, think about why. Have you had little, no, or bad experiences with discussion? If so, you may already have a mental inventory of things not to do which will aid you when you start leading discussions. Do you share many student teachers' initial fears of their students staring at them in stony silence or students running amuck, out of control? If so, try not to worry ahead of yourself. Focus on developing the skills needed to facilitate discussion.

Context

In chapters 1 and 3, we examined three kinds of contexts that surround every communicative exchange: physical, temporal, and social/psychological (climate). Think about these contexts in relation to your students and consider how to make them supportive of discussion.

Physical. How can you make your room physically inviting to discussion? Return to chapter 3 on nonverbal behavior and review the "Spatial Arrangements" section. Think of the different options in terms of how many people you want participating in a particular discussion. For example, modular works well when you divide the class up into small groups, with each group having its own independent discussion.

Temporal.   Using discussions takes a commitment in time—time for you to learn how to plan and to lead a discussion, time for your students to develop their confidence and skills in discussing ideas, and time for each particular discussion to unfold. Recitations can be faster because they are teacher-dominated and deal with recall. Discussions involve thinking, and thinking takes time. Keep in mind that the amount of time an individual discussion needs depends on your plan, how you facilitate the discussion, and the students' responses.

Climate.   Positive, supportive, and talk friendly environments are conducive to discussions. Recognize that you also need to develop a spirit of inquiry. This means an openness to questioning everything, an investigative turn of mind. Inquiry thrives on genuine questions, enthusiasm, and respect for everyone's questions and comments. If your students are accustomed to discussion as guessing the right answer, then discussion as raising questions and sharing ideas requires developing a new orientation. The latter type of discussion is riskier because it requires more personal participation than simply stating facts. Students may be confused, resistant, or suspicious that you are asking trick questions. Be patient, persistent, and model the discussion behaviors that you expect. Dillon (1988) says how answers are handled enables students to come to realize the possible diversity that answers may have: There is no right answer; there may be several good answers; and there may be different useful answers for different people and situations.

Students

It is important that you understand what your students' pragmatic background has taught them about questions and answering in order to understand what their discussion behavior means. If there are differences between their referent group's norms and the traditional school norms, you need to take these differences into account when planning discussions. Rubin (1986, pp. 163–69) points to four possible differences that could affect participation:

1. *Norms of Loquacity.* Cultures vary in the amount of talk that is appropriate. Hymes (1974) suggests thinking of each culture as falling somewhere along a continuum of loquacity that varies from verbose at one end to concise, terse at the other end. Schools expect verbosity in response to questions. Students from cultures like middle-class Anglo and inner-city African American do well. Students whose loquacity norms are more passive, such as Native

Americans and Chinese Americans, may be penalized.

2. *Norms for Discourse Structure and Sequence.* Traditional school norms for organizing talk involve: turn-taking (a comment is followed by a response, questions by answers), one person speaks at a time, and a question should be answered by the person to whom it was addressed. Phillips (1970) reports that in some Native American groups questions do not carry an obligation for an immediate response. If there is a response, it may be a behavioral act performed at some later date.

3. *Norms for Participant Relations.* These are norms that define what is or is not an appropriate situation for speaking based on the roles of participants. Rubin cites studies of Cherokee children, whose norms define cooperative groups as appropriate and the singling out of an individual to speak as inappropriate. These children work well in groups because that is how their referent group is organized. They are comfortable talking when they are allowed to answer questions as a group, with group members elaborating, correcting, refining, creating—giving a group response.

4. *Ways of Construing the Functions of Questions.* We tend to base our interpretation of and response to questions on our own cultural background. However, cultures vary in what constitutes a question. The questions teachers traditionally ask are typical of Anglo middle-class culture. These types of questions include: genuine questions seeking information, quasi-questions designed to test student knowledge, directives masquerading as questions designed to get students to do something ("Can you put your coat away?").

Greek and Puerto Rican cultures presume questions are motivated by needs other than informing. Quasi-questions are rare in Asian, African-American, and Hispanic culture (Powell and Andersen 1994). Children unaccustomed to knowledge-testing questions may know the answer, yet not respond because they are confused by teachers asking questions when they already know the answers. Rubin speculates some children may interpret teachers' directive questions as accusations or threats. When this occurs, he suggests that teachers use a more direct form of request ("Hang your coat in your locker.").

Step II: Identify Objectives for the Discussion

Some people criticize discussion because they feel it is a "waste of time," never rising about the level of a "bull session." When such criticism is justified, it points to a discussion that lacked a plan: no pre-conceived thoughts about how to get from here to there and no clear idea of where "there" is. According to the *Webster's Collegiate Dictionary* (1976, p. 647), a *plan* is a "method of doing something, a procedure, [and it] always implies a mental formulation." Beware of recommendations not to plan, to "wing it," because, after all, it's just talking. Such comments are symptomatic of a lack of knowledge about discussion. Such talk sessions pass the time but do not produce thoughtful responses. You should always keep the thinking-speaking connection in mind and make a plan.

Good listening is crucial to meaningful discussion. In creating a workable discussion plan, then, you need to recall the planning guidelines from chapter 5 on listening. Four of those suggestions are major elements in a discussion plan: clear objectives that you share with students, an introduction, a logical sequence that students can follow, and a conclusion. The logical order in which to consider these elements when planning a discussion is first the objectives and then the sequence of questions that constitute the substance or body of the discussion. Once you have planned the questions that you want to ask, then it is time to think about what you need to do during the actual discussion: how to introduce it, how to respond during it, and how to conclude it.

Start with your educational goal for the lesson. Why do you want to have a discussion? Since the point of discussing is to think: thus, what do you want your students to think about? Why? To what purpose? The details of your plan will be created around your answers to these questions. Often, the questions are answered in terms of some object (a story, an experiment, or an experience such as the death of a classmate, communicating on the Internet, or listening to a speaker), a particular idea (censorship, ethics, communication), or a real or hypothetical problem (drugs in school, violence in society, how to clean up the environment).

Do not be misled by the use of the phrase, "a discussion plan." There is no generic, all-purpose discussion plan appropriate for all occasions. There is only a discussion plan created for particular students on a specific day to meet objectives appropriate for them at that time. Thus, each discussion plan will look different. Each one is your creative act tailored to your students. The questions in the preceding paragraph must be asked each time you plan a discussion, and your answers determine the details of each plan.

Creating a plan involves planning questions that you believe are likely to provoke responses that meet your thinking-discussing objective(s). Think of these planned questions as initial questions, which start lines of thought. Your plan is a guide that provides focus and shape to the discussion. Because a discussion is a dynamic event, the plan must be utilized flexibly. It is not a check-list, nor should it act like a straitjacket limiting your responses to what actually occurs during the discussion. As you discuss, some of your prepared questions may become irrelevant. Additional questions from you and your students will grow out of what is said. The group may delve deeply in a direction you could not have anticipated ahead of time. We will examine what you should do after you pose an initial question later in this chapter.

Once you establish your thinking-discussing objective(s) (what and why you want your students to discuss), you are ready to plan your initial questions.

Step III: Plan Appropriate Questions

Although we are concerned at this point in writing questions for a discussion plan, keep in mind that what follows applies to questions anytime, in any place, whether they are planned or spontaneous. *Functions* and *form* matter no matter who is asking the questions (teachers or students) or what the setting is (interpersonal, spontaneous questions during discussion, whole class, or small groups).

There are benefits to both teachers and students understanding how questions operate and what a *good* question sounds like. Teachers are in a position to create clear, reasonable questions that their students are likely to understand and respond to. Students develop skill in phrasing their own questions and can interpret the meaning of other people's questions.

Functions

How a question **functions** depends on the kind of thinking it requires to make a relevant response. Bloom's *Taxonomy of Educational Objectives–Handbook I: Cognitive Domain* (1956) provides a framework for understanding varying degrees of cognitive complexity. It provides a way to analyze the cognitive level of objectives and also supplies a way to think about the relationship between questions and different kinds of thought processes, so you can write appropriate, feasible questions for your students.

When this relationship is unclear, the discussion is hampered. Several studies found only about half of the students' responses were at the same cognitive level as the teachers' questions (reported in Gall 1984).[1] Of the incongruent responses, one-third to one-half were at a lower cognitive level than the teachers' questions. The researchers speculate students did not answer the questions appropriately because they did not understand the kind of mental activity required to answer the questions. The researchers suggest teachers give clear verbal cues to prompt students about the kind of thinking needed and to explain the relationship between questions and thinking levels.

Bloom's *Cognitive Domain* (1956) identifies six major classes of objectives that are arranged in a hierarchy from simple to complex. Each succeeding level involves more complex cognitive activity. The first two levels provide a foundation of "knowing" a subject, while the next four contribute to "owning" it (Richmond and Gorham 1992, p. 6). Here are explanations for each level and typical question wording that signal it.

Knowledge.   Questions requiring responses that recall information are called **knowledge questions**. An appropriate response to a knowledge question involves remembering something that has been previously learned, such as facts, observations, or definitions. Knowledge level questions may deal with anything from the simple and concrete ("How many stars are there in the American flag?") to the abstract and complex ("What is a market economy?").

Clue words: define, recall, recognize, who, what, when, where

Comprehension.   Questions requiring responses that demonstrate a personal grasp of the literal meaning and intent of information are called **comprehension questions**. Comprehension can be shown through:

translation (put into other terms): "In your own words, what point was the character trying to make?"

interpretation (reordering of the ideas): "What are the differences between the Democrats and the Republicans on the environment?"

extrapolation (see implications or make inferences closely connected to information). "What conclusions can you draw from this news story?"

Clue words: describe, compare, contrast, paraphrase, summarize

Application.   Questions requiring responses that demonstrate appropriate identification and use of comprehended information in novel situations are called **application questions**. For example, "According to our definition, which of these animals are mammals?"

Clue words: apply, classify, choose, solve, relate, which

Analysis. Questions requiring responses that identify constituent parts of something, recognize the relationships among the parts and how they are organized are called **analytical questions**. Analysis questions encourage a fuller understanding of the information and are basic to critical thinking skills (Hunkins 1989). Analysis may involve:

- identifying elements implicit or explicit in material (facts, assumptions, motives, hypotheses, conclusions, bias, claims). For example, "What are the unstated assumptions behind competency testing for teachers?"
- recognizing relationships between the identified elements (such as consistency of part to part), relevance of parts to the central idea, forms of evidence to each other, and connections between hypotheses, evidence, and conclusions. For example, "What evidence supports the conspiracy theory in President Kennedy's assassination?"
- discovering the organizing principles (form, pattern, structure, point of view, purpose) in material. For example: "How do the media depict teenagers?"

Clue words: identify motives or causes, determine evidence, distinguish, analyze, why, support, logical, conclude

Synthesis. Questions requiring responses that draw upon elements from different sources and combine them to create something new are called **synthesis questions**. Synthesis questions require creative thinking and involve all the previous kinds of thinking. The new creation may be:

- a unique communication product that expresses personal meanings and communicates ideas, feelings, or experiences to others (speeches, relating a personal experience, essays, media productions, a song, poetry, telling a story: "What was it like the day you became a citizen?")
- a plan or proposed set of operations that meet specified criteria or solve a problem, for example, "How would you help your students develop community spirit?"
- a set of abstract relations, a statement or conclusion that explains or classifies information. These questions may begin with data or phenomena or start with propositions or conclusions in order to deduce propositions. For example, "What explains the increasing violence in the United States?"

Clue words: predict, produce, write, construct, design, develop, what would happen if, how can we solve or improve, combine, create

Evaluation. Questions requiring a response that makes a value judgment about something according to some identifiable criteria or standards, which may be objective or personal, are called **evaluation questions**. Bloom places it last because it involves all the other behaviors to some degree, but he says it is not necessarily the last step in thinking or problem solving. The evaluative process may precede any of the other processes: knowledge, comprehension, application, analysis or synthesis. A sample evaluative question is, "How do you evaluate public education in the United States?"

> Clue words: evaluate, critique, select, assess, judge, compare and contrast (in this context emphasizing relative worth and use of criteria)

Relating the Functional Question Types to Your Plan

Although the levels of thinking and questioning are arranged in a hierarchy of complexity, this does not mean that you must always cover all six levels in each and every discussion. The taxonomy also does not imply an ideal number of questions to be asked at one level before pressing on to the next level. You can plan questions proceeding all the way up the hierarchy in one discussion if you want to. You could plan a discussion with questions focusing on one or more particular levels. You might want to plan a series of discussions on a topic or problem that would extend over days, weeks, or months. The individual discussions would focus on different thinking levels and eventually lead up the hierarchy.

Which and How Many? Deciding which type of questions you need depends on your objectives for a given discussion. A general rule of thumb is to plan questions for the cognitive level of your objective(s), including questions for the levels beneath it. For example, if the objective is to check students' understanding, then plan knowledge- and comprehension-level questions. If the objective is to apply some principle or procedure already mastered, then knowledge and/or comprehension questions are needed to review, followed by application questions.

How many questions you need to plan is affected by your objective(s), as well as how much time you are allotting to the discussion and how it fits in the lesson plan. Is the discussion the entire lesson or does it follow or lead into other activities (lecture, group work, seat work)? Lower-level cognitive questions need less time for appropriate responses than do higher cognitive-level questions. Dillon (1988) suggests that a recitation may stem from a few questions, while an hour's discussion may be promoted by one good higher-level question. "But to conceive of that question will require thought; to formulate it requires labor; and to pose it, tact" (p. 127).

There are several cautions that you need to keep in mind as you consider which and how many questions to prepare.

Caution #1: Although you may have discussions that feature lower cognitive-level questions, beware of having discussions with only this focus.

Caution #2: Questions may begin at any level. What you must decide is whether your students are ready to pick up at that point—that is, if they have sufficient background and motivation to become engaged at that level. If they are not ready, then you need to consider what you will do about it—plan other activities first? review? motivate the question? phrase lower-level questions? Remember, sometimes starting at a higher level can rouse interest in gathering facts, analyzing connections, and then synthesizing new answers.

Caution #3: Spontaneous questions that occur during discussion may ricochet up and down the taxonomy and be relevant, exciting, and productive. Your planned questions still provide the overall shape or focus, your reference point. The spontaneous questions and your students' responses provide you with insights about their thinking. These insights can help you facilitate the discussion while it is occurring and later enable you to plan future activities and discussions.

Sequencing. Questions need to be arranged in a logical order or sequence that makes sense. The order operates like a flow chart of key ideas. Good and Brophy (1994) say the focus should be on sequences of questions that help students develop connected understandings, rather than the cognitive level of individual questions considered in isolation from one another. Answers to questions should be integrated, not simply dropped. For example, questions that move students up the hierarchy move in an inductive sequence (review basic facts and understandings, apply to a new situation, evaluate). If the questions start at a high cognitive level and proceed downward, then they are moving in a deductive sequence. Questions focusing on application may need a chronological sequence to make sense. Questions emphasizing knowledge and comprehension may need to be organized by topic areas with subordinate questions planned under each topic.

Once you have your rough draft of feasible questions and are satisfied with their logical relationship to each other, then you are ready to examine the shape of the question.

Form

A question is an oral-aural event. Therefore, a question's **form**—how it is phrased, how it sounds—is important. There is no instant replay. If the people who hear the question cannot decipher what it means, they may not ask for clarification. Instead, they either will not respond at all or respond in some irrelevant way. When roles are unequal in status, people in the lower position rarely ask clarification questions. There are apprehensions about such questions from both points of view. Teachers may feel students are being disrespectful, attacking their teaching ability. Students have a host of possible fears, including: appearing too interested in front of their peers, the teacher's wrath at being questioned, and admitting confusion. You need to model asking your students clarification questions as needed, so they will learn to feel comfortable asking them of you and each other. We need to aim for clear, precise, and concise questions in the first place.

Critique your draft questions against the following indicators of good form, and revise as necessary. By using these guides consistently when planning questions, you will eventually internalize them. Then you will find yourself thinking of questions, including spontaneous ones, in a listenable form.

State Questions as Interrogatives, Not Directives. It is important to understand the distinction between interrogatives and directives. **Interrogatives** are genuine questions that *ask* for a response. **Directives** are imperative statements that demand an answer. They masquerade as questions, camouflaged with a question mark. Tharp and Gallimore (1988) explain the difference this way: Questions, logically and socially, request a reply in language. They reflect a genuine perplexity and set up the expectation for an appropriate response. Directives, acting like instructions, request a reply in action. They presume compliance and emphasize the authority to demand.

This distinction does not matter when writing questions for a written test, because testing situations are command/demand/evaluative performances. However, in the world of speech, blurring the two intents in your planned questions matters in terms of the social and cognitive interaction. Interrogatives set up a different atmosphere than directives. If you mean a question, then phrase it in an interrogative form: "What do you think it means to be gifted?" If you mean a demand, then phrase it in the form of a directive: "State three criteria that define giftedness."

Consider the Type of Response the Question Invites. How the question is phrased can affect the length and complexity of the responses. Phrasing that limits is one reason why questions intended to produce more complex thought do not get much response. Let's consider what kind of phrasing invites a limited or expanded response.

All questions can be divided according to their timing in a discussion into *primary* (initial or first in a line of thought) or *secondary* (second or next questions that follow-up on a response to a primary question). Although your plan is composed of primary questions, you might also plan some possible secondary probing questions.

Depending upon how they are phrased, primary questions may invite a limited *closed*, response or an elaborated, *open*, response.

1. **Primary Closed Questions.** These questions set up narrow, restrictive choices from which a respondent must choose or ask for a specific, correct response. They often deal with lower-level cognitive activity. This type of phrasing is useful when reviewing facts, determining procedures, or as a base for higher-level follow-up questions. Their danger lies in forcing agreement, limiting possible responses, and encouraging guessing

   • **Yes/No**. The choice is limited to yes or no. Words signalling these questions include: would, should, do, are, is, don't. "Do you all have your workbooks?" "Don't you think that teacher education programs should require Red Cross certification?"

   • **Recall/Short Answer**. There are correct answers to these questions. "Who wrote the Constitution of the United States?" "When did the California Gold Rush occur?"

   • **Forced Choice**. Limits choices to suggested possibilities (a multiple choice format). "Would you rather have the quiz first or meet with your groups?" "Is it through society that prejudice is promoted or is it an individual's choice to be prejudiced?

2. **Primary Open Questions**. These questions bring up a topic and set general boundaries within which any response is appropriate. There are no right and wrong answers. Respondents create their own responses. Questions phrased this way invite longer, elaborated, personalized responses; in short, they encourage more complex thinking. Here is an open question that a student prepared for a discussion about special needs students: "How can we promote positive interaction between handicapped and non-handicapped students?"

3. **Secondary Questions**. There are three different types of secondary questions. Although some possible probes may be anticipated in your plan, secondary questions occur in response to what happens in the actual discussion. Knowing about them as possibilities alerts you to forming them when needed.

   • **Probe**. Probes follow-up and explore the first response. They can occur after any other question type, including primary closed questions. They provide the direction to find out more about what the asker wants to know. For example, assuming a possible response to the sample open question, a probe would be, "How do you think having handicapped students talk about their handicap will help?"

- **Mirror**. These questions paraphrase and reflect back what a person heard. They sound like a statement, except for the rising intonation at the end. "So you are saying . . ." and "in other words . . ." are two phrases that signal this type of question. They are appropriate when you want clarification or want someone to keep elaborating. For example, "You think it would help the other students to be less fearful of them?"

- **Loaded**. Although it is structured as a yes/no question, it produces a longer response because it is weighted against some idea likely to be controversial. This is the type of question referred to as "playing the devil's advocate." It stirs up responses when you know the people involved well enough to load it properly, and it is placed at an opportune moment in the discussion. If these two conditions are not met, the asker may be perceived as sarcastic or seriously advocating the content of the question. An example would be, "So you think handicapped students should be given preferential treatment?"

Check for Clarity: Eliminate Semantic and Syntactic Noise.

Read each question from the perspective of your students. Is the intent of the question clear? Does the present wording have sufficient focus to indicate the territory of a relevant response or is it obscured by linguistic noise? Specifically, check for signs of:

- *Vagueness*. The territory is the universe. You need to narrow it down and be more specific. "What do you think the theme of the movie was?" is more helpful than "How about that movie?"

- *Multiple Directions*. The listener cannot tell what the focus of the question is. Avoid overloading questions with too many ideas and clauses that either do not clearly relate to each other or point in different directions. Separate out the different ideas and write them as separate questions. In doing this, you may discover some of them are redundant or are actually probes of other questions. Choose one focus for each question to prevent confusion. For example, a student submitted this draft question for a discussion on poverty: "In what ways do you agree with the cause-effect relationship between poverty, drug use, and lack of education?" One possible way to focus it is, "What relationships do you see among poverty, drug use, and lack of education?"

- *Wordiness*. Be direct. Avoid using unnecessary words to convey your meaning. Do not use "weasel words," which are filler words that take up space but do not contribute to clarity. Named for the weasel who sucks the life out of eggs in other animals' nests, weasel words kill the life in a question. Consider this student-drafted question, "Since many people that live in rural areas are considered to have poor economic status and their children often go to schools that have inadequate finances, what disadvantages may these students face that students from more prominent school districts often don't face?" The following rewrite is less wordy: "What are the possible disadvantages from attending poorly financed rural schools?"

- *Bias*. Avoid biased language that indicates what you think because it skews responses. Do not editorialize by disguising your opinion as a question. If you want to make a statement, then make a statement. If you do so, however, consider the effect of timing. Starting with your opinion constrains the range and nature of the students' responses. Look at this student-drafted question for biased wording. "How can we provide a substantial education for average students when we are forced to deal with so many special cases (mainstreamed, handicapped, and gifted students)?" To eliminate bias, remove "substantial"; substitute "the majority of" for "average"; and substitute "must deal" for "are forced to deal."

- *Chaining Questions*. Asking several different questions one right after the other or repeating the same question several times with different wording is known as **chaining questions**. In either case, each question acts like a link in a chain. Discussants do not know which part of the chain to attack first. Ask one question at a time. Rewrite or choose the best question in terms of the territory it rules in, the clearest phrasing, and appropriate timing. A student asked these two questions together: "What feelings did we have concerning the handicapped students in our classes? How do these feelings relate to what our students may be feeling about disabled students in our classroom?" The ideas behind these two questions could have been combined into one clearer question, "How can we use our experiences with handicapped classmates to understand our students' feelings about their disabled classmates?"

Check for Listenability. Questions that are listener friendly have **listenability**. A question may look good on paper, but fail to fly when spoken. "Oralize" each question. Read it out loud. Is it easy to *listen through* and understand? The ideas discussed in the listening chapter about the effect of short, direct statements on listening also apply to questions. Listener friendly questions are concise and precise. Be suspicious of long questions. If you cannot easily read the question out loud (slowly, in one breath, so the meaning is clear), then it is too long and should be revised.

If you have a length problem due to preambles and prefatory statements setting the stage for the actual question, you may have a question for which your students lack sufficient background. If so, consider your options: Write a question at a more appropriate cognitive level or design an activity or experience that prepares them for the question you want to ask (minus the exposition).

Once you are satisfied with the function, sequence, and form of your questions, then it is time to discuss.

Step IV: Facilitate Participation

Remember, discussions are dynamic, interactive, fluid events, like the confluence of a mighty river. Both can be channelled, be dammed up, flood over their banks, or run a natural course, but neither can be confidently predicted or totally controlled.

Suggestions on how to facilitate a discussion are guidelines, not rules or steps. Whether a suggestion is appropriate to implement can only be decided by you moment by moment as you interact with your students. To mix a metaphor: You must be on your mental toes to recognize what the discussion needs for it to continue breathing.

Being able to recognize the opportune moment requires alertness to the two levels of any discussion: the *content* (what is or is not being said, comments and questions raised, gaps in thought, leaps that need to be made) and *process* (the dynamics, who is or is not speaking to whom about what). Discussion leaders need to monitor and critique what is occurring on these two levels, and then make a decision about what is likely to further the content and stimulate the process.

Learning to moderate a discussion rather than dominate it requires motivation, effort, practice, and thoughtful reflection. Self-reflective practice needs to happen now, in student teaching, and when you have your own classroom. See every discussion as an opportunity to develop your skills as a facilitator. Experiment thoughtfully with your students to discover what helps them to become involved in discussion. Realize that what they need may vary with the topic and changes as their discussion confidence and skills develop. As you begin any discussion, you need to be alert to what kind of assistance your students need *this* time.

Let's look at the discussion from the perspective of what you need to consider in its introduction, body, and the conclusion.

Introduction

Students need to know what is to be discussed, why they need to discuss it, how it relates to them, and how the discussion will proceed. In other words, they need focus, purpose, motivation, and procedures. There is no necessary order for meeting these needs. To determine what to say, think back over your decision points in creating your plan. Be creative and relevant.

- *Focus*. What are we going to talk about? What is the issue, problem, idea, dilemma, controversy, topic, circumstance?
- *Purpose*. Why are we going to talk about it? What is our target? Are we going to evaluate evidence or positions? Apply ideas? Develop ideas? Review? Come up with a plan?
- *Motivation*. The introduction should create attention and generate interest in students. Relate the topic area to them and what has gone on, and will go on in class. Find a way to answer or get them to answer the question, "Why should we care?" Help them develop connections between themselves, the focus, and the purpose.
- *Procedures*. How are we going to discuss? (Where? With whom? For how long? In what order, if any?) For example, must students move into a circle or direct their attention to some part of the room? Do they have to raise their hands or can they just jump in when they have a comment? Do they need to do something individually or in small groups before the entire class gathers to discuss?

The Body

Wait Time. Ask your first question and then wait for an answer. As we examined in chapter 3 on nonverbal behavior, the amount of time given to someone or something communicates meaning. **Wait time** is the amount of time a teacher gives a student to respond. There are two wait times: "*Wait Time 1*" is postquestion wait time, the pause between the teacher's question and a student being expected to respond. "*Wait Time 2*" is postresponse time, the pause after the student's response and before the teacher reacts. The average teacher waits one second in either case, regardless of subject or grade level (Rowe 1987). When so little time is given for a response, possible meanings are all negative: "Give me a quick answer"; "I don't care what you think"; and "I don't care about you."

Increasing wait times to 3–5 seconds produces remarkable effects on the students' and teacher's discussion behavior. Wait time is thinking time. Keep in mind that 3–5 seconds is the amount of time it takes to sing silently, "O-oh say, can you see?" or "Baa-baa black sheep, have you any wool?" (Dillon 1987, p. 63). The effects of increased wait time on students are (Rowe 1987, p. 97–99):

- The length of student responses increases between 300 and 700 percent.
- More inferences are supported by logical evidence.
- Speculative thinking and student-generated questions increase.
- More and more elaborated responses are given (particularly during wait time 2).
- Classroom discipline improves. (Short wait times produce restlessness, withdrawal, and disruption. Longer wait times influences perception of caring and motivation for productive participation.)
- Student-student exchanges increase.
- The variety and number of students voluntarily participating increases.
- Students gain confidence in their ability to discuss.
- Achievement on cognitively complex test items improves.

Teachers' behavior is affected by increased wait time in several ways (Rowe 1987):

- Teachers understand students' reasoning better.
- Teachers need to ask fewer questions because students are asking more questions.
- Expectations become higher for some students based on their more frequent and productive participation.

The Basics of Teachers' Responses.   Facilitators must be responsive to what is occurring. Appropriate verbal and nonverbal responses spring from what you know and your application skills. We need to review the major ideas that you need to apply when leading a discussion:

- Think about the connections among self-concept, perceptions, learning styles, and expectations. Concentrate on your students. Remember how they are affected by how people (you) communicate toward them and how their self-concept and expectations affect what they perceive and how they communicate.

- Eliminate potential noises or deal with them as they occur.
- Monitor your nonverbal behavior, especially kinesics (eyes, facial expression, posture, movement, gestures), proxemics, and paralanguage (vocal variety, volume, rate). Keep in mind how they affect the feedback you give and the "affect" you create with your students.
- Practice the guidelines for improving teacher listening. Remember the importance of providing positive nonverbal feedback cues (attending behaviors, back-channeling cues). Remember the important distinction between judgmental and critical listening. Avoid judgmental responses.
- Hold in mind the interpersonal needs that you and your students continually seek to meet (inclusion, control, and affection) and how they affect behavior. Students are more likely to become involved in discussion when their needs are met—their participation is sought, they are encouraged to express their personal ideas and questions, and they are supported as a valued participant.

Other Teacher Response Behaviors. The following list is a repertoire of other possible teacher behaviors. Only you can decide what is appropriate at any given moment by listening carefully to your students, remembering the discussion's purpose, and using your plan flexibly. Choose and monitor responses.

1. Encourage involvement by as many students as possible. Communicate your expectation that everyone has ideas worth sharing and will participate. Think in terms of "participant," not volunteer or nonvolunteer. Watch the faces, eyes, and posture for the nonverbal clues that someone has something to say.
2. Acknowledge and accept the students' feelings. Listen "therapeutically," reflecting back what you think the feelings are without adding any judgments.
3. Encourage student-to-student interaction:
   - Let comments flow among students without you intervening with a comment after each student speaks.
   - Ask students to comment on or relate to the ideas of other students: "What do the rest of you think of Chris's idea?"
   - Encourage students to ask spontaneous and planned questions. Student response to student questions is longer and more complex than to teacher questions (Dillon 1987). Discuss what makes a good question at the beginning of the term.

- Redirect (repeat) a question back to the class: "How can you answer the question Pat raises?"

4. Ask questions judiciously. Seek quality and relevance. For instance:
   - Ask probing and mirror questions when necessary for clarification and elaboration.
   - Ask *perplexing questions* that occur to you during the discussion (Dillon 1988). Dillon calls these genuine questions, as opposed to the quasi-questions teachers usually ask.
   - Do not repeat or answer your own questions. Notice this is a *non-behavior*—something you should not do. People new to discussion leading frequently start chaining a question or immediately answer it. They fear no one will say anything. Remember wait time is thinking time.

5. Tend the shape of the discussion as needed, so the discussion develops and moves toward the objectives. Shaping statements involve focus, direction, or progress. Examples involve summaries of progress or of positions thus far: pointing out similarities, differences, or connections among the ideas presented; or a reminder of the question or issue at hand. These statements may be made by teachers and/or framed as questions for students to answer: "How can we sum up the several positions that have emerged?"

6. State the thought that occurs to you in relation to what a student has just said.

7. Trust silence (Dillon 1987). Maintain an attentive, appreciative silence until a speaker resumes or another student speaks.

8. Model and encourage the giving of constructive, supportive verbal and nonverbal feedback among all participants.
   - Practice the nonverbal behaviors that signal listening and interest.
   - Avoid judgmental responses. Reflect on the problems with and correctives for praise discussed in chapter 6.
   - Realize that commenting on, questioning, and building on the students' remarks are forms of verbal feedback.
   - Do not let any student's comments or questions be ignored by the group, particularly those of students who have low peer status, are reticent, new to the class, rarely participate, are members of a minority group, or have controversial ideas.
   - Support students helping each other out, whether supplying facts, trying to express what they mean, or phrasing a question.

Conclusion

A conclusion cannot be planned ahead of time because you do not know what will be said during a discussion. However, time needs to be allotted for a conclusion to occur. Students need a sense of what has happened during a discussion and what it means in terms of the purpose and the focus. Discussions, even good ones, should not be ended by the bell for the next class. They need sense of closure. Teachers may provide the conclusion or enlist students in creating the conclusion together.

- *Summary.* "What have we gained from this discussion?" "What main points (ideas, opinions, questions raised, plans, themes, solutions, hypotheses, etc.) have we raised?" If the teacher or a student has kept track on the board of points during the discussion, this is the time for the class to review the list.
- *Reflective Interpretation.* The following kinds of questions stimulate thought about the meaning of the discussion. "What does the summary mean?" "Have we accomplished our purpose?" "If not, why not?" "Have we discovered new purposes?" "What is our view of our focus now?" "What questions have we raised?" "Where do we need to go from here?"
- *Connectors.* The teacher needs to make clear how the discussion "connects" to what comes next. If a discussion is part of a class session, then you need a transition to the next part of the lesson. If the discussion is the session, then link it to tomorrow's session, future plans, or thinking.

Step V: Evaluate the Discussion

Sit down with your plan, review your fresh impressions of what happened, and evaluate the discussion. Recollect what occurred with what consequences. Analyze the content and the process dimensions. The following questions are only suggestive of the kind of questions you need to ask yourself:

Content. How do I rate what was accomplished by the plan? Of my planned questions: Which ones did I use? Why? Which ones got the best response? Why? Of the student questions: What were they? What do they tell me about their thinking? What can be said about the depth and the breath of the comments? How do I evaluate what I did to aid thinking? What else could I have done? How can we build on this discussion?

Process. Who did not join in? Why? What can I do to get them in next time? Were there patterns in who talked to whom? If so, what do the patterns mean? Did I acknowledge and use (or encourage the class to use) each comment? If not, why not? Was the tone positive and supportive for everyone? If not, why not? What can I do so the next discussion is more encouraging?

Asking yourself such questions will help you get the discussion in perspective and plan the next one more effectively. Decide what you learned about your students' thinking and discussion skills and about yourself as a facilitator. Jot notes to yourself. Set specific goals for what you need to work on in your next discussion.

Discussion: Coming to Know

Discussions are vital to students' learning. A discussion is an arena in which students practice critical thinking, listening, and expressing themselves clearly. Good discussions do not happen by accident. They require planning, and they take time—time to truly listen and respond to each student's comment in a constructive way.

Note

[1] Gall cites the following studies:

Dillon, J. T. 1982. "Cognitive Correspondence Between Question/Statement and Response." *American Educational Research Journal* 19:540–51.

Mills, S., C. Rice, D. Berliner, and E. Rousseau. 1980. "The Correspondence Between Teacher Questions and Student Answers in Classroom Discourse." *Journal of Experimental Education* 48:194–204.

Willson, I. 1979. "Changes in Mean Levels of Thinking in Grades 1–8 Through Use of an Interaction Analysis System Based on Bloom's Taxonomy." *Journal of Education Research* 49:1350.

References

Andersen, J. 1982. "Acquisition of Cognitive Skill." *Psychological Review* 89:369–406. Cited in J. Bransford and N. Vye, "A Perspective on Cognitive Research and Its Implications for Instruction." In L. Resnick and L. Klopfer, editors, *Toward the Thinking Curriculum: Current Cognitive Research*. Washington, DC: Association for Supervision and Curriculum Development, 1989.

Andersen, J. 1987. "Skill Acquisition: Compilation of Weak-Method Problem Solutions." *Psychological Review* 94:192–210. Cited in J. Bransford and N. Vye, "A Perspective on Cognitive Research and Its Implications for Instruction," In L. Resnick and L. Klopfer, editors, *Toward the Thinking*

Curriculum: Current Cognitive Research. Washington, DC: Association for Supervision and Curriculum Development, 1989.

Bloom, B., editor. 1956. *Taxonomy of Educational Objectives—Handbook I: Cognitive Domain.* New York: David McKay.

Bransford, J. and N. Vye. 1989. "A Perspective on Cognitive Research and Its Implications for Instruction." In L. Resnick and L. Klopfer, editors, *Toward the Thinking Curriculum: Current Cognitive Research.* Washington, DC: Association for Supervision and Curriculum Development, 1989.

Britton, J. 1982. "Shaping at the Point of Utterance." In G. M. Pradl, editor, *Prospect and Retrospect: Selected Essays of James Britton.* Montclair, NJ: Boynton/Cook.

Dembo, M. 1991. *Applying Educational Psychology in the Classroom,* 4th edition. New York: Longman.

Dewey, J. 1933. *How We Think—A Restatement of the Relation of Reflective Thinking to the Educative Process.* Boston: DC Heath.

Dillon, J. 1984. "Research on Questioning and Discussion." *Educational Leadership.* November: 50–56.

———. 1987. "The Multidisciplinary World of Questioning." In W. Wilen, editor, *Questions, Questioning Techniques, and Effective Teaching.* Washington, DC: NEA.

———, editor. 1988. *Questioning and Discussion—A Multidisciplinary Study.* Norwood, NJ: Ablex.

Gall, M. 1984. "Synthesis of Research on Teachers' Questioning." *Educational Leadership* (2): 40–47.

Gall, M. and J. Gall. 1976. "The Discussion Method." In N. Gage, editor, *Psychology of Teaching Methods.* Chicago: University of Chicago. Cited in M. Gall, "Synthesis of Research on Teachers' Questioning." *Educational Leadership* (2): 40–47.

Glatthorn, A. and J. Baron. 1985. "The Good Thinker." Developing Minds. Washington, DC: Association for Supervision and Curriculum Development.

Good, T. and J. Brophy. 1994. *Looking in Classrooms,* 6th edition. New York: HarperCollins.

Goodlad, J. 1984. *A Place Called School: Prospects for the Future.* New York: McGraw-Hill. Cited in A. Costa and L. Lowery, *Techniques for Teaching Thinking* (Pacific Grove, CA: Midwest Publications, 1989).

Hulit, L. and M. Howard. 1993. *Born to Talk: An Introduction to Speech and Language Development.* New York: Macmillan.

Hunkins, F. 1989. *Teaching Thinking Through Effective Questioning.* Boston: Christopher-Gordon Publishers.

Hymes, D. 1974. *Foundations in Sociolinguisitics: An Enthographic Approach.* Philadelphia: University of Pennsylvania Press. Cited in D. Rubin, "Nobody Play by the Rules He Know." In Y. Kim, editor, *Interethnic Communication: Current Research.* Newberry Park, CA: Sage, 1986.

Klinzing, H, and G. Klinzing-Eurich. 1988. "Questions, Responses, and Reactions." In J. Dillon, editor, *Questioning and Discussion: A Multidisciplinary Study.* Norwood, NJ: Ablex.

Lesgold, A. 1988. "Problem Solving." In R. J. Sternberg and E. E. Smith, editors, "The Psychology of Human Thought." New York: Cambridge University Press. Cited in J. Bransford and N. Vye, "A Perspective on Cognitive Research and Its Implications for Instruction." In L. Resnick and L. Klopfer, editors, *Toward the Thinking Curriculum: Current Cognitive Research.* (Alexandria, VA: Association for Supervision and Curriculum Development, 1989.)

Lindsay, P. and D. Norman. 1977. *Human Information Processing*, 2nd edition. New York: Academic Press. Cited in R. Owens, *Language Development—An Introduction* (New York: Macmillan, 1992).

Lippman, M. 1988. "Critical Thinking—What Can It Be?" *Educational Leadership*. 46:38–43.

Owens, R. 1992. *Language Development—An Introduction*. New York: Macmillan.

Paul, R. 1984. "Critical Thinking: Fundamental to Education in a Free Society." *Educational Leadership* 42:4–14.

Phillips, S. 1970. "Acquisition of Rules for Appropriate Speech Usage." In J. Alatis, editor, *Bilingualism and Language Contact: Anthropological, Linguistic, Psychological, and Sociological Aspects.* (Monograph #23). Washington, DC: Georgetown University Press. Cited in D. Rubin, "Nobody Play by the Rules He Know." In Y. Kim, editor, *Interethnic Communication: Current Research.* Newberry Park, CA: Sage, 1986.

Piaget, J. 1964. "Development and Learning." In R. Ripple and V. Rockcastle, editors, *Piaget Rediscovered: A Report on the Conference on Cognitive Skills and Curriculum Development.* Ithaca, NY: Cornell University, School of Education. Cited in M. Dembo, *Applying Educational Psychology in the Classroom*, 4th edition (New York: Longman, 1991).

Powell, R. and J. Andersen. 1994. "Culture and Classroom Communication." In L. Samovar and R. Porter, editors, *Intercultural Communication: a Reader.* Belmont, CA: Wadsworth.

Resnick, L and Klopfer, L., editors. 1989. *Toward the Thinking Curriculum: Current Cognitive Research.* Alexandria, VA: Association for Supervision and Curriculum Development.

Richmond, V. and J. Gorham. 1992. *Communication, Learning, and Affect in Instruction.* Edina, MN: Burgess.

Roby, T. 1988. "Models of Discussion." In J. Dillon, editor, *Questioning and Discussion—A Multidisciplinary Study.* Norwood, NJ: Ablex.

Rowe, M. 1987. "Using Wait Time To Stimulate Inquiry." In W. Wilen, editor, *Questions, Questioning Techniques, and Effective Teaching.* Washington, DC: NEA.

Rubin, D. 1986. "Nobody Play by the Rules He Know." In Y. Kim, editor, *Interethnic Communication: Current Research.* Newberry Park, CA: Sage.

Stodolsky, S., T. Ferguson, and K. Wimpelberg. 1981. "The Recitation Persists, But What Does It Look Like?" *Journal of Curriculum Studies* 13:121–30. Cited in J. Dillon, "Research on Questioning and Discussion." *Educational Leadership.* November, 1984: 50–56.

Swift, N., C. T. Gooding, and P. Swift. 1988. "Questions and Wait Time." In *Questioning and Discussion—A Multidisciplinary Study.* Dillon (ed.). Norwood, NJ: Ablex.

Tharp, R. and R. Gallimore. 1988. *Rousing Minds to Life—Teaching, Learning, and Schooling in Social Context*. Cambridge, England: Cambridge University Press.

Vygotsky, L. 1978. *Mind in Society*. Cambridge: Harvard University.

Webster's *New Collegiate Dictionary*, 7th edition. 1976. Springfield, MA: G. & C. Merriam Co.

Wertsch, J. 1985. *Culture, Communication, and Cognition*. Cambridge, England: Cambridge University Press.

Whitehead, A. 1929. *The Aims of Education*. New York: Macmillan. Cited in J. Bransford and N. Vye, "A Perspective on Cognitive Research and Its Implications for Instruction." In L. Resnick and L. Klopfer, editors, *Toward the Thinking Curriculum: Current Cognitive Research*. Washington, DC: Association for Supervision and Curriculum Development, 1989.

Wilen, W. 1987. "Effective Questions and Questioning: A Classroom Application." In W. Wilen, editor, *Questions, Questioning Techniques, and Effective Teaching*. Washington, DC: NEA, 1987.

———. (editor). 1987. *Questions, Questioning Techniques, and Effective Teaching*. Washington, DC: NEA.

Wilen, W. and A. Clegg. 1986. "Effective Questions and Questioning: A Research Review." *Theory and Research in Social Education*. 14(2): 153–61.

Suggested Reading

Engaging Students—Thinking, Talking, Cooperating, by Carolyn Temple Adger, Maya Kalyanpur, Dana Peterson, and Teresa Bridger. Thousand Oaks, CA: Corwin Press, 1995.

Practical classroom-tested, research-based ideas that engage students in learning through thought and talk and facilitate their thinking and communication development. Explains how to incorporate "Think Trix," a thinking topology that guides the students' analytical reasoning and helps teachers move beyond asking recall questions. Ideas apply across content areas and the grade levels.

Turning the Soul—Teaching Through Conversation in the High School, by Sophie Haroutunian-Gordon. Chicago: University of Chicago Press, 1991.

Two classrooms grapple with *Romeo and Juliet* through meaningful discussion. The classes are in very different school contexts. One school is private, integrated, and urban, while the other school is public, largely African-American, and poor. The students in the former class are accustomed to discussion, while the students in the latter class are not.

Chapter 8

Small Groups

Ideas to Remember

* Small groups are defined by the following characteristics:
  Small number of members who can interact easily
  Mutually interdependent goals
  Mutually understood public procedure
  Individual responsibility and accountability
  A sense of cooperation among members
* Classes may be structured so students work individualistically, competitively, or cooperatively.
* Competition can be motivating, but it also has the potential to create negative effects on academic achievement, personal feelings, and social relationships.
* "Cooperative learning" refers to a number of cooperative approaches, which operationalize the characteristics of small groups differently.
* Cooperative learning can accelerate learning under certain conditions and contributes to more positive feelings about self, school, the subject, and classmates.
* Students have experience as members of social groups but need instruction in how to work effectively in task groups.
* Before starting to use groups, you must consider yourself, your students, and the context.

✻   The basic elements in the group process suggest questions that you must answer each time you plan a small group assignment.

    Goals: What is my purpose?

    Procedures: How do I need to structure the task?

    Time frame: How does time need to be structured?

    Group Composition: Who do I put in which group?

    Physical Arrangements: Where do I want the group to work?

    Norms: What rules do we need?

    Roles: What functions do we need?

    Decision making: How should group members make decisions?

    Output: What outcome do I want from this task?

✻   There are eight basic types of task groups:

    Learning (Enlightenment)

    Research

    Problem solving

    Role-play

    Game

    Simulation

    Short-term groupings

    Public discussion: panel

✻   The teacher's role is to set up the group activity and then to serve as a supportive guide and resource to facilitate task accomplishment.

✻   Teachers need to introduce the group activity, monitor the students' doing of the task, and then wrap up what has been accomplished in a conclusion.

How did your small group experience cause you to react to the endorsements given groups in the preceding chapters? In chapter 6, "Communicating Interpersonally," the intrinsic motivating qualities of small groups were explained by the students' preference for active involvement in their own learning and for opportunities to interact with their peers. In chapter 7, "Discussion," interactive small groups were cited as natural settings for the social construction of knowledge to occur.

Most of my students remember little or no experience with groups in K–12, and what memories they recall are bad. This has left them with mixed, mostly negative attitudes about small groups as an instructional strategy. Some are still intimidated by the idea of being in a small group and are initially suspicious of using groups in the classroom when they teach. Some think groups are a waste of time. They remember feeling frustrated because the goals and directions were unclear, and they had to guess what they were supposed to do. Since there was little guidance or supervision, students socialized until the deadline, at which point, the person(s) who cared most about the grade ended up doing all the work. Students who found themselves in this position resented it and vowed to avoid groups in the future. They are skeptical about using groups based on their past experiences. They agree groups are fun but doubt meaningful learning can occur.

Actually, what they (and perhaps you) have experienced is "bunching," not small groups. Bunching exhibits what may be called the banana approach to groups. Put a bunch of people in a group (like bananas) with a vague task and leave them alone to talk. This method is based on the false assumption that working in a group is easy and instinctual, people just automatically know what to do. Actually, group interaction possesses the same characteristics of any purposive communication interaction. It is dynamic and complex, involving mutual influence in the creation of meaning and simultaneous content and relationship messages. Working effectively in a group is learned behavior. People who are bunched experience a negative fate, like bananas left out on a counter. The fruit goes bad. People feel unproductive and personally frustrated.

Effective small group experiences, the kind in which learning occurs, start with understanding the difference between a bunch of people and a small group.

Definition of Small Group

Small groups are defined by the following fundamental characteristics and expectations (Drawn from Brilhart and Galanes 1989 and Wood, Phillips, and Petersen 1986). Each of these elements will be examined later in the chapter. Groups have:

1. *A small enough number of members so each person may communicate easily (verbally and nonverbally) with all other members.* Although research suggests a range from no less than three to no more than fifteen, estimates of reasonable numbers imply

adult group members. Brilhart and Galanes say three to seven is typical. Wood, Phillips and Petersen recommend five to seven for problem solving. The number of members for any specific small group should be defined by the purpose, situation, and students.

2. *Mutually interdependent goals.* Members share a common, mutual goal, and they need each other to accomplish it. They must collaborate, work together collectively, to attain the goal. The success of any one member is contingent upon the success of all members.

3. *Mutually understood public procedure.* All members of the group share an understanding of the procedure they are to use in moving toward accomplishing their goal. The type of group task determines what kind of procedure is needed.

4. *Individual responsibility and accountability.* Each member is expected to participate fully in achieving the group's goal and is held accountable by the group. This means each member recognizes his or her personal responsibility, as well as that of other members. If any member abdicates his or her responsibility, the group's outcome is diminished. Silent members or members who speak infrequently are depriving the rest of the group of their ideas.

5. *Cooperation among members.* Members perceive themselves as working together for the good of the group goal. They cooperatively assist each other, working with and for each other. They recognize that the **synergistic effect** of working together (synthesizing individual contributions and creating new possibilities together) produces greater outcomes than an individual working alone. In other words, the whole is greater than the sum of the parts. Disagreement over specific ideas or opinions is treated as a normal part of the communication process and as the way to evolve more thoughtful or useful responses that lead to more effective completion of the task.

Small groups are, by their nature, collaborative and cooperative. Their interaction is focused on joint accomplishment of common goals. To understand how groups function in the classroom, we need to examine where they fit within possible classroom goal structures.

Classroom Goal Structures

Goal structures determine how students will relate to each other while working to accomplish instructional goals (Johnson and Johnson 1991). According to the Johnsons, teachers must choose which of three possible goal structures are appropriate for particular learning activities: individualistic, competitive, and cooperative. All are effective under certain conditions and relevant to specific goals and objectives (Dembo 1991). The Johnsons (1991) state that in an *ideal classroom* all three would be used appropriately.

Each goal structure promotes different interaction patterns, which, in turn, can affect achievement, personal attitudes (about self, others, and motivation), teacher expectations, and climate.

Individualistic

In this structure, students work independently. Their achievement of the instructional goal is unrelated to the other students' achievement. Interaction is restricted with peers and is promoted with teachers, so positive affective outcomes are minimized. Students are told to work by themselves, not disturb their neighbors, and to ask the teacher for help when they need it (Johnson and Johnson 1991). Students have personal sets of materials and work at their own pace.

Individual goals are assigned and efforts are evaluated and rewarded according to a criteria-referenced basis (fixed set of standards). Students judge their ability by their improvement over their past performances, so they believe individual effort is worthwhile and confidence increases (Ames and Ames 1985). These positive attitudes do not occur, however, if students work independently but their performance is compared to others in the class.

Competitive

Students work against each other to obtain scarce, often artificially restricted rewards, such as a set number of A's and B's. Students are graded on a norm-referenced basis (a curve), which means they must work faster and better than their classmates (Johnson and Johnson 1991). This approach encourages teachers to perceive students in dichotomized ways, such as success versus failure, able versus unable, high versus low expectations (Ames and Ames 1985).

The competitive structure promotes a win-lose orientation. Students assess their ability based on social comparisons with the performance of others: If they win, their ability is high; if they lose, their ability is low (Ames and Ames 1985). Students handle competitive situations in a number of ways. Some study harder in order to do better than classmates, while others give up. Others celebrate their classmates' failures. Some students increase their odds of success through spreading misinformation ("No, that isn't going to be on the test.") or obstruction (hiding material, tearing pages out of books).

Competition needs to be considered in the context of life outside the classroom. The Johnsons (1991) point out that competition permeates the fabric of our society. A win-lose orientation (first, best, only, most) defines success and status for many people personally, socially, professionally, and nationally. They point out that some activities are necessarily competitive, such as sports, games, contests, and tournaments. These activities are structured so participants are comparatively ranked, yet people engage in them because they are fun and enjoyable. However, the Johnsons conclude that in any society that stresses winning, " . . . it is no wonder that competition often gets out of hand and barriers arise to competing appropriately" (Johnson and Johnson 1991, p. 10).

The connection between rampant competition in society and the need for competition in schools is controversial. Many people believe students need to exercise their competitive muscles in school, so they will able to compete successfully in the real world. As was pointed out in the chapter 6, Brophy (1987) thinks rewards and competition are best used with tasks whose purpose is to accomplish mastery of basic skills and when speed or quantity of output matters. He also thinks appropriate competition can be an incentive. *Appropriateness* depends on depersonalizing the competition. This can be done by emphasizing the content being learned rather than who wins and loses and by using handicapping systems, so students have an equal chance of winning. Dembo (1991) thinks a limited amount of competition can be motivating, such as for bored students to complete an assignment or for similar-ability students to work harder. However, he believes competition is overused in the classroom. He states that evidence confirms that the extensive use of competition does not produce many of its intended motivational effects.

Kohn (1986) critiques the use of competition in the schools on several grounds:

> *Competition does not promote achievement.* According to Kohn, University of Texas researchers have studied the relationship between achievement and competitiveness using appropriate achievement measures for different populations. Their subjects included scientists, business people, pilots, psychologists, undergraduates, and fifth and sixth graders. The researchers found an inverse relationship between competitiveness and achievement: the more competitive, the lower the achievement.

> *Competition causes anxiety.* The psychological stakes always are high and important even when the tangible rewards are not. Tension caused by the possibility of losing interferes with performance.

> Students handle the anxiety caused by competition in different

ways. Early, unsuccessful competitive experiences may cause students to avoid competition in the future. Some students want to avoid failure more than maximize success. These students "play it safe," avoiding any academic or creative risks that might jeopardize their winning. Richmond and Gorham (1992) report that some students develop a fear of winning out of guilt for doing better than others or fear of the reactions of the people whom they outdo. Such students may choose not to compete or intentionally do a poorer job than they are capable of doing.

Competition fosters suspicion and isolates people. People who rely solely on their own resources and perspective may miss opportunities or not think of alternatives. They regard others as barriers to their success, not as allies.

"Competition does not promote excellence because trying to do well and trying to beat others are two different," incompatible goals. We do best at what we enjoy, because we are intrinsically motivated. Trying to beat others is an extrinsic motivator. Recall chapter 6's examination of potential negative effects of extrinsic motivation: Extrinsic motivators may undermine existing intrinsic motivation. The consequence, not the activity, is the reward. In the case of competition, the rewarding consequence is beating someone else.

Cooperative

In this structure, students work together to accomplish shared goals to maximize their own and each other's learning (Johnson, Johnson, and Holubec 1994). Since the goals are shared, personal success depends on the success of other group members. Ideas and materials are shared, although subtasks may be divided among members as the group moves toward accomplishing the goal. Members both feel responsible to the group and benefit from each other's efforts. This positive interdependence provides an incentive for students to help, assist, and encourage each other. Peer tutoring appears naturally. The cooperative goal structure promotes a positive, supportive climate. Kohn (1986) makes the interesting observation that cooperation is so rare and undervalued in our schools that its spontaneous appearance is called "cheating."

Everyone in the group is rewarded for successful completion of the task. A criteria-referenced evaluation system is used. Assessment focuses on group performance information and the degree to which effort was related to both individual and group achievement (Dembo 1991). This multiple faceted approach—group outcomes, effort, personal achievement—helps insulate low-achievers from the negative effects of failure on their self-esteem (Dembo 1991). In a cooperative setting, teachers place more emphasis on effort and try to help more students in the class (Ames and Ames 1985).

Although there is one goal structure called "cooperative," it is important to realize that there are many different approaches to operationalizing cooperative/collaborative learning in the classroom. The broad term "cooperative learning" covers diverse viewpoints that differ significantly in their details. Johnson, Johnson, and Holubec (1994) point out that some cooperative learning procedures actually contain a mixture of cooperative, competitive, and individualistic efforts, while others contain "pure cooperation" (p. 20).

Cooperative/Collaborative Learning. Since "cooperative learning" is an umbrella term that covers many different approaches, methods, and activities, beware of semantic noise. When the phrase is used, inquire how it is being used and what its means in that instance. "What approach is being referred to? How are its attributes defined?"

Cooperative learning is often used synonymously with the term "collaborative learning," but they may have different meanings. According to Davidson (1994), **cooperative learning** refers collectively to the many approaches emphasizing interdependent, cooperative learning among students in small groups, while the collaborative approach is one such approach. Davidson sees the differences between the cooperative and collaborative learning approaches revolving around the degree of structure. Cooperative learning procedures tend to be more structured and focused on specific behaviors and rewards. Methods following the collaborative approach are less structured, usually do not provide rewards, and emphasize interdependence and individual accountability less.

Davidson (1994) identifies six major approaches to cooperative learning:

1. *Student Team Learning* (STL). Developed by Robert Slavin and his associates at the Johns Hopkins University, the key features are individual accountability and either group rewards or goals. Examples of STL are: Student Teams Achievement Divisions (STAD), Teams-Games-Tournaments (TGT), and Jigsaw II.

2. *Learning Together.* Developed by David and Roger Johnson at the University of Minnesota, this approach emphasizes positive interdependence, face-to-face interaction, direct teaching of interpersonal and small group skills, and individual accountability.

3. *Group Investigation.* Based on the ideas of Thelen and investigated by Sharan and Sharan, this approach involves dividing a complex topic into subtopics to be studied by different groups.

4. *Structural Approach.* Developed by Kagan, in this approach teachers learn a number of simple structures, such as Think-Pair-Share, Roundtable, Three-Step-Interview, Numbered Heads Together, that they use immediately. The goal is for teachers to combine them in different ways to form more complex lessons. There are structures for practice and mastery, thinking, and information sharing among others. This approach incorporates procedures from the first three approaches.

5. *Complex Instruction.* Originally developed by Elizabeth Cohen and associates for instruction in math and science and now used in other subjects. Multiple-ability tasks are designed to incorporate other kinds of performance besides cognitive. Cooperative management techniques are used, including delegation of authority to students and group decision making.

6. *Collaborative Approach.* Associated with theories about language and learning developed by James Britton and Douglas Barnes, "Its intention is to focus on the creation of personal meaning and internally persuasive understandings through dialogue and discussion" (Davidson 1994, p. 23).

Davidson (1994) views the diversity of cooperative learning approaches as healthy, stimulating each other and the ongoing dialogue about methods. Davidson says all six approaches share the following attributes: a common task suitable for group work, use of small groups, cooperative behavior, interdependence, and individual responsibility. Notice these are the same as the characteristics and expectations for small groups. He sees variations in how each approach structures the following attributes: group composition, how interdependence is structured (tasks, resources, roles, leadership, rewards), group structure, teacher's role, explicit teaching of communication skills, reflection on group process and what was learned, and climate setting (team building, trust building, etc.).

Outcomes. Since the 1970s, much innovative practice and research have been done on cooperative learning, variously defined and measured against differing criteria. In summarizing the major areas of agreement within the research, Robert Slavin (1990a) reports important outcomes in both the academic and interpersonal areas.

- *Academic Outcomes.* Cooperative methods accelerate student Learning When The Following Three Conditions Are Met: (1) Group goals and individual accountability are present. (2) Basic skill objectives are the focus. Most studies have focused on basic skills in math, language arts, and reading. Although some studies have involved higher-level skills, the appropriateness of cooperative learning for higher-level conceptual learning is still being studied. (3) The elementary and middle/junior high school levels are involved. Slavin says there is ample evidence cooperative methods are effective grades two through nine, but few studies examine grades ten through twelve.

* *Interpersonal Outcomes.* Cooperative learning has the following kinds of effects: (1) increases liking and respect among group members of different racial and ethnic backgrounds; (2) increases "the social acceptance of mainstreamed academically handicapped classmates"; (3) "increases friendships among students"; and (4) personal benefits include improved self-esteem, greater liking of school and the subject, more time spent doing learning tasks, and improved attendance.

Goal Structures and Groups

Since groups are cooperative and collaborative, they belong within the cooperative goal structure. The cooperative goal structure itself makes extensive use of small groups. The different cooperative learning approaches, which have generated many kinds of learning activities, all depend on the use of groups.

To further understand the place of small groups in the classroom, it is important to remind ourselves of the connections between small groups and communication.

The Role of Groups in Communication

Small groups are specialized settings where interpersonal communication and discussion occur. All interpersonal relationships occur either in the context of a group or reflect individuals' group memberships. Our lives are lived in groups, and what we learn in our real groups (outside school) affects what we bring to small group experiences in the classroom.

Everyone's first small group experience is the family. Interpersonal communication is first experienced in the context of the family group, the transmitter of cultural, referent group meanings. It is where we are introduced to what becomes a lifelong communication pattern: setting goals, meeting role expectations, behaving, and receiving feedback. How effectively, and appropriately, we are enacting this pattern affects what people think of us interpersonally and as a member of the group. Initially, this pattern enables us to begin forging our identity and learning linguistic and pragmatic behavior. Throughout our lives it is the means to revising and sustaining our identities and navigating relationships and groups.

It is also in the family group where we first encounter the basic dynamics that are present in all groups. All groups have one or more goals and must develop ways of operating to accomplish them. Time constraints and physical arrangements affect what happens in the group. Group interaction is also affected by the roles that are present (who does what), norms that develop (what do members expect from each other), and procedures (how we do what we need to do). All groups develop ways to make decisions, to handle conflict, and to evaluate outcomes.

Although we can assume all students have had experience with groups on the social level, we do not know what they have learned about groups that might usefully transfer to working effectively and appropriately in task groups. No matter what students' backgrounds or grade levels are ("they should know how to work in groups by now"), we cannot assume that they know how to work effectively in groups. If they have been in instructional groups in the past, we do not know if they experienced bunching or actual group process. Learning to work effectively in task groups requires guidance, encouragement, and supervision. If group experiences lack these ingredients needed for success, then groups will fail to achieve their potential as cauldrons for creative and critical thought, development and practice of communication skills, and positive, supportive relationships.

The chapter is about helping you structure group experiences, so they promote your students' active learning. Keep in mind that these ideas are of practical, personal value to you right now, as well as in the future, as a group member and leader. In the rest of the chapter, we will examine the options and choices available to you in creating and conducting useful small group experiences.

Setting the Stage for Groups

Getting ready to use groups is similar to preparing to discuss. It requires thinking about yourself, your students, and the context. Teachers' and students' attitudes and past experiences color initial expectations and performance. Understanding everybody's starting point enables you to make more effective choices when you plan and conduct group activities.

Yourself

Think about the task-oriented small group experiences that you have had in and out of school—the group projects that were completed, the committees on which you served. Sort them into two piles: the successful, pleasant experiences and the frustrating, unproductive ones. Analyze each pile and recall specific behaviors that cause you to assess these groups as you do. What did or did not happen that should have? How do your experiences compare and contrast with those of my students discussed at the beginning of the chapter?

Attitude is still everything. Depending on whether your past group experiences were more positive or negative affects your present attitudes toward groups, whether using them as a teaching strategy or being in them as a teacher. If you have had good experiences, then you are probably enthusiastic about trying groups. If you were the one left holding the bag, stuck doing the group's work, then groups are not on your list of things to try. Keep in mind that the failure of task groups is usually traceable to poor planning and managing. Think about the potential positive benefits from working in groups and focus on the behaviors that promote successful outcomes.

Students

Differences in the students' pragmatic backgrounds and experiences affect their attitudes and expectations for groups. The students' socialization and cultural backgrounds affect whether they are field dependent or field independent, which, in turn, may affect their initial attitudes about groups. Students who are socialized in field-dependent cultures, for instance Mexican Americans, African Americans, Hawaiians, and Native Americans, prefer group work. (Dembo 1991, p. 99).[1] Field-independent students prefer working alone, so may need coaxing into group work. Students who are reticent are more comfortable talking in a small group. Students, depending on their experiences with bunching, may expect fun and a free ride with others doing the work, anticipate frustration, or dread the whole idea.

Context

Group contextual dimensions, particularly physical arrangements and the amount of time needed, are tied to the specific task of the group. There are many types of small groups. Each type focuses on different tasks and outcomes and needs to structure interaction in a certain way to accomplish its task. This means physical and temporal considerations need to be dealt with after you choose the group task.

Groups need the same kind of classroom climates to thrive that discussions need: positive, supportive, and talk friendly. Groups also develop their own personal climate. Although groups are by their nature cooperative and collaborative, they do not all automatically have positive climates. A group's climate evolves from the dynamic interaction among members as they work toward task accomplishment. What kind of a climate develops depends on what happens in the interplay among members (efforts, communication, attitudes), the complexity of the task, and the amount of time to do it. Groups with simple tasks may meet for too short a time for a climate to develop.

How you structure and assist the group's work affects climate. A group's climate is more likely to be positive when students know how to work effectively in task groups in general and also what to do when working on specific types of tasks.

Planning the Small Group

All groups share basic, constituent elements, although they vary as to task. If you know what these descriptive elements are, then you can use them as tools to aid your work with groups in four ways: (1) to describe any group that you are in or observe; (2) to frame questions in order to understand how a new group method or activity is supposed to work, for example: "What are the procedures? What is the expected output?"; (3) to analyze why a group is having trouble, for example, "What elements are inhibiting the group's work?"; and (4) to plan group experiences that are effective and productive. Each basic element suggests a general question that you need to answer specifically when planning a group activity.

Goals: What Is My Purpose?

A group is brought together around a common purpose in the belief that people can accomplish more together than individually. In the case of task groups in the classroom, students are brought together to help each other learn; the cognitive and social domains are brought together.

Start with your educational goal(s) for the lesson and ask yourself, "Why do I want to put them in groups?" "What do I want them to learn?" "How will a group experience help them do it?" Consult Bloom's *cognitive objectives*, which were examined in the previous chapter, for help in understanding what kind of thinking you want students to do.

Once you answer these questions and clarify your educational goal(s), then consider the different types of small task groups: learning discussion, research, problem-solving, role-play, game, simulation, short-term groups, and panel discussion. Each type will be explored later in the chapter.

Procedures: How Do I Need to Structure the Task?

Groups need to have some orderly way to attack the task that is before them. Although it is possible for procedures to be discovered inductively ("Let's see what works."), such an approach is time-consuming, often frustrating, and usually associated with bunching. Procedures are usually given deductively or explicitly ("Here's what you are to do.") to save time, for greater clarity, and so all group members have the same understanding of how they are to proceed. Deductive procedures come in two primary forms: **directions** (who does what, when), and an **agenda** (systematic plan or list of topics to guide group action). All group tasks need directions, but some tasks require an agenda, too.

Both forms of procedures can run along a continuum that provides varying degrees of structure ranging from general guidelines to minute detail. The amount and complexity of procedures needed in any given assignment depend on your students. Have they ever been in this kind of group before? Whether or not they have and what their group experiences have been determine what kinds of procedures you need to give them. They need enough structure so they can succeed at the task; too few or too many procedures may confuse students, provide insufficient guidance, overwhelm them, or inhibit their responses.

It is important to structure the procedures, so they promote each member's active participation and individual responsibility. There are many possible ways to encourage individual and mutual effort, such as:

- Keep the groups small. Fewer members allow more opportunities for individual contributions.
- Allow choices whenever possible. For example, let students suggest or choose from among possibilities for the subject matter of the task.
- Build in check-points for written or oral progress reports about what the group has accomplished so far.
- Have students keep individual journals about what they do in the group.
- Monitor the groups while they work.
- Give individual quizzes or tests (Johnson, Johnson, and Holubec 1994).
- Divide up resources, information, materials, or labor among members, so each member has a specific responsibility toward accomplishing the group task (Johnson, Johnson, and Holubec 1994). Teachers, students, or students and teachers could decide who is responsible for what.

- Give all members the same grade.
- Give all members a group grade and an individual grade.
- Give bonus points for group effort and/or group performance.
- Students evaluate each other's group performance using a checklist or scale of behaviors for an effective group member. The evaluation criteria are drawn up before the group meets, so everyone knows what is expected. Results serve as feedback to each group member and the teacher. Bonus points could be awarded to students who are perceived as effective by their group mates.

Time Frame: How Does Time Need to Be Structured?

You need to decide how much time to allot for working on the group task. Some groups may meet for just a few minutes, while others may meet for part or all of a class period. Complex group assignments may be structured to meet over several days, weeks, or even months. Students need answers to the following questions: "When do we get into groups?" "How long do we have to work in our groups?"

Group Composition: Who Do I Put in Which Group?

There are many ways to group students. Your criteria for choosing which method for an individual assignment should include: the nature of the task, your students' needs and abilities, what is most likely to facilitate doing the task, and the feasible number of students to work on the task. In other words, consider what resources each individual student would bring to the task and what the task demands.

Students may wonder why they are in a particular group and may otherwise place some negative, self-critical interpretation on their placement. Teachers should be able to tell their students the basis for composition. Being open about the basis for the grouping decision is respectful of the students' feelings, alleviates worry, and builds trust.

Some students like the security of always being in the same grouping. Keep in mind that varying group composition presents a more realistic communication practice. Students have to speak and listen to people with differing perspectives and learn to work cooperatively with different people. Heterogeneous groups of students engage in more elaborate thinking and give and receive explanations more frequently (Johnson, Johnson, and Holubec 1994). Changing who works with whom helps students get to know everyone in the class, rather than just the same few classmates. They develop more positive feelings about more people, which helps build a more supportive classroom climate.

Let's look at the options for group composition and consider their pros and cons:

Students' Choice. Students generally pick their friends or people they perceive as "smart" for graded assignments. This option may work well for simple tasks and short-term groups, however, in the long term, socializing may interfere with doing the task. Students might not be chosen because they are: new (no one knows them), different (handicapped, mainstreamed, in terms of race or ethnicity), reticent, or do not fit in socially.

Random Methods. When who is in the group does not matter, but how many there are does, this option works well. There are many ways to achieve randomness, such as:

Numerical: "I have twenty students, I need five groups, so count off by fours. The people with the same number are a group."

Clump: "Form a group with two neighbors."

Rows: "Each row is a group."

Variation: "Find two people you have not worked with yet and form a group."

Teacher's Choice. The teacher prearranges who is in which group for some reason relevant to the task. For example, a teacher might want to put highly motivated and less motivated students together on a project, so they stimulate each other. In some types of cooperative learning groups, groupings must be mixed in terms of achievement, sex, and ethnicity (Slavin 1990b). The preselection basis could be anything relevant to the impending task, such as to get students working with classmates with whom they have not worked, male and female students working together, or higher achievers working with lower achievers (based on tests or quizzes).

Physical Arrangements: Where Do I Want the Group to Work?

Groups need a place to work where they will not be disturbed or distracted and a spatial arrangement that facilitates talk. Since most teachers are restricted to keeping their students within the room, this means directing them to their place in the room. The modular arrangement allows everyone the opportunity to communicate easily with everyone else in the group.

Norms: What Rules Do We Need?

Groups need operating guidelines to help them manage their inter-action in a manner all members find constructive. **Norms** are informal rules about what people expect from each other in certain circum-stances. Think of them as the *shoulds* and the *oughts*. When they are violated, members exert peer pressure to reestablish compliance.

Norms may be implicit or explicit, formal or informal. They may evolve informally in a group that meets over a period of time. No one writes them down, but everyone is aware of what they are, and viola-tions are dealt with informally. Or, norms may be consciously con-structed when a group forms, and written down so members remember their responsibilities to the group. Most classroom norms are implicit and reflect the cultural biases of the teacher and the school. Students from different cultures often are censured because they do not know these implicit norms. Recall that one of our tips for a talk friendly environment was to set up clear, explicit norms for classroom interaction.

When you use small groups in the classroom, you need to address with the students what norms are needed for group work. The class-room talk norms are one jumping-off point for deciding what norms are needed for groups. For example, "Everyone must participate," or "No interrupting each other." Keep in mind that norms, once agreed upon, can be amended and revised when experience proves that they need to be. Groups that stay together for a protracted period of time may develop additional, idiosyncratic norms. Here are several basic principles useful in establishing and maintaining group norms (Johnson 1970):

1. *Clarify Relevance.* Members accept and internalize norms that they see as useful in helping them accomplish their goals.
2. *Ownership.* Members support and accept norms that they have helped set up.
3. *Enforcement.* Norms should be enforced consistently and imme-diately.
4. *Practice.* Members should be helped to understand the norms through examples, models, and practice.
5. *Flexibility.* Norms should be amended, added, or deleted as nec-essary.

Roles: What Functions Do We Need?

People generally think of group roles as being divided into members and leaders. Based on their bunching experiences, most people have vague ideas of what to do in either role. For many, leadership, is a mystical quality conferred at birth, you either have it or you don't. Membership is just talking. Neither idea is of much practical use to you or your students when you face actually participating in a group.

Role embraces a set of behaviors which perform some function in the context of the group (Brilhart and Galanes 1989). Each act of a member is a behavior. **Function** is the meaning the behavior has to the group, or the purpose it accomplishes for the group. For example, a member asks a question (behavior). The question functions to reorient the group to its agenda. "A member's role represents the constellation of all the behavioral functions performed by that member, just as an actor's role consists of all the lines and actions of the character in the play" (Brilhart and Galanes 1989, p. 172).

A member's role, the behavioral functions performed, is worked out in interaction with the rest of the group. A member's behavior is in response to the dynamic interaction among all the members. What functions each member performs depends on his or her communication skills, who is present, what functions the other members perform, the task, and what the group needs. This means a person's role can vary group to group or at different meetings of the same group. So you could describe what a person's role was (functional behaviors performed), at one meeting or at several meetings or in several groups over an extended period of time.

The behavioral functions needed in small groups involve the same two levels that operate simultaneously in all communication: the *content* (task-related) and the *process* (the social-interpersonal relationship). The two dimensions are intertwined in their effects. Success or failure on either level affects the other. When interpersonal communication becomes negative, task performance suffers. Good task performance encourages more positive interpersonal attitudes. Effective groups perform both types of functions well. Students need to learn to think about both dimensions when they are in a group.

Functions in a Small Group. The following classification system identifies the functions that a small group needs to accomplish its goals (drawn from Brilhart and Galanes 1989). Since they are stated in behavioral terms, they are specific about what groups need as well as *not* need to do (non-behaviors) in order to work well. The approach is practical; rather than vague directives to "Just get in the group and talk," the terms are specific and describe what kind of talk facilitates task accomplishment. The functions are classified in three groupings: (1) Task; (2) Group Building and Maintenance (the positive process functions that members need to do); and (3) Self-Centered (the negative process functions that members need to avoid).

Task Functions: Behaviors that affect the doing of the task

Idea Initiating. Propose new ideas, goals, plans of action, activities.

Seeking Information. Ask for information or clarification of information.

Seeking Opinion. Ask for beliefs, opinions, judgments, interpretations.

Giving Information. Offer facts and information, and evidence.

Giving Opinion. State beliefs, opinions, judgments, interpretations.

Elaborating. Develop an idea previously expressed (by self or another member) by giving examples or additional explanations.

Coordinating. Describe, integrate, or clarify relationships between or among ideas.

Orienting. Clarify the goal(s) of the group; define the position of the group in relation to the goal(s); or suggest the direction or purpose of the group.

Energizing. Stimulate the group to greater activity.

Recording. Keep track of what the group has done, often in the form of reports or minutes (important in groups with complex tasks and/or that meet over a long period of time).

Group Building and Maintenance Functions: Behaviors that build and maintain cooperative, positive interpersonal relationships and a group-centered orientation

Gatekeeping. Encourage others to speak; stop the overly talkative from monopolizing the group's talk.

Supporting. Indicate respect for other members and their ideas; be diplomatic when disagreeing (recall the ways to verbally and nonverbally show support).

Norming: Suggest standards of behavior needed in the group; challenge unproductive behavior; insist norms be followed.

Tension-Relieving. Put others at ease by stressing common interests and experiences, joking, and talking informally.

Harmonizing. Mediate differences; find common ground; suggest compromise.

Self-Centered Functions: Behaviors that satisfy personal needs at the expense of the group, harm group orientation, and interfere with group accomplishment should be avoided. If they occur, use group building and maintenance functions to deal with them.

Blocking. Prevent progress toward the goal by raising irrelevant objections or by repeatedly bringing up something the group has finished discussing (it is not blocking to raise an idea the group has not yet really heard or considered).

Attacking. Make personal attacks; engage in name calling; make fun of others or their ideas; belittle.

Dominating. Insist on one's own way; interrupt or cut others off, prevent them from speaking; give orders to the group.

Horseplaying. Engage in irrelevant joking around that interferes with doing the task.

Status Seeking. Call attention to oneself in ways disruptive to doing the task; brag to the group.

Ways to Use the Functions.   Here are six suggestions about how to use the task and process functions for improving group skills, your students' and yours:

1. To observe role emergence and performance. Who is performing which functions?

2. As a diagnostic checklist to analyze groups when they are having trouble. What functions are not being performed?

3. To help your students identify and practice useful group skills. Students need to know what functions they need to do for a task, so start with the relevant ones. Analyze what functions students already perform and introduce others as needed. How to bring the functions to your students' awareness can be handled in a variety of ways. For example, functions may be identified inductively through discussion with the whole class after groups have met ("What did people do that helped the group do its task?" "What interfered with getting the job done?"). Or, functions could be introduced deductively before groups meet ("These are the functions that our task needs.") and then discussed after the groups meet ("What did we discover from trying to do these functions?"). In this case, remember students need examples, models, and practice to understand the roles before they begin. Keep in mind that the more group experience students have, the more practice they get in developing their group communication skills.

4. As a way to give specific feedback to students about their participation, such as what functions their comments accomplished.

5. As an inventory of what functions you perform when you are in a group.

6. To identify and cope with functions that are harmful to the group process.

Members need to learn to recognize which function is needed and how to meet the need by doing the function. The more functions an individual member can perform appropriately, the more valuable that member is to the group. Keep these points in mind:

- Some functions are performed by many members, while others may be assigned or done by a limited number of members.
- Some functions are more important in some task groups than in others, while some functions may not be needed at all. For example, groups that only meet once do not need recording (someone to take minutes).
- Which functions are needed at the moment depends on where the group is in the doing of its task. For example, from the start, all groups need to get focused, so orienting, idea initiating, and gatekeeping are needed. As groups become involved in the task, more task functions (number of and frequency of occurrence) are needed. When there is conflict, there is a need for more elaborating, coordinating, and harmonizing. When groups are finishing up (with a part of the task or the entire task), then coordinating tends to be important.

How Do Functions Relate to Leadership? The task and process functions can be used to understand the role of leader. The functional approach to leadership states that leadership consists of certain functions that must be performed by someone if the group is to be effective (Brilhart and Galanes 1989). These functions can be learned by anyone. Leaders, then, are people who are able to do what the group needs to have done. The more functions a member can perform when they are needed, the more leadership that person is demonstrating.

It is important to distinguish between being called a leader and actually knowing what to do that constitutes leadership. There is no inherent ability conferred in the title, "leader." A person may be designated leader but have no idea what to do. A member, who frequently and consistently does the behavioral functions that the group needs, actually leads the group.

If you decide a task group needs a leader, then you need to make sure that everyone understands what the leader is supposed to do and is able to do. What functions you want a leader to do depend on the task (purpose, complexity), your definition of the assignment, and your students (age, group skills). For example, in one group assignment you may expect a leader to be responsible for recording, coordinating, orienting, and gatekeeping. In another group, the leader may be responsible only for recording. Let's look at the options for determining the leader:

- *Designated.* Either the teachers or students decide who the leader is. This person is responsible for the effectiveness of the group.
- *Elected.* Students vote for their leaders. It is likely students will pick the most liked or highest status person unless criteria are developed for what the leader needs to do.
- *Appointed.* Teachers announce the leaders. They often pick the "best" academic students or leaders. Students who are not (or ever) chosen perceive this as favoritism, or criticism or dislike of them. For them leadership becomes something they are incapable of doing. In the interests of trust building, climate, and developing group skills, vary whom you choose to lead and tell students the basis for the selection.

  Consider the leadership needs of the task. With some groups, you may want the highest achievers in the subject or skill relevant to the task. In other groups, you may want the most imaginative student to be the leader.

  Consider, also, whether you have the long-term goal of all your students having opportunities to develop leadership skills. If you do, you may use a rotation system, so everyone eventually serves as leader in a task group. Serving as leaders helps students develop leadership skills, empathize with the leadership position, and view group effort from a fresh perspective, often resulting in more cooperativeness.
- *Emergent.* No single person is designated leader. The member who helps the group the most evolves as the leader during the doing of the task.
- *Shared.* Each member is equally responsible for doing the necessary functions. All members are co-leaders. This method works well with members who are comfortable working in groups and have developed basic group skills.

Decision Making: How Should Groups Make Decisions?

Task groups have to make decisions during the course of accomplishing their purpose. Since there are different people, there will be different ideas, opinions, and answers that have to be meshed and focused into group action. Individual differences are the source of the strength of group effort. However, conflict is inevitable. In effective groups, conflict's consequences are constructive, reflecting a win-win orientation. Students need to realize how to reconcile their individual differences in the interests of the group task.

There are three alternative methods for making decisions. Each is useful under certain circumstances. Students need to be aware of these options, so they choose the appropriate one. They may all be needed in one group or one meeting of a group as circumstances alter.

Consensus occurs when everyone agrees. Agreement is arrived at through discussion of everyone's ideas. It is important that all members contribute their ideas and consider other members' ideas. Similarities and differences are considered. Evidence and reasoning are examined. Students need to listen, give feedback, and utilize critical thinking skills in order to arrive at consensus.

Negotiation/Compromise occurs when members bargain to reach agreement that honors each person's position in some respect. Members individually give up something that they do not care as much about in order to get something that matters more. For example, consider the basis for negotiating and compromise in a group that is planning a presentation to the class. One student may not care who goes first but wants to introduce everyone. Another member does not want to speak in front of the class but wants to make the poster. A third member may want to go first but does not want to give the entire report. The fourth student does not care in what order they speak but is worried about what to say.

Voting occurs when agreement is reached through majority rule. Whatever idea gets the most votes is what the group does. Voting is quick and easy. It should be preceded by discussion of what is to be voted on. If it is not, the members who are in the minority may feel disgruntled, which may negatively affect their participation.

Output: What Outcome Do I Want from This Task?

Purpose defines procedures and output. From the students' point of view, output is the target, the point of the activity. From the teachers' point of view, output is the means to an end, the end being learning.

Assigning a specific output to a group helps focus student attention and effort. Students should know from the beginning what they are expected to produce, what shape it should take, and what will happen to it. In other words, students want to know what *done* will look like.

Clarity about output is important to the morale and productivity of the group. Sometimes you may totally define the nature of the output. With other assignments you may let the students choose among alternative possibilities or make decisions about aspects of the output. In any event, you need to address the following areas of concern:

Shape. What is to be produced (a list of something, an answer, a paragraph, a solution, an opinion, ideas, a project, a paper, a presentation, a position)? What form must it be? Oral or written? How long is it expected to be? Who is to speak it or write it? Is there a certain format that must be used?

Audience. Is the output for group members, to be shared with other groups and/or the teacher, or to be presented to the whole class?

Response. Who will react to the output (other group members, group members and the teacher, the rest of the class, just the teacher)? What will be the nature of the reaction (constructive feedback, interested reactions, evaluation in the form of a grade)?

No matter what group task you pick you will have to make decisions about how to handle these elements appropriately for your students. Think of these elements as building blocks, the mechanics for planning an effective small group assignment. While this section examined these basic group process elements with the options they present for planning, the following section looks at the types of task groups and relates how the elements operate with the different tasks.

Types of Task Groups

There are eight basic types of task groups: learning, research, problem solving, role-play, games, simulations, short-term groupings, and panel discussions. Although it is necessary to examine each type of task group one at a time in order to understand it, realize that they need not be used singly. They may be used in different combinations to achieve your learning objectives. Also, keep in mind how task groups relate to lesson plans and other instructional strategies. Any type of group may constitute the entire class session, precede or follow a lecture or a discussion, or continue over several lesson plans (alone or with lectures and discussions interspersed).

Anyone of the task groups can be used on any level if it is adapted and crafted appropriately for specific students—age, interests, abilities, discussion experience, and communication skills—to ensure a successful learning experience. It is best to start with short, structured assignments and move toward longer, more demanding assignments as group skills and confidence develop.

Learning (Enlightenment)

The purpose of a **learning discussion** is the personal learning or the "enlightenment" of the group members (Brilhart and Galanes 1989, p. 302). According to the *Webster's Collegiate Dictionary*, "enlighten" means to illuminate. Learning discussions are a format for students to illuminate their thinking and to develop insights about a particular topic. What is sought is a fuller understanding, a wider grasp of information, or consideration of a problem from as many points of view as possible. There is no need for decision making. Small group learning discussions are similar in purpose to whole class discussions in that they create an opportunity for students to share and question ideas and opinions—theirs and the other members. The point is understanding, exploration, and appreciation.

Participation in learning discussions is more motivated when topics are of interest and/or relevant to the students involved. When possible, let them choose the topic or make choices from among possible topics. Ask students for suggestions and observe what topics are of the most interest to them. Each learning discussion group can have a different topic as its focus.

Groups should be small (three to five students) to ensure everyone the opportunity to talk and a diversity of opinions. When deciding who goes in which group, remember that diversity and interest are both important factors and need to be balanced. One way to achieve diversity is to poll the students' stances toward various topics and then form groups representing different positions. Interest could be the criterion for forming groups by letting students choose the topic, thus becoming a group. Changing the composition of the group for each new learning discussion topic promotes motivation through different topics and sets up a more realistic communication practice.

The procedures for learning discussions involve an agenda and directions. Agenda items may be written by teachers, solicited from students by the teacher, or created by the students themselves. Directions need to lay out the time frame, physical arrangements, group composition, leadership (if any), and output.

There are three general principles to keep in mind when planning a learning discussion (Brilhart and Galanes 1989):

1. *Keep the focus on common experience.* Group members must share a common experience relative to the topic. This means they should all see the same movie; read the same story, chapter, or article; study the same problem; or hear the same speaker. Meaningful discussion evolves from their differing perceptions, thoughts, opinions, and past experiences.

2. *Limit the number of issues and topics.* Learning discussions seek thought, so it is better to have a few issues that can be explored in depth, rather than many topics covered superficially. Judge the number of issues by your students' discussion skills and your time frame. Learning discussions can be of any length, as long or as short as you want, but the length affects how many

agenda items your students can discuss in depth. The issues or topics should be written as open-ended questions. One topic may be enough when students are in the initial stages of their learning discussion experiences, while they are developing skills and familiarity with the format.

3. *Be guided by the nature of the subject.* The pattern for a learning discussion is usually inherent in the subject. The issues should be arranged in a logical sequence. Basic issues on a topic would follow a topical or classification pattern. If sequence is important in understanding the issues, then a chronological arrangement makes sense.

Students need to prepare by contemplating whatever the common experience is from as many angles as possible. They need to consider what they see, hear, understand, feel, or think in response to it. You might ask students to jot down brief notes and bring them to the group discussion as a possible springboard for comments. You might have students prepare a probe question(s) for each agenda item for possible use during the discussion. The following functions occur frequently in learning discussions: information and opinion seeking and giving, elaborating, supporting, and gatekeeping. Since each learning discussion is another topic, there is no need for a recorder.

Here is an agenda created by a group of my students after they had all read a pool of articles on a subject of their choosing (school violence):

1. How do we think violence is impacting the schools?
2. What do we think causes school violence?
3. What impact do the media have on school violence?
4. What can we do about violence in the schools?

With learning discussions, *the process is the output.* The thinking that the group members do together is the goal. Groups often meet simultaneously in modular arrangements in different parts of the room. It is possible to have one group discuss with the rest of the class observing, using the fishbowl seating arrangement discussed in chapter 3. The output of individual groups may be shared in a variety of ways: each group makes a brief oral report on its responses to the agenda (this is interesting whether each group has the same or a different agenda; the groups' reports may lead into a discussion by the whole class); students record reactions in individual journals.

Research Group

The purpose of a **research group** is to explore a subject or topic through cooperative research. The subject is divided into subtopics, which are assigned to different groups. Each group's subtopic is further divided into subtasks, so each member has a research task to do. When the tasks are completed at the group level, then each group presents its findings to the rest of the class. The time frame for a research group depends on the subject, your students, available resources, and how deeply you expect them to delve into the topic. A research group could meet daily for a week or for several days or regularly over several weeks.

"Group Investigation," one of the six cooperative learning approaches, presents a model of how a research task can be organized. The model has six stages (Sharan and Sharan 1992):

1. A broad problem of common concern to the class is identified. The class decides subtopics and then organizes into research groups.
2. The groups plan what they will study and decide how they will divide up the work.
3. Members of the group research their subtopics.
4. Members share their data and plan how to present their information to the rest of the class.
5. All members of the group participate in the group's presentation.
6. The group investigation is evaluated individually, in the groups, and by the class.

In this method, groups are limited to four or five members, and a variety of grouping procedures are used: random assignment, common interest in a topic, and student or teacher selection. Positive interdependence is promoted through the planning of the division of labor at the class and group levels, the sharing of resources between groups, and the intrinsic motivation of working together on the task. Shared leadership occurs as students plan together and select their tasks in the investigation.

Problem Solving

The purpose of a **problem-solving** group is to systematically investigate a problem and decide on an effective solution to it. An agenda is used to steer the group through the process in a logical, rational, and thorough sequence. The sequence in group problem solving is based on John Dewey's *How We Think* (1910), which describes the steps of reflective thinking, that is, what rational thinkers do when confronted with a problem. It is known as the "Standard Agenda for Group Problem-Solving," referred to simply as the standard agenda.

The Purpose of the Standard Agenda. The **standard agenda** ensures that the group's talk is focused on the task in a systematic way. It also facilitates helpful criticism and constructive conflict. It provides standards by which progress can be judged and decisions made about what remains to be done. A group working with a standard agenda clearly knows what it has to do and can fit its work within the time frame set by the person or organization that convenes the group. The standard agenda considers the following steps. Note that the questions included in each step must be answered by the group in order to complete that step in the process (Wood, Phillips, and Petersen 1986).

1. *Understanding the charge.* Everyone in the group must understand what the group is to do. In organizational settings, the reason the group is convened is "the charge." In a school setting the charge is the purpose and specifics of the assignment.

   What is the group supposed to do? What form does the output take? Who gets it? What is to be done with it? How much time to we have?

2. *Understanding and phrasing the question.* The group must agree on what the problem is and phrase a question that indicates who is to do what about what. A well-worded question guides the group through the next step.

   What is the group to examine or inquire about? What do the words in the question mean? Are all technical words and issues clear to the members? Is the group supposed to fact-find, evaluate conditions, set policy, propose a solution, or do all of these?

3. *Fact finding.* The group must gather, understand, and store the relevant, informed opinions of experts, which have been confirmed for accuracy. At the conclusion of fact finding, the problem should be summarized and the problem question rephrased if necessary.

   What are the symptoms of the problem? What are the causes of the symptoms? What is or is not happening that should be? Who is affected and how? What will happen if the situation is not remedied?

4. *Setting criteria and limitations.* The group must develop standards against which possible solutions can be tested. It is necessary to determine what is needed and what must be avoided.

   What is possible (as opposed to what is desirable)? What are the legal, moral, financial, practical, and logistical limits on decision making? What would a good solution have to do?

5. *Discovering and selecting solutions.* The group must propose and examine as many solutions as possible and select an opti-

mum solution or construct one from among possibilities.

What are the alternatives? How does each meet the criteria and limitations? Which provides more of what is wanted with the least harm? Which one should be selected? Who is to do what about what, when and where, with what projected effect? How will it be paid for? What evaluation plan can be used to measure the effectiveness of the solution?

6. *Preparing and presenting the final report.* Many organizational groups are finished at step 5 when they submit the solution. Whether a group needs a formal, persuasive report depends on the charge to the group. Whether your students need to do step 6 depends on how you structure the assignment.

   What must be written down? What must be said? When, where, and to whom? How can the final report be most persuasively presented?

Using the Standard Agenda. The standard agenda supplies an objective approach to group problem solving that is systematic and produces practical results. Knowing how to use the standard agenda is an important asset to anyone in a problem-solving situation. If someone understands the logical steps along the way in solving a problem, then he or she is more likely to be an active participant and to make constructive contributions to the group effort. Since the preliminary form of the standard agenda was first introduced in 1939, its usefulness and flexibility in group problem-solving situations has been demonstrated in public planning, and in other administrative and organizational settings (Wood, Phillips, and Petersen 1986).

The standard agenda provides the most comprehensive method for problem solving, but it is also flexible. This means it can be modified to suit specific circumstances. Since it presents the full range of possible steps in the problem-solving process, it gives members an informed basis for deciding how thoroughly to apply each step—in other words, how to allot time and effort given the nature of the problem before the group.

When deciding on possible problems, there are several factors that you must consider. Choose real problems that are interesting and relevant to the students because they will be more motivating. Consider these interrelated factors at the same time: the problem's complexity, available resources, time frame, and what your choice means in terms of using the standard agenda. If the problem is complex and rich resources are available (for example, investigating a pollution problem in a local river or park), then the group will need more time to work on the problem. All steps in the standard agenda will need to be done in detail. If the problem is simpler, perhaps a case study which presents all the facts, then less overall time may be needed. The group will not need to spend time on fact-finding. Or, in another instance, you may want the group to reach a solution but not write a final proposal. In which case, the group would not need to do step 6.

Since each step in the standard agenda builds on the preceding step(s), it is important that members and leaders (if you choose to use leaders) understand what their responsibilities are for each step. Problem-solving groups generally function with leaders who may be selected in any of the ways already listed.

Role-Play

As we have seen throughout this text, our unconscious role-playing—learning to meet the role expectations of others—creates and sustains our interpersonal relationships and memberships in groups. However well or ill we play the roles expected of us, they define our identity. The play of children illustrates this informal social learning as they play the roles they see around them, such as mommy, daddy, power rangers, teachers, and service workers (firemen, police). Sometimes people consciously "play a role" when trying to make a particular kind of impression on someone.

Purpose of Role-Play. The purpose of **role-play** is to explore imaginatively and spontaneously what it would be like to be someone else in a particular set of circumstances. During a role-playing activity, each participant acts "as if" he or she is such-and-such a person in a particular situation; the participants play out the situation together to see what happens. The results depend on the dynamic interaction of each member's imaginative improvisation. Endings are open-ended. There are no right or wrong answers, only plausible or implausible ones based on what happens in the situation.

Role-playing is at the heart of communication and drama. Drama is, at its most basic, characters in conflict: Characters (roles), who have differing goals, are in a dramatic situation in which they seek to accomplish their goals. Drama roles, however, unlike roles in life, are created ahead of time by a single author, which makes them carefully crafted, scripted, and compressed in terms of time.

Role-playing is used for many purposes and known by many names. "Psychodrama" deals with the therapeutic use of role-playing by psychotherapists as a technique to deal with mental and emotional problems. "Sociodrama" refers to the educational use of role-playing and focuses on the situation being explored. "Creative dramatics" is the term used with younger students to refer to informal dramatics; "improvisation" is a term used with older students to refer to the same thing.

It is important to understand that role-play in the classroom is dramatic, but it is *not* theatrical. When you choose to do role-plays, you are not doing theater. This means you do not need the trappings of conventional theater, such as costumes, lights, scenery, blocking, a director, a script, memorization, a stage, or an audience. The focus is on the process for the participants, what the experience means for them in terms of personal thinking and feeling.

The essence of role-playing, wherever it is found, is the improvisation. "Improvisation" comes from the Latin *improvisus*, which means unforeseen, to see ahead. **Improvisation** asks participants to pretend, to try on new roles, and to create what might be. Think of it like a short, imaginative trip into an alternative reality as someone else. The situations used as the basis for a role-play may or may not be like situations students face in their own lives. The important distinction is that they are not being asked to be themselves. They are playing a role. This creates an emotionally safe place to experiment, to improvise, and to try out new behaviors and ideas. This aspect places role-playing in contrast to the other types of groups, which ask students to be themselves doing things in the here and now with real consequences.

In educational settings, there are many advantages to using role-play. Since roles give students the chance literally to assume other people's perspectives, they identify more with others and develop a dual perspective. Students learn to work cooperatively as they learn the give-and-take needed among participants in role-playing. Role-plays give students opportunities to think creatively and critically. They think of new possibilities and consider alternative ideas, motivations, and behaviors.

Role-plays are a natural way to develop verbal and nonverbal communication skills. Dialogue created while doing a role-play is like everyday communication, " . . . they must think on their feet and handle the skein of language as it unravels" (Ladousse 1987, p. 6). Both verbal and nonverbal behaviors are driven by purpose, spontaneously improvised in interaction with others, dependent on effective listening, judged for relevancy, and interpreted for meaning. Even when doing a role-play, there is a need to be clear, cogent, and relevant to what is occurring. For these reasons, doing role-plays tends also to increase skill in concentration, as students strive to "stay in character."

Setting Up a Role-Play.   Role-plays may be used many ways in a lesson: as motivation, as pre-writing experiences (act out various ideas and then write a personal version), as post-writing experiences (students meet in groups and write down ideas, so they have ideas for role-plays), as well as independent experiences. Role-plays sometimes follow work in a research group. Based on their research, students might role-play people whom they have studied at critical junctures in their lives. ("What did Columbus say to Queen Isabella and King Ferdinand to secure funds to seek a new route to the East?"). A variation of this idea was used as the format in Public Broadcasting's *Meeting of the Minds*[2] and could be adapted for class use. Each weekly show brought together four famous people from different historical eras to talk about their lives. (The program had a moderator who asked questions, but in a classroom setting, questions could be asked by other students.)

Role-plays must be adapted to your students (age, interests, familiarity with doing role-plays, comfort level, and communication skills). They need directions that make clear the usual basic elements. Consider time frame in light of the complexity of the situation(s) you are using. The more complex the role-play situation, the more time is needed. Groups may vary in size (two to seven). Smaller groupings are recommended at least until students become accustomed to doing role-plays. Varying group composition is important whether reenacting the same situation or doing different situations. **Replay** (redoing, trying a role-play with different people) is a key ingredient of role-playing. Different combinations of people produce different ideas and outcomes.

Directions also need to be clear to students and can be explained on the basis of the **Three Ws**: *who* they are (who each role is and who they are in relation to the other roles), *why* they are in the situation (what they are doing or want, such as goal, motivation, or perspective), and *where* (environment) the scene is taking place. "Why" is critical. Remember there must be some conflict or difference in goals at the center of a role-play, so something happens. The role-plays may be written out on a sheet and given to each group, put on individual cards and given to members, or described orally to the group(s).

Whether you create your own role-play situations or use published role-plays, keep in mind that the content can vary along two dimensions: information and realism. "Information" involves the amount of information given and the degree of specificity about the Three Ws. It may vary from general and sketchy with a minimum of details to specific with a maximum of details. "Realism" refers to the degree to which the "three Ws" are like the students' actual lives (age, life experience, culture, circumstances). It may vary from very similar, slightly different, to very different.

Anything is a possibility for the content of a role-play if a "what if . . . ?" question is worth exploring about it. For example, the following are likely sources: a news story, historical happenings, community events, school or school happenings (conflicts, problems), novels, myths, poetry, or short stories. The imagination of you and your students is the limit. When starting, choose simple situations. With experience, students will develop the ability to handle more complex situations.

The pattern is: set up the role-play (the Three Ws), get students in groups, play out the situation, and then discuss. The cycle can then repeat itself with the same or a different role-play with students taking different parts. Remember, the emphasis in discussion about the role-plays is on "descriptive," not evaluative or judgmental. Comments (yours and the other students) should talk about the group's work or what a "character" did, not the individual personally. For example, acceptable questions would be, "What do you think of how the group resolved the situation?" or "What might have changed the outcome?" Create a norm that rules out comments and questions like, "How did you like Pat's job?" or "You did a bad job." Choose from among these possible options as ways to proceed:

1. Groups that are spaced out all over the room may work simultaneously on the same role-play. Afterward, the class discusses what happened in the groups. (This arrangement is one way to reduce the self-consciousness many students feel when first introduced to role-plays.)

2. Do one role-play (as in 1 above) but *ask* if any groups would like to redo their role-play for the class, and then discuss.

3. Do one role-play (as in 1 above) and then have each group do its role-play for the whole class. Discussion follows each group. (Watch the clock. Make sure you get in all the groups and all the discussions on the same day.)

4. One role-play situation may be played out by several different sets of people during the same class. One group at a time does its role-play for the class and then the class discusses. The focus in the replays could be the same for each group (purpose to get other people's ideas, how it might come out with different people), or could change for each group (complicating factors added or different perspectives or other characters added).

5. Groups work simultaneously on a different role-play. For example, each group does a different scene from the same story or works on original prequels or sequels to a story. Each group could plan its scene and then do it for the class, followed by a discussion.

A role-play that I used with fourth graders to celebrate Martin Luther King Day illustrates the suggestions in this section. We began by talking about what started the Montgomery, Alabama, bus boycott and who Rosa Parks was. We decided together who we would need to role-play the event that began the boycott (Rosa Parks, the bus driver, police, other passengers, the person who told Mrs. Park to move). In terms of the directions (the Three Ws), the information was general and sketchy and the realism was different from the students' lives (age, circumstances), although the adults were recognizable in their experience (bus driver, passengers, police). The procedures were organized as described in option #4, and discussion followed each replaying with different students. With redoings, the simple storyline developed depth, and characters became multidimensional. Characters argued among themselves about the unfairness, and the bus driver and police questioned what they were doing. There were different reasons in different groupings, but the students' endings had Mrs. Parks staying in her seat.

Game

The purpose of a game can best be understood by looking at its definition. "(A game is a) contest (play) among adversaries (players) operating under constraints (rules) for an objective (winning, victory or payoff)" (Abt 1965, as quoted in Heitzmann 1987, p. 7). People play games to win. Students like games because they are a break in the usual routine, they are fun, they allow students to interact, and students like to win. Teachers use games for these reasons, but what they want students to win is knowledge. Teachers choose or create a game to facilitate learning about a topic or subject.

A **game**, by definition, has clear directions, rules, penalties for infractions, and endpoints. These basic game elements are defined for you when you use commercial educational games. If you wanted to create a game for your students, you would need to use the basic elements as guidelines in creating it.

There are two kinds of educational games. The first type involves individuals playing with other people but not as a group. They are *in* a group, but they do not constitute a group (no common goals, interdependence, cooperation). They are individuals playing to win for themselves, who happen to be grouped together for the sake of the game. There are learning games like this in every subject for every level.

The second type of educational game is a group game, in which members work together to win a common goal. "Student Team Learning" (STL), one of the six cooperative learning approaches mentioned at the beginning of this chapter, utilizes this kind of game. There are many forms of STL, but "Student Teams Achievement Division" (STAD) is the simplest and one of the most extensively used forms. It emphasizes team success through all members mastering the material.

According to Slavin (1990b, 1991), STAD works in the following manner:

1. Students are assigned to four-member learning teams mixed in performance levels, boys and girls, and ethnicity. Group leaders are not specified.
2. Each week the teacher introduces new material in a lecture or a discussion. Students receive work sheets (study questions or practice exercises).
3. Teams work toward mastery, doing any of the following activities: coach each other, do problems together, quiz each other, discuss exercises as a group.
4. Students take individual quizzes, which determine their grades. Teams earn points based on individual members' improvement over their previous performance. Teams meeting a preset standard of improvement earn public recognition.
5. Recognition takes place primarily through class newsletters, but bulletin boards, posters, small prizes, and special privileges are used also.

Slavin (1990b) points out that this activity is most appropriate for teaching well-defined objectives with single, correct answers, such as mathematical computations, language usage and mechanics, geography and map skills, and science facts and concepts.

A very different example of this type of learning game is "Learning Together," another one of the six cooperative learning approaches (Johnson and Johnson 1991). This approach, too, focuses on team success through all members mastering the material. According to Johnson, Johnson, and Holubec (1994), considerable research has demonstrated that this approach can be used with confidence at every grade level, with any subject, and with any task (mastering basic skills and facts and developing higher cognitive processes).

This approach does not involve specific strategies applied in detailed or structured ways, but its attributes include (Davidson 1994, pp. 16–17):

1. Groups have two to four members who are usually mixed as to gender, race/ethnicity, social class, and achievement levels.
2. Positive interdependence is achieved through requiring students to agree upon answers and be able to explain their group's reasoning or strategies. It is also encouraged through groups being given one copy of resource materials or each student having different materials that they must share.

3. Roles essential to the group's functioning are assigned and rotated frequently, such as reader, checker, accuracy coach, summarizer, elaborator, and confidence builder.
4. Interpersonal and small-group skills are explicitly taught, and reflection upon the group work is emphasized.
5. Individual responsibility is emphasized through individual work sheets, randomly selecting one member to explain what the group is doing, or individual quizzes or tests.
6. Bonus points are given if all group members reach preset criteria.

Simulation

The purpose of a **simulation** is for students to experience vicariously a dynamic model of a situation (social, mathematical or physical). Simulations incorporate elements of role-playing. The students are placed in a simulation and asked to act "as if" they were in an actual situation. For example, business technology classes may simulate a real office with students behaving like actual employees. Simulations are designed to operate as a genuine model of a situation, a complete system in operation. Simulations do not need to look exactly like the real situation, but they must react like it, that is have the elements and processes essential to its operation. Think of simulations as reality simplified.

Simulations are distinct from **simulation games** which integrate the characteristics of a simulation with those of a game. The main difference between the two is the use of incentives to motivate the participants. In simulation games, the players' objectives are described in terms of observable, quantifiable criteria. There must be clear rules for determining winners and losers.

Most simulations used in education can be referred to as "behavioral stimulation," which emphasizes role-playing, interpersonal interactions, and scaled down versions of actual life-like situations (Letson 1981). Commercial simulations, which are available for all subjects and levels, lay out all the basic elements needed to conduct the simulation. If you design your own, then you would need to decide on the specifics of your target situation.

There are many advantages to using simulations. Students may acquire and improve skills that they need in the real world: skills specific to a particular situation, communication skills, and skill at working with others. Simulations give students a chance to try out a slice of reality in a protected environment without real behavioral consequences. Since simulations are experiential, they provide a way for students to grapple with complex or abstract material in a concrete, direct manner. They encourage precision and practical decision making. As Letson expresses it, "Simulations provide a setting where theory and practice meet" (1981, p. 45). According to Letson, simulations are powerful in developing higher cognitive processes and less useful for acquiring factual knowledge. Examples of simulations used in schools are: model workplaces (offices, stores) and governmental bodies (city councils, state legislatures, Congress, and the United Nations).

Short-Term Groupings

Short-term groupings meet briefly (for a few minutes, during part of a session) to accomplish very specific tasks. The number of members varies, and the criteria for group composition can be whatever you choose. All three may be used as part of the task groups already examined or utilized independently

Brainstorming. Meaning literally to storm the brain, **brainstorming** involves all members in generating as many responses as possible. It is useful whenever a group needs more of something, such as more ideas, topics, suggestions, or options for solutions. Brainstorming can be useful at different points in all of the other types of groups. It is especially useful in problem-solving groups for steps two through five. Brainstorming may also be useful for you while speaking with the whole class. For example, you may ask students to brainstorm as a motivator in your introduction to a lesson or a group activity. Or, you may ask students to brainstorm during class discussions.

There are three basic rules when brainstorming: (1) No criticism is allowed during brainstorming. Reaction or evaluation of what was suggested only occurs after brainstorming is completed. (2) Quantity is wanted. Members should be encouraged not to keep their ideas to themselves, no matter how wild, improbable, or silly. The more ideas, the greater the likelihood of good ideas. (3) Keep track of the group's ideas on the board or on paper.

Buzz Groups. When a large group has been divided into many small groups to work concurrently on a task, the small groups are called **buzz groups**. Their purpose is to stimulate personal involvement and thinking by members of a large group (Brilhart and Galanes 1989). The task might be to generate questions, answers, solutions, or to identify issues. You might use buzz groups during a whole class discussion or during a lecture.

"Phillips 66" was developed and popularized by Donald Phillips for use in conference settings, although it works in the classroom, too.

Groups of six meet for six minutes to discuss the target task. The steps are (drawn from Brilhart and Galanes 1989, p. 320–21):

1. The leader presents a target task in specific, concise terms.
2. The large group is divided into groups of six by a quick, random method.
3. A recorder-spokesperson—who writes down all ideas—is appointed for each group.
4. The group comes up with as many ideas as possible in five minutes. The leader then announces that the groups have one minute to decide whether to eliminate any of the ideas and to rank order the ideas that are left.
5. The small group responses are shared with the whole group in some way. For example, they may be:
   a. Collected, edited to eliminate repetition, duplicated, and distributed at a subsequent session.
   b. Read aloud. Each spokesperson is asked to read one new item. Someone writes the items on the board.

Huddles. Small, ad hoc groupings that are asked to accomplish a specific task in a brief amount of time are called **huddles**. Their purpose is to facilitate learning, involvement, and motivation. Picture a football team's huddles between plays. The huddles allow the team to focus and decide what to do next. Academic huddles help students focus, too, through assigning tasks that encourage relating and integrating what they have just done or are about to do.

Students can be asked to huddle for a variety of reasons: to produce a question, an example, an answer; to review; to summarize; to discuss; to coach each other; to create something together; and so forth. Johnson, Johnson, and Holubec (1994, p. 49) use the term "informal cooperative learning" for this type of grouping. They suggest three- to five-minute focused discussions before and after a lecture and two- to three-minute turn-to-your-partner discussions during a lecture (Teacher randomly chooses two or three students to summarize their group's discussion.)

Huddling to create a response not only aids learning, it can increase the likelihood of participation from reticent or silent students or students who lack academic self-confidence. Huddles provide an opportunity for peer support and assistance. Students can check personal understanding and help generate an appropriate response. Once students have a group response ready, it is an easier step to speak out in class.

Panel Discussion

Many teachers believe their students are having panel discussions when they are actually giving oral reports. The confusion occurs at the process (doing) vs. product (outcome) levels. Panels are both the process and the product occurring simultaneously, while oral reports report on the product, which was produced previously in the task group. Understanding the difference between the two activities opens up the possibility of using another type of group.

A **panel discussion** is a public discussion conducted for the benefit of the audience listening to it, not for the small group doing it (Brilhart and Galanes 1989). The discussion occurs in front of an audience among invited panel members, who are knowledgeable about the topic and represent different viewpoints. The goal is a spontaneous, stimulating informal discussion of ideas about a particular topic. A moderator, who invites the panel of experts, leads the discussion with the use of an outline (introduction, sequence of questions about the topic, and a planned conclusion format). It is the moderator's job to keep the discussion on track and to make sure all the speakers are heard. Panelists know what the questions are ahead of time and interact spontaneously. Teachers might arrange or let students arrange panel discussions by outside guests on topics of interest to them. Or, if students have done research on a topic (either independently or in a task group) and have reached differing points of view, a panel discussion of students could be set up.

Oral reports are individual informative speeches about work *previously done* in a group. They report on the goals, experiences, findings, and accomplishments of the group. Members divide up the group's report in some logical manner, and each member sums up his or her portion for the rest of the class. For example, a research group might have each member report on one of the subparts, while a problem-solving group might have each member report on one step. There is no group interaction, instead each member reports part of the output.

Now that we have examined the basic types of task groups and how to plan for them, let's turn to what you need to do when groups meet.

Doing Groups

This is when to remind ourselves that groups are for the participants—members must do their own interacting and learning. Teachers must suppress any urge to become part of the group and direct what is happening. They belong outside the group, looking in. The teacher's job is to present the group activity and then to step back and trust the group process to unfold. From this neutral vantage point, the teacher serves as a supportive guide and resource person to facilitate task accomplishment.

In order to assist students, teachers need to provide focus and guidance throughout the time task groups meet, each time they meet. Let's look at what the teacher needs to be doing in the beginning (introduction), during (the body or substance of the experience), and at the end (the conclusion).

Introduction

Students need the same kinds of information to orient them to a small group activity that they needed to prepare them for discussion: focus, purpose, motivation, and procedures. When students understand what they are to do and why, they become more involved and gain more from the experience.

What is actually said in the introduction depends on how many times a particular group meets to accomplish its task. If the group meets once, then the introduction focuses on what is to happen during that one session. However, if a group meets repeatedly, as research and problem-solving groups usually do, there should be an initial introduction to the entire activity at the outset and then an introduction before each subsequent meeting. Each of these must introduce that day's activity, as well as link it to previous and future meetings. These connections provide continuity and relevance and help students focus on how subtasks contribute to the doing of the overall task.

In either circumstance, introductions need to let students know:

- *The Focus.* What is the group's content (topic, issue, problem)? What is the group working on?
- *The Purpose.* Why are we going to get into groups to deal with it? What is suppose to happen as a result? What is the expected output or outcome?
- *The Motivation.* Generate interest in the assignment by showing how it relates to them personally, to what has or will go on in class, or to life beyond school. As with discussion, the question to answer or involve them in answering is, "Why should we care?"
- *The Procedures.* This is where you explain the definition of the basic elements that you have chosen for the assignment (time frame, group composition, physical arrangement, directions, roles, and norms). Explain the procedures as concisely and clearly as possible. Ask students if they have any questions.

After you answer their questions, then let them move to their groups and begin work. Once they are in groups distribute (or let students get) needed materials or resources.

Body

Since the teacher's role is that of facilitator, his or her primary function is to monitor the groups while they work. **Monitoring** means the teacher remains attentive and vigilant about what is happening in the groups and ready to offer supportive guidance where needed. The teacher is watchfully poised to assist a group in successfully accomplishing its task, whatever that might mean at any given moment. When the teacher perceives a need or members have a question, the teacher moves in to assist strategically and unobtrusively. This means the teacher targets his or her comments to what is at issue. This might involve asking a probing question, making a suggestion, or answering a question. The teacher intervenes for as short amount of time as possible, so not to disrupt the group or swamp it with his or her ideas.

When teachers monitor groups, they circulate around the room observing and listening to each group—briefly, repeatedly throughout a session. Some teachers observe while sitting near a group or even in a group (for a brief time if it does not interrupt the group), but wherever the teacher is, he or she is alert to what is going on in the other groups, as well. If the teacher perceives a question or a need, then the teacher moves to that group to see what is going on. What the teacher is not doing is marking papers, planning lessons, or walking out of the room.

When monitoring, watch the nonverbal cues for indications of frustration, confusion, involvement, and apathy. Review chapter 3 on nonverbal behavior to remind yourself of what kinesics (eyes, facial expressions, posture, body orientation, gestures) and paralanguage (rate, volume, vocal variety) can mean. Keep in mind that groups develop according to a rhythm. Groups start slowly because everyone feels a little awkward at first. Comments may be few and far between during this warm-up period. As the group agrees on what it is to do and begins doing it, the tempo picks up and more comments are made. When involvement is high, there are many comments. Lulls in the talk may mean a variety of things: for example, thinking is going on, the group is at a "stuck" point, the group has completed the task, or the group is disengaging. Once a group's task is done, the tempo slows down and comments usually become social.

Part of monitoring is helping students keep track of the time in relation to the task and reminding them what output is due when. For example, a teacher might say, "Remember to have one copy of your group's solutions in ten minutes."

Monitoring has many advantages. It communicates to the students that their teacher has high expectations for them. Coming around to see how the groups are doing and working with them demonstrates teacher interest. Monitoring provides opportunities to catch errors or misunderstandings about directions, check progress toward the goal, and for students to ask questions. It allows the teacher to assist the group's effort and reasoning in a supportive way. The teacher's presence and notice may also encourage some students to get or to stay involved with the task.

Monitoring the students' progress can be accomplished through means mentioned earlier in this chapter—establishing check-points for student written or oral progress reports and individual student journals—which work well with groups that meet over a period of time. At the end of a class session you might ask each student to give you some feedback either about the assignment or their group's handling of it. Always be specific about the format for the feedback. Structure focuses students' thinking, saves time, and gives you specific ideas about how to help the groups. For example, ask students to write one question they have or one thing they thought their group did well or one thing the group had trouble with or needs to work on. You might choose to share the separate groups' responses in a general summation to the class. Or, you might let the members in each group read each other's questions or comments, so the group can react to them.

Conclusion

Small group activities need conclusions that recognize what has been accomplished, tie the activities and accomplishments together, and provide closure. As with discussions, conclusions cannot be planned ahead, although time can be set aside for a conclusion to be constructed between you and the groups. When you define the basic elements of your small group activity, you determine the task, the time frame, the number of groups, procedures, and the output. These details enable you to decide how much time you need to set aside for a conclusion.

The substance of the conclusion will vary with the type of group task, but must, in some way, address three issues:

- *Summary.* What have we gained from our group experiences? At this point each group might share its output in the manner prescribed in the assignment. Since role-plays engage in discussion following each "playing," this might involve the class summarizing the major insights or ideas from all the role-plays.

- *Reflective Interpretation.* The class discusses what each group's summary means in terms of the focus and purpose. What has been learned? Were the purposes achieved?
- *Connectors.* How does this group activity relate to what we have done and what we will do? It is important that students make a connection between the group experience and their learning, to see beyond "groups are fun." Also, if the groups are part of a class session, then a transition is needed to the next part. If the group activity is the session, then it needs to be linked to what will happen in the future.

After the Group

After the group activity is completed, review what happened and evaluate the assignment's effectiveness. Was your purpose achieved? Were the outcomes achieved? Look at the choices you made for each element in the planning process and reflect on students' responses. Whether you think something was or was not effective, it is important to figure out why, so you can improve your planning skills for future task groups.

- Keep a record of the ideas that worked and did not work.
- Brainstorm alternatives for whatever was problematic. What do you wish you had done instead? How else might you have handled it?
- Think about what you learned about yourself as a facilitator and monitor. What could you say or do differently to better assist students in this type group?
- What did you learn about your students as group members? What problems did they have in completing the task or working together? What roles emerged? What input do they need from you about group work before the next group assignment?

To Group or Not to Group, That Is the Question

Groups do not have to be a waste of time. Small groups can be meaningful learning experiences when they are well planned, encouraged, and guided in a supportive manner. Use the types of groups and the options examined in this chapter as a guide to your decision making when planning your small group activities.

Be patient. Working effectively in task groups is a learned behavior, and it takes time to learn for both students and teachers. It is not fair to judge the worth of small groups as an instructional method based on one or two tries. As teachers and students become more familiar with how to work in groups, participation skills develop, confidence increases, and productivity blossoms.

Notes

[1]Dembo cites the following sources:
Gallimore, R., J. Boggs, and C. Jordan. 1974. *Culture, Behavior, and Education: A Study of Hawaiian-American*. Beverly Hills: Sage.
Kubany, E., R. Gallimore, and J. Buell. 1970. "The Effects of Extrinsic Factors on Achievement Oriented Behaviors: A Non-Western Case." *Journal of Cross-Cultural Psychology* (1): 77–84.
Shade, B. 1982. "Afro-American Cognitive Style: A Variable in School Success." *Review of Educational Research* 52:219–44.
Wax, M. 1969. *Indian Education in Eastern Oklahoma* (Research Contract Report No. O. C. 6-10-260 and B/A No. 5-05650-2-12-1). Washington, DC: U.S. Department of Education.
[2]Series developed by Steve Allen. Available on audio cassettes from the *Mind's Eye Catalogue* (phone number: 1-800-949-3333).

References

Abt Associates, Inc. 1965. *Game Learning and Disadvantaged Groups*. Cambridge, MA. Quoted in W. Heitzmann, editor, Educational Games and Simulations, revised edition. (Washington, DC: National Educational Association, 1987.)

Ames, C. and R. Ames. 1985. "Goal Structures and Motivation." *Elementary School Journal* 85:40–51. Cited in M. Dembo, *Applying Educational Psychology in the Classroom*, 4th edition (New York: Longman, 1991).

Brilhart, J. and G. Galanes. 1989. *Effective Group Discussion*, 6th edition. Dubuque, IA: Wm. C. Brown.

Brophy, J. 1987. "Synthesis of Research on Strategies for Motivating Students to Learn." *Educational Leadership* 45:40–48.

Davidson, N. 1994. "Cooperative and Collaborative Learning: An Integrative Perspective." In *Creativity and Collaborative Learning—A Practical Guide to Empowering Students and Teachers*. Baltimore: Paul H. Brookes.

Dembo, M. 1991. *Applying Educational Psychology in the Classroom*, 4th edition. New York: Longman.

Dewey, J. 1910. *How We Think*. Boston: DC Heath.

Johnson, D. W. 1970. *The Social Psychology of Education*. New York: Holt, Rinehart & Winston.

Johnson, D. and R. Johnson. 1991. *Learning Together and Alone: Cooperative, Competitive, and Individualistic Learning*, 3rd edition. Englewood Cliffs, NJ: Prentice Hall.

Johnson, D., R. Johnson, and E. J. Holubec. 1994. *The New Circles of Learning—Cooperation in the Classroom and School*. Alexandria, VA: Association for Supervision and Curriculum Development.

Kohn, A. 1986. "How to Succeed Without Even Vying." *Psychology Today*, Vol. 20, September: 22–28.

Ladousse, G. 1987. *Role-Play*. Oxford, England: Oxford University Press.

Letson, R. 1981. *Simulation and Gaming Activities in the Classroom*. Tucson, AZ: University of Arizona, College of Education.

Richmond, V. and J. Gorham. 1992. *Communication, Learning, Affect in Instruction*. Edina, MN: Burgess.

Sharan, Y. and S. Sharan. 1992. *Expanding Cooperative Learning Through Group Investigation*. New York: Teachers College Press. Cited in N. Davidson, "Cooperative and Collaborative Learning: An Integrative Perspective." In *Creativity and Collaborative Learning—A Practical Guide to Empowering Students and Teachers*. Baltimore: Paul H. Brookes, 1994.

Slavin, R. 1991. *Student Team Learning: A Practical Guide to Cooperative Learning*, 3rd edition. Washington, DC: National Education Association.

———. 1990a. "Research on Cooperative Learning: Consensus and Controversy." *Educational Leadership*. 47:52–54.

———. 1990b. *Cooperative Learning: Theory, Research, and Practice*. Boston: Allyn & Bacon.

Wood, J. W., G. Phillips, and D. Petersen. 1986. *Group Discussion: a Practical Guide to Participation and Leadership*. New York: Harper & Row.

Suggested Reading

Role-Play by Gillian Ladousse. Oxford, England: Oxford University Press, 1987.

A wide array of techniques that range from very structured, teacher-directed role-play activities to simulations devised and written by the students. User friendly to teachers at all levels and with varying degrees of experience. Each activity contains the following information: brief description, level, time frame, purpose, language skills involved, group size, preparation, warm-up, procedure, follow-up, comments to the teacher, and variations.

Group Discussion: A Practical Guide to Participation and Leadership by Julia Wood, Gerald Phillips, and Douglas Petersen. New York: Harper & Row, 1986.

A thorough, detailed guide of how to use the standard agenda to maneuver through the intricacies of problem-solving discussion. Chapters on each step of the standard agenda with goals, outcomes, member tasks, and leader obligations. Separate chapters on the group as a system, making effective choices when leading and participating, managing conflict, and presentational speaking and report writing. Material can be adapted to your students.

Education Index. Check this index in the reference room of your school's library for titles of articles about how small groups are used in your context area. Depending on the format your library has (CD-Rom, on-line system through the computerized library catalogue or print), abstracts may also be available. Do a "subject search" for the type of group in which you are interested. For example, I searched "educational games" and found articles geared to the elementary and secondary levels for history, geography, biology, chemistry, math, art, and English.

Chapter 9

Lecturing:
Giving Information

Ideas to Remember

* Common beliefs about lecturing, which interfere with our under-standing of what lecturing is all about, are that lectures are:
  Uninterrupted talk by one person
  Long
  Impersonal
  A way to cover large amounts of information
  The most efficient use of teaching time
  Inappropriate below the high school level
  Good lecturers are born, not made
* The purpose of lecturing is to present information in a planned, organized way likely to lead to listeners' understanding.
* The teacher's role is central information-giver, while the students' role is receiver or audience.
* The twelve steps for lecturing are divided into: planning, giving, and after the lecture.
* Planning the lecture:
  1. Understand your goals and objectives.
  2. Analyze your students as listeners.
  3. Analyze your situation.

4. Narrow down your topic.

5. Get organized.

6. Support your ideas.

7. Create an introduction and a conclusion.

8. Create your speaking outline.

9. Incorporate listening aids.

*   Giving the lecture:

10. Practice out loud.

11. Give the lecture.

*   After the lecture:

12. Do a self-critique.

We are so familiar with lectures that the word itself instantly conjures up images from our past experience. These memories form the base for what we assume and expect about lecturing and, subsequently, our behavior when using lecturing as a teaching strategy. As is the case with other aspects of communication, when we lecture, our assumptions and expectations powerfully affect our communicative behavior, yet we are generally unaware of what they are or their impact on behavior.

To help you understand your own assumptions and expectations about lecturing, let's examine seven common beliefs about lecturing for their factual basis and classroom implications.

Common Beliefs about Lecturing

Belief #1: Lectures are uninterrupted talk by one person. This statement describes the traditional format of a lecture at the college level, but it is not a defining characteristic. The format is malleable and can be shaped to serve the needs of the students who will hear the lecture. Lectures can be used with other teaching strategies in one lesson plan. For example, short lectures can be interspersed with questions (Good and Brophy 1994). Lectures can precede or follow discussions or small groups, or lecture material can be spread over several days, so it can be interspersed with other instructional strategies (Richmond and Gorham 1992).

Belief #2: Lectures are long. In practice, especially at the college level, lectures are long; however, length is not an inherent, defining characteristic. Lectures can be any length, short or long. Some people prefer the term "mini-lecture" to describe short lectures. The important point about length is that lectures should not exceed the students' attention span. Adults' and secondary students' attention wanders after fifteen to twenty minutes of uninterrupted lecturing (Cooper 1995; Kindsvatter, Wilen, and Ishler 1988). Think about this time length in light of the age of the students whom you plan to teach.

Belief #3: Lectures are impersonal because there is no interaction between the speaker and the listeners. If you look in on a typical lecture, what you see is the teacher talking to the whole class. Normally the class will follow the mainstream cultural norm for lecture/public speaking situations—the audience (listeners) remains silent until the speaker (teacher) asks for an oral response. In this sense, lectures are less personal and more formal than small groups or discussions.

However, personal interaction does occur in lecturing. Recall from chapter 6 that the dyad is the fundamental unit of communication. Each dyadic connection has both content and relationship dimensions. The teacher sees a big class, yet each student sees one teacher. Students relate to the teacher personally and understand the content individually. In lecturing, each student engages in a private, silent dialogue with what the teacher is saying. In this verbally silent dialogue, students try to make sense of the content and react personally to the teacher. If they are paying any attention at all, then they are actively thinking about and reacting to both the teacher and the content of the lecture.

In lecturing, as with other communicative situations, the creation of meaning is dynamic and involves mutual influence. The teacher may be in control of the talking, yet the listening students react nonverbally. Their reactions give feedback to the teacher about the content and delivery of the lecture. Teachers respond by adjusting what they are saying and how they are saying it.

Belief #4: Lectures cover large amounts of information. This is true. However, it is potentially both an advantage and a disadvantage of lecturing. Covering a lot of information is efficient for the teacher but does not necessarily mean that a lot of learning has occurred for all, or even some, of the students.

Width of coverage is usually achieved at the sacrifice of depth of coverage and at the price of speed. When this happens, especially when Belief #1 is also operating, teachers may get through a lot of information, but students drop by the wayside overwhelmed and confused. Stating one idea after another without taking time to develop each one is announcing, *not* effective lecturing. Lectures need to focus on a few ideas and develop them in sufficient depth, so the people listening understand and remember them.

Belief #5: Lectures are the most efficient use of teaching time. The word "most" is problematic. The question is "efficient" for what? Lectures are efficient in the sense that a lot of information can be communicated to a maximum number of students without special equipment. Students do as well or better on tests of factual recall when the facts have been delivered by lecturing rather than taught by discussion methods (Richmond and Gorham 1992). However, lectures are not as effective as other methods in promoting higher levels of learning (application, analysis, synthesis, and evaluation) (Richmond and Gorham 1992).

Belief #6: Lectures are inappropriate below the high school level. It depends on how you define "inappropriate." The typical college level lecture is inappropriate at lower educational levels because it is too long, does not involve active learning, and covers too much complex material. However, an appropriate lecture can be created for students of any age as long as what is put in it is adapted to their educational needs, abilities, attention spans, and interest levels.

Belief #7: Good lecturers are born, not made. This belief rests on the assumption that skill at speaking to an audience is innate—you either have it or you don't. The number of uninspired lecturers supports a corollary to this assumption, that is, most people do not have it. However, anyone committed to learning how to lecture can do it. What goes into planning and delivering an effective lecture is known. It can be learned with effort and practice.

What Is Lecturing?

Lecturing is not defined by length, uninterrupted format, amount covered, age appropriateness, or suitability for higher cognitive learning objectives. **Lecturing** is defined by its purpose: to present information in a planned, organized way likely to lead to listeners' understanding. Lecturing is informative speaking (Cooper 1995). Richmond and Gorham (1992, p. 23) say that lecturing happens when a teacher assumes the role of "information-giver" and speaks with a "structured agenda" (they mean agenda in the sense of a planned presentation). This means that a lecture is like an informative speech. When informative speeches occur in classrooms with students, they are called lectures.

Lectures need to be adapted to the students who are to hear them. Although the format is more formal than other teaching strategies, lecturing does link lecturer and listeners. Finally, the skills of effective lecturing can be mastered if the motivation is there to work on developing them.

Let's look at lecturing in the context of public speeches for a moment. A **public speech** is one person speaking a prepared message to a specific audience (Kougl 1988). Public speeches can have one of three **general purposes**: (1) to give information; (2) to persuade agreement about belief or action; or (3) to meet the needs of a special occasion. Most of your speaking to an audience will be informative speaking (lecturing) to your students in your classroom. However, there will be times when you will be called on to speak to groups for the other purposes, too. For example, teachers speak to persuade when they speak to the public about voting for school levies or when they ask civic groups for money for special school projects (band, drama, forensics, sports, academic field trips). Teachers speak to meet the needs of special occasions when they speak at awards banquets, give commencement addresses, or speak at retirement dinners.

It is important to understand this connection among the different speech purposes because the steps are similar in constructing and presenting any speech. Audiences, situations, and general and specific purposes may differ, but the creative process is the same. In this chapter, the focus is on informative speaking as it occurs in classroom lectures.

The key to the effectiveness of a lecture, and other kinds of public speeches, is how well-adapted it is to the audience who hears it. Effective audience analysis is critical in guiding you at every step of the creative process, from planning through delivery.

The Role of Lecturer

One way to understand the teachers' role as lecturer is to contrast it with their role in the other teaching strategies that we have examined. Think of who is doing what to whom. With discussion, teachers lead students to do their own thinking. With small groups, teachers monitor and assist students in cooperatively completing tasks together. In both of these strategies, teachers and students are part of the process as it unfolds. With lectures, teachers create a product that they present to students. The teachers' role becomes one of central (usually solo) performer, while the students' role shifts to that of audience.

Some people initially respond to the solo nature of lecturing in a favorable way. They feel in control. They feel powerful and like being able to make all the decisions. They are relieved at not having to worry about the students' participation, as they do with discussion and small groups. They think they are free to do whatever they want.

Unfortunately, such attitudes by-pass the whole point of lecturing: getting a message across in a clear and interesting way to others. The lecture is meant to appeal to the listeners, not be an occasion for the speaker's idiosyncratic self-expression. A lecture is not a monologue. It is more like a dialogue. The teacher's input begins the dialogue, initiating the students' response, which completes the dialogue. As noted in the previous section, students' responses may be expressed silently (as in the traditional format) or orally (as with active response invited by the teacher).

Rather than freeing the speaker from the constraints of ordinary communication, lecturing requires more detailed planning and attention to listeners. The speaker's solo control is also solo responsibility for maximizing the match between his or her intended meaning and listeners' perceived meaning. Speakers must analyze the students' present relationship to the topic, anticipate potential reactions and trouble spots, and plan around them. Decisions at every step must be made with the best interests of the listeners in mind. For teachers, the question that needs to be asked continually when planning is, "What can I do to help my students understand this?"

This chapter is about helping you learn what to do when you are in the role of lecturer and give information. We will examine what needs to be done step-by-step when planning and delivering a lecture. As we go through each step, think about the age of the students and subject that you plan to teach. Consider how you will operationalize each step for them.

The Twelve Steps for Lecturing

Planning the Lecture

Each step in this phase is accompanied by a companion question to help you think in planning terms.

Step 1: Understand your goals and objectives: What information do my students need from me?

Begin by examining your educational goals for the proposed lesson. These goals specify what you want your students to learn in terms of behavioral objective(s) and a topic or subject. Since the general purpose of a lecture is to give information, your goal(s) should involve the first two levels of Bloom's cognitive objectives, knowledge and comprehension, which focus on knowing and understanding information. If the goals aim at higher cognitive objectives (where some other teaching strategy may be more appropriate) you should evaluate whether students have the information that they need to achieve the higher cognitive goals.

Once you are sure your goals are informational, look at your topic. There are many ways for students to get information depending on what the topic is, and what the available resources are. For instance, students can read independently, work in research groups, work in problem-solving groups, or use the Internet. Lecturing is another option to acquire information.

When Is Lecturing Appropriate?[1]

For the nature of the situation

1. When the objective is to give information
2. When information is not available in a readily accessible form
3. When the material must be organized in a particular way
4. When the information is original or must be integrated from different sources
5. When curriculum materials need updating or elaborating
6. When the teacher wants to provide supplementary explanations of material that students may have difficulty learning on their own

In relation to teaching strategies

7. When it is necessary to arouse interest in the subject
8. When it is necessary to introduce a topic before students read about it on their own or to provide instructions about a task
9. When information needs to be summarized or synthesized (following discussion or inquiry)
10. When the teacher wants to present alternative points of view or to clarify issues in preparation for a discussion

---

Notice the recurring theme. Lecturing is appropriate when students need supplemental or additional information. Teachers need to give information when it is not accessible to students for physical or cognitive reasons (numbers 2–6 and 10) or needed for other activities (numbers 7–9). Nothing on the list suggests lectures are designed to give students all the information that they need all the time.

As the list makes clear, the teacher's role as information-giver focuses on support. Lecturing is a bridge leading to or from something. Teachers use their subject matter expertise and their more sophisticated perspective to help students acquire and manipulate information appropriately. Their lectures help provide the base for and aid thinking.

Examine the list of ten occasions in which lecturing is appropriate and ask, "Which applies in my situation?" If none of them do, then reconsider your choice of teaching strategy. If one of them explains your personal objective or rationale, then lecturing is the best means to convey the needed information. Move on to step two.

Step 2. Analyze your students as listeners: What affects my students listening to this topic?

Effective lecturing starts with making appropriate choices adapted to your students and your circumstances. Doing a thorough analysis of your students and the situation is critical. What you discover in steps 2 and 3 will guide all your subsequent planning decisions.

Realize this means that you must consider listeners and situational variables each time you plan a lecture. It is not an activity done once in September and then applied to every subsequent lecture until June. As the preceding chapters demonstrate, communication is always dynamic, involving a transaction of meaning, especially in classrooms. Students and teachers change, and these changes are brought into the classroom environment. Developing interpersonal relationships affects teacher-student communication. *What* and *how* students learn affect their responses later to new topics. Each topic presents different challenges and obstacles. Think of each lecture as a unique event, the shape and substance of which must be tailored to students at that time.

Since the goal is getting students to understand information, we need to figure out what might hinder or expedite their listening and understanding on two different levels. We need to begin with what affects students (or people) in general, and then move onto analyzing your students specifically in relation to the topic.

Students in General

In a lecture, the students' role is that of listener and the teacher's expectation is that students will listen and learn. Perception, listening skills, and motivation affect how students enact this role and whether the teacher's expectations are met. It is important to recall from earlier chapters how this trio interrelates and impacts everyone's communicative behavior, including that of students.

Perception is always selective, and listening is one aspect of perception. What we select to pay attention to are stimuli that are personally meaningful (meet a need, relate to our background, concern self-concept), grab attention (intense, novel, repetitive, have variety), or are motivating. Students are most accustomed to listening passively to entertainment media that do not demand close attention or deep, thoughtful responses. This means many students may have undeveloped listening skills. Students are intrinsically motivated by their own interests, active involvement, novelty, choice making, peer interaction, game-like features, and a sense of accomplishment (as in completing projects).

This brief review suggests several practical ideas that you need to keep in mind when planning a lecture:

1. Since traditional lecturing places students in a passive role, it may be their least favorite teaching strategy. Its reliance on listening skills may also make it the one they are least prepared for in terms of the skills needed to do it.

2. Whenever possible, use personally relevant material, such as to their life experience (neighborhood, referent group), age group, and interests.

3. Whenever possible, use interesting or novel material that is intriguing, mentally stimulating, or has emotional impact.

4. Organize the lecture clearly and obviously to aid students' listening. Do whatever you can to help them identify what is important and to follow the progression of ideas.

5. Plan to allow opportunities for students' active responses, such as answering questions, asking questions, or brief small group tasks (huddles).

6. Plan for variety in your content and delivery.

Your Students Specifically

With your actual students, you need to discover two types of information: "What do they respond to and how do they relate to the topic?" As a new teacher, perhaps with little experience with students this age except through student teaching, this task may seem daunting. Recall from chapter 6 how communication changes as relationships develop. Analyzing your students becomes easier the better you get to know them because you have more to go on.

You can learn what elicits their response through experimentation and observation.

- What kind of response do you get to what you try? When do they become responsive and attentive? A social studies teacher gave the example of a class that became riveted each time photographs were used.

- How long can they listen at a stretch? What do their questions and comments reveal about their comprehension skills?

- Notice students' patterns of how they prefer learning. Students who learn aurally will have an easier time learning from lectures than students with the other modality preferences (visual, kinesthetic/tactile). Find ways to accommodate other modality strengths. These "other ways" encourage all the students to learn, not just students with other learning styles. For instance, visual aids help everyone understand, not just the visual learners.

Finding out how students relate to a topic involves you answering the question: "How does this topic relate to them?" What you are looking for is how to connect the new information to their present knowledge. What you need to avoid is talking over their heads (they lack background or foundation), telling them things they already know (they feel bored, patronized), or failing to show relevance or importance.

- What levels of interest, motivation, and comprehension have they demonstrated up to this point in the course?
- How does this topic relate to other material covered in this class or previous classes or grades?
- What do they probably know about this topic? Have they experienced it or anything similar before? If so, how, where, and what? It is important to determine what they know and its connections, even though they may know little or nothing.
- What do they probably think or believe about the topic? How does the topic look through their eyes? For example, an American history teacher said his students think of the 1960s as ancient history. He said any history earlier than that, for them, is whatever images the media provide.
- What new terms or concepts might create semantic noise?

Step 3. Analyze your situation: What circumstances do I need to deal with?

Physical, temporal, and climatic aspects of the classroom situation all need to be considered because they affect the content and delivery of your lecture.

Physical

Whether students can easily and comfortably hear a lecture affects their listening. Inventory the physical environment and eliminate obstacles to listening or control them as much as you can. Noise in the hall can be reduced by closing the door. However, if your room is next to a noisy furnace, you may have to settle for short lectures. Seats should be arranged facing wherever you intend to stand while lecturing. Each seat should have clear sight lines, so all students can see visual aids, demonstrations, and your nonverbal delivery.

Temporal

The time of your class period relative to other events can affect students' response to a lecture. For example, after lunch students are relaxed and drowsy. Students, who come in upset from another class, are distracted. After a long day at school last period classes often are snappy. As one teacher expressed it, "After a long day they do not want another adult coming at them." Timing in terms of the school calendar can also affect the students' concentration. Recall classes you were in before a holiday, after a holiday, and during the spring you were graduating.

Climate

The climate that develops in a class is expressed in different emotional styles. Classes may be warm and supportive, yet the style is low-key and quiet. Another class's closeness may be expressed in a loud, boisterous, and playful style. Classes where there is apathy or hostility may be silent and emotionally guarded.

Climate (and how it manifests itself on any given day) affects the choices you make for shaping a lecture (active participation or not), delivery choices, and what norms you establish for lecture listening. For example, some teachers set a norm of having students bring up questions as they occur to them, while others prefer that students save questions until the lecture is over. Some teachers plan to involve students actively (questions or guided activities of some kind). You may decide a class needs a more energetic delivery one day to hold their attention, while on another day they need a low-keyed delivery.

Step 4. Narrow down your topic: What is my specific purpose?

You begin this step with a clear educational goal (topic and informational objective that needs to be met with a lecture) and an analysis of your students and the situation. You know how your students relate to your general topic, how long it is reasonable to speak at one time, and what kinds of involvement will probably elicit your students' response. Now, it is time to decide exactly what you intend to say. The task of this step is to narrow down the general topic to a specific focus.

A **specific purpose** is a narrowing down of your general topic to a focused statement of what you want to accomplish with your listeners (Kougl 1988). It is a short declarative sentence that targets what you want your students to understand and to remember. It is based on what you decided about how your students relate to the topic (what they know and believe) and what they need to know and can use.

To write a specific purpose you must answer the question, "What are the few ideas that I want to develop in a clear and interesting way?" The format for a specific purpose has three parts:

1. Begin with the phrase, "I want my students to . . ." This opening keeps you focused on whom the message is for as you work through the planning process.

2. Next, choose a verb that reflects your informational goal, such as understand, know, or remember. You might select from among the clue words suggested for the different levels of Bloom's cognitive objectives. For lectures, the first two levels are relevant. Recall the suggestions for the knowledge level: define, recall, recognize. The suggestions for the comprehension level included describe, compare, and contrast.

3. Finally, end the statement with the points you want to get across. Write them as specifically as you can. How you word your specific purpose is critical because it determines your focus, what your main points will need to be, and which structure will be appropriate for organizing the points. For example, ". . . the five steps in resolving conflict." The following is an example from one of my students: ". . . why so many Hispanic students drop out of school."

Step 5. Get organized: What is the clearest way to structure my ideas?

Once the focus of your speech is clear, then you are ready to identify your main ideas and to arrange them in the way most likely to aid your students' listening. What we know about perception and listening emphasizes how important this step is. When you ask students to learn new information through listening to you, an orderly presentation of ideas literally structures their listening for them (Zolten and Phillips 1985). The structuring of listening helps focus and sustain attention.

If you think of your specific purpose as the destination of your speech, then identifying and organizing your main points is like making a map for listeners to follow. Main points serve as landmarks, so listeners perceive what is important about the trip rather than remembering whatever catches their fancy. Main ideas are identified by examining your specific purpose. Answer the question, "What ideas do I need to cover to accomplish my specific purpose?" List the ideas in whatever order they occur to you. If your specific purpose is indeed specific, then you may have already identified the main ideas. The step

4 example, "I want my students to understand the five steps in resolving conflict" indicates what five ideas have to be covered.

Sometimes specific purposes are clear in focus, yet do not state main ideas in an obvious way. The second example in step 4 falls in this category. "I want my students to know why so many Hispanic students drop out of school." What ideas would you have to cover for this to happen? Yes, causes. You would need to identify the main causes that you want to cover, and they would be your main ideas.

This example also illustrates how to use the boundaries set by your listener and situation analysis in planning. There may be thirteen different causes for Hispanic students dropping out of school, but you are not obligated to speak about all of them. Refer back to what you learned in steps 2 and 3 about your audience and situation and decide which causes to include. What do your students need, and what are they able to understand at this point? There are a number of ways to decide specific focus using your analysis information. Emphasize the most important one(s) for your students to understand. Choose the causes that are unfamiliar to them. Or, try regrouping the causes into larger, more inclusive categories, such as language difficulties, cultural differences, and poverty.

After you decide what your main ideas need to be, arrange them in a logical sequence that will be easy for students to follow.

Organizational Patterns

There are seven basic structures for organizing points into patterns. You are familiar with them already. We all use them in our everyday speaking and writing for the same reason we need them when lecturing: to enable recipients to follow what we are talking about.

The **time structure** organizes points in chronological order. This pattern is used when points must follow a necessary sequence to make sense. Think of when this kind of careful ordering of points is critical to the understanding of ideas: giving directions, demonstrating how to do something, and telling a story. When using this structure, make sure that you include all the necessary points and the points are considered in the correct order. The specific purpose about the steps in conflict resolution would need a chronological structure.

The **classification structure** organizes points that are parts or subdivisions of a subject. This structure is used whenever the points can be grouped or divided into separate classes or categories.

When organizing points this way, examine the subject and think carefully about what the subgroupings are. Stringing individual facts about the subject together or trying to cover the entire subject do not constitute subdivisions. Make sure information does not overlap between the categories. Since sequence is not the focus, it does not matter in what order you cover the groupings. It is important to cover all the groupings that you say you are going to cover.

This structure is probably the most common way to organize ideas. People frequently talk about aspects or parts of a subject in everyday communication. For example, parents or teachers signal this pattern when they say, "There are three reasons why doing homework is important." One of my student's specific purposes that needed to use this structure was, "I want my listeners to understand the three goals of teacher empowerment." Each goal was a sub-division of the subject, "Goals of Teacher Empowerment."

The **space structure** organizes points that are interrelated to each other in terms of spatial relationships. The whole is understood by talking about each point or part in relationship to all the other parts. The location and direction of the points in relation to each other matter.

This structure is used when describing objects, systems or organizations, or places. The "locations" may be geographic or physical-concrete, or on a page, chart, or map. The "direction" should be whatever makes sense for the subject and used consistently (left to right, top to bottom, east to west, close to far, clockwise, etc.)

The **cause-effect structure** is used when trying to make causal connections between points A and Z: A causes Z to occur or Z is an effect of A. There are many variations with this pattern depending upon how many causes or effects the speaker chooses to focus on, for instance:

One cause leading to one effect. Remember, there may be many causes, but you are choosing to focus on this one causal relationship at this time for these students.

Several causes leading to one effect. The Hispanic dropout specific purpose—why so many Hispanic students drop out of school—follows this variation of the pattern.

One cause leading to several effects. If there are few effects, you may focus on all of them. Or, there may be other effects, too, that you are choosing not to speak about in this lecture. For example, air pollution has many effects, but you may focus on particular health-medical effects.

The **comparison structure** is used when comparing two things (ideas, events, places, objects, people) to show how they are similar. Comparison is very useful when students are familiar with one of the things but unfamiliar or less familiar with the other. It links the new information that you are giving them with what they already know.

When using this structure, you must clearly establish your criteria for comparison. The criteria must be relevant and involve features common to both. Otherwise, similarities do not emerge and students are confused. For example, if you were comparing how one place is like another, then criteria like geography, natural resources, and climate make sense. Deciding on how many points of comparison to use is up to you. You may choose to lecture on one criterion. In another lecture on another topic, you may have two or three points of comparison.

The **contrast structure** works in the opposite direction from the preceding one. This structure is used to show how two things differ (ideas, events, places, objects, people).

What is true of the preceding structure also applies to this one. It is useful when students are familiar with one thing and unfamiliar or less familiar with the other. You must use a set of criteria, features both things have, as your points of contrast. For example, if you were contrasting one political system with another, relevant criteria would be items such as economic base, organization, and obligations of citizens. As with the comparison structure, this pattern can vary in the number of points in your criteria to suit your topic, students, and situation.

The **problem-solution structure** organizes information based on a specific problem with its solution(s). First, the problem must be clearly identified and explained. This can be done in a variety of ways depending on what the problem is, such as giving historical background, causes, magnitude, and impact. Then, the solution or possible solutions must be presented. Solutions should be relevant to the problem: practical (can be done) and desirable (solves the problem without causing other problems).

Guidelines for Choosing an Organizational Pattern

1. Remember, a lecture aims to develop a point or a few points in depth. You must choose one structure to organize your main points. It becomes the overall organizing pattern for the whole lecture.

2. Each structure involves a different focus that organizes ideas in a particular way. Select the structure that allows you to organize your points in the simplest and most direct way to aid your students' listening.

3. How you state your specific purpose determines what your main point(s) need to be and which structure will be appropriate. There needs to be a match between the wording of your specific purpose and the structure that you select. If there is no match, something needs to be adjusted. Sometimes you revise your specific purpose because you realize it does not express exactly what you mean. Other times you may have to use a different structure than the one you initially thought you would need.

Organizing Substructures and Making Outlines

After you choose the most appropriate structure to organize your main points, then you need to consider what your subpoints should be. The structure you chose to arrange the main points is your *overall* structure. For example, if my specific purpose were, "I want my students to understand the four steps in making a paper lantern," then I would need to use a time pattern as my overall structure. Each main part of your overall structure is a **substructure**. For example, each step in making the lantern is a substructure of the overall structure. The information in each substructure must be organized in a clear, direct way to aid listening. Substructures are also organized by one of the seven basic patterns:

- *Time*—each step in the sequence
- *Classification*—each subdivision or category
- *Space*—each part within the whole
- *Cause-Effect*—each cause(s) and each effect(s)
- *Comparison or Contrast*—each criterion
- *Problem-Solution*—the problem and the solution

How you organize each substructure depends on what information you have in it, and what you decide to say about each main point (substructure) are your subpoints—what you need to say to make the main point understandable. The subpoints define which organizational pattern is needed to arrange them. It's a question of fit. Let's look at the example of the four steps in lantern making. The first step is gathering materials, so the subpoints are the needed materials. This substructure needs to be organized by classification. The second step is cutting. The subpoints describe the steps in sequence, so a time pattern is needed. The third step is shaping, so the subpoints describe a sequence (time pattern). The final step is pasting and also has to be explained in sequence, so must be organized with the time pattern.

At this point, it is easy to make an outline, a record of how ideas relate to each other. A formal outline follows traditional organizational rules and expresses its content in one of two forms: (1) topical outline—ideas are indicated by words and phrases in condensed notes, and (2) sentence outline—ideas are written out word for word in complete sentences. Each form produces different types of speaking notes and supports different delivery styles. Topical outlines are preferable for teachers because they lead to the kind of speaking notes you will need when you lecture. The relationship between these forms, speaking notes and delivery styles will be discussed in Step 8.

Structures and substructures translate easily into traditional outline form. Each subpoint is supportive of the main point above it. Follow these guidelines:

1. Roman numerals designate the main points of the overall structure. Each Roman numeral is a substructure of the main topic.
2. Capital letters are used to indicate the subpoints of each main point or substructure.
3. Arabic numbers (1., 2., 3.) are subpoints that support the idea represented in the capital letter above it.
4. The next level of subpoints is lower case letters (a., b., c.) followed by arabic numbers with a parenthesis (1), (2), (3), followed by lower case letters with a parenthesis (a), (b), (c).

Here is a topical outline of the four steps (Roman numerals I.–IV.) in making a paper lantern. Keep in mind that topical outlines work when you are very familiar with what you want to say and help you pull your ideas together and organize the information. Also, before you give your lecture you will have practiced expressing your ideas out loud from your brief notes (practice will be discussed later in the chapter in Step 10). Thus all you need are brief reminders of what to say and where you are in the explanation.

I. Gather materials
   A. Construction paper
   B. Scissors
   C. Paste
II. Cutting
   A. Position paper
      1. Flat
      2. Line up: long side/front edge of desk
   B. Cut handle
      1. Long side: 1" strip
      2. Put aside
   C. Cut lantern
      1. Fold paper
         a. Short side: right ——> left
         b. Crease
      2. Cut design
         a. Hold
            (1) 1 hand—scissors
            (2) Other hand—paper (open edge facing palm)
         b. Begin cut
            (1) 1" from bottom (at fold)
            (2) Horizontal cut—to 2" (from open edge)
         c. Repeat pattern
            (1) 1" intervals
            (2) Stop 1" from top edge

III. Shape
    A. Unfold—lay flat
    B. Line up—long side/front edge of desk
    C. Top edge down ——> bottom edge (form cylinder).
IV. Paste
    A. Overlapped edges
    B. Handle
        1. Apply--both ends/same side
        2. Pick cylinder end for handle
        3. Attach 1 end
            a. On inside
            b. 1" down
        4. Repeat "3" above
            a. Other pasted end
            b. Across from first end

Step 6. Support your ideas: How can I make these ideas clear and interesting?

With main points identified and arranged, it is time to choose ways to make the ideas clear, interesting, and memorable. This step takes a series of assertions and builds support for each one of them, so they can be understood. If you think of the organized points as the skeleton of the lecture, then supports are the flesh on the bones. A **support** is anything that helps explain, clarify, elaborate or dramatize a point for listeners.

Where Do I Find My Information?

Since your topic search for material has a clear direction, and is focused, you will save time in looking for effective, appropriate supporting material. There are many resources available to teachers in their search for supporting material. For instance:

Subject Matter Expertise. The more you know about your subject, the more information you have readily available. As a new teacher, you will have achieved a certain basic level of knowledge. As you continue teaching and pursue continued study in your subject, the depth of your expertise will grow.

Curriculum Resources. Schools supply materials to support the curriculum in the form of textbooks, teachers' guides to textbooks, resource libraries for teachers, and media specialists. You will become familiar with your school's resources through doing your unit planning.

Personal Professional Stockpile. Most people who enjoy teaching are continually scouting for material that they can use in the classroom. They perceive the world through the units that they are teaching. They save anything that might be useful—articles, brochures, transparencies, maps, diagrams, books, pictures. Some people refer to this preoccupation as the "pack-rat" syndrome because pack-rats save everything. Probably you are have already begun doing this. Your stockpile will function like a bank full of possibilities from which you draw for particular lesson plans.

Collegial Resources. Subject matter colleagues share ideas from their personal stockpiles. Ask colleagues what supports work for them for particular points or ideas. As a rookie, do not hesitate to ask for advice from experienced teachers. Learning to teach is a process, and veteran teachers remember what it was like as a beginning teacher.

What Am I Looking For?

You are looking for any means to explain your points in a meaningful way to your students. You are familiar with the possible ways to support ideas because you already use them in your speaking and writing. You need them here for the same reason that you need them in your daily communication: to be sufficiently clear and interesting so your recipients understand what you mean.

Use your listener and situational analyses to guide your decisions about what kind of supports are appropriate for your lecture. You want supports that work with your students. Let's look at the possibilities.

Example. A particular item or incident that represents a group is called an **example**. It is usually in the form of an expository or descriptive passage. Its specific details provide a "for instance" of the larger point and make it come alive. There are three types of examples:

- Real—It happened to you or someone else.
- Hypothetical—It did not actually happen, but it does accurately represent what tends to happen or might happen in a given situation.
- Fictional—It is made up to illustrate a point. These are often the spur-of-the-moment examples made up in response to listeners' nonverbal feedback or questions.

Examples are little stories. All people respond to stories because the narrative impulse is intrinsic to human nature. Humans are *homo narrans*, the storytellers (Fisher 1984, p. 6). We live our lives as narrative, assimilating our daily lived bits of experience into our personal stories. This is why we identify with stories. The story helps us understand the point that it illustrates.

Definitions.   A statement of the meaning of a word, phrase, concept, object, or symbol is its **definition**. You need them whenever you think your students might not know what you mean or might have another meaning than the one you intend. Consider what your analysis revealed about possible semantic noise when deciding what, if any, definitions to use.

If you decide to use definitions, choose the kind that meets your students' information needs. Use as many types in combination as you need to achieve understanding. There are five types of definitions:

1. A *dictionary* definition states the unique characteristics that identify a term. There are specialized dictionaries for specialized and technical words.
2. An *operational* definition uses sensory words to describe how something appears to an observer. It describes how an object operates or an idea is actualized in terms of specific behaviors. Operational definitions help define abstract words because they translate them into specific behaviors that can be visualized.
3. A *comparison* definition defines something unfamiliar by showing how it is similar to something students know.
4. A *contrast* definition defines something unfamiliar by stating how it is different from something students know.
5. *Derivations* tell the origin or history of a word. This type of definition is helpful in making a complex term less intimidating by breaking it down into smaller, more comprehensible parts. It also builds vocabulary.

Testimony.   Evidence from a **testimony** is a qualified source about an object, event, person, or circumstance. "Evidence" is something that gives proof about the subject (observations, conclusions). "Qualified" means the source has expertise, experience, or data relevant to the subject. What constitutes evidence or qualified varies with the subject, the speaker, the situation, and the listeners. In classrooms, teachers are considered a qualified source for the subject, and younger students regard what they say as evidence. As students grow older and develop their critical thinking skills, they expect evidence from other sources, too.

Generalizations.   Broad conclusions based on specific instances of something are called **generalizations**. Allness generalizations, such as "always" and "never," do not work because they are vague. When it is clear what specific instances lead to the conclusion, then generalizations have substance. There are two kinds of generalizations. Their conclusions are reached in different ways:

- Enumerative—The conclusions are based on counting individual instances of something.
- Statistical—The conclusions are based on collected numerical data that has been analyzed according to the principles of the statistical method.

Figurative Language Devices. Words that are put together in an out-of-ordinary way, creating a more dramatic impact than ordinary language, are known as **figurative language**. Students notice and remember the point because the device calls attention to it in a vivid way.

Choose devices and craft them to fit your students. The content must be recognizable for the device to work for your students. Figurative language devices are usually considered to be from literary sources (stories, novels, speeches, plays, poems), but in our media age, their content often comes from popular culture, particularly television shows. If not adapted to your students, they will not support your point and may create semantic noise. Choose from among these frequently used literary devices:

1. A *simile* is a comparison between two things to create a strong visual image or to highlight similarities. Similes are signalled by words such as: like, as, then, and similar to (for example, a lecture is like a speech).

2. A *metaphor* is also a comparison between two things, but it says "A" is "B". The one thing has the same qualities as the other.

3. An *allusion* is a reference to another source to intensify the students' reaction to the point. Their connotative meanings for that source become associated with the point.

4. A *rhetorical question* is a question that is raised to provoke thought but is not meant to be answered out loud. Give clear speaker signals when asking this type of question because you may also be asking questions in your lecture that you want answered. When asking a rhetorical question, you could say something like, "I am going to ask a question that I want you to think about."

5. A *literary (media) quotation* (exact words) can be used to illustrate or intensify a point. Use short quotes because it is hard for students to listen to long ones.

Demonstrations. Exhibitions that illustrate what you are talking about are **demonstrations**. They appeal to the senses by giving listeners something they can see, hear, touch, or do. Their content frequently illustrates an example, definition, or a generalization. Demonstrations aid the understanding of all students, but they are especially helpful for students whose perceptual modality preference is visual or psychomotor (kinesthetic/tactile).

There are three types of demonstrations: visual aid, aural aid, and psychomotor aid. The word "aid" highlights their status as supports for a main point. They cannot stand alone. They need verbal explanation accompanying them to make their meaning clear and to relate them to the point which they are supporting. Demonstrations must be accessible for all students—that is, easily seen, heard, or done. If they are not, then they will be ineffective as supports. Let's look at the possibilities and how to use them:

A **visual aid** is any kind of physical representation that can be seen.

1. *Objects.* Showing the actual object clarifies and creates interest. However, sometimes it is neither practical nor desirable to use objects (too big, unavailable, expensive). Passing small objects around while you are speaking distracts students from what you are saying. To avoid this problem try a "walk-by." Introduce the object, stop talking, walk among the students so everyone can see the object, and then resume your talk. When possible, later display the object so students can examine it on their own.

2. *Models.* A three-dimensional representation of something, a model is a concrete stand-in for reality and makes a good substitute for an unavailable object. Very often, departments have a pool of models pertinent to their subjects, such as models of DNA, the human skeleton, castles, pyramids, and so forth.

3. *Chalkboards.* Best-suited for simple, short, and direct messages. For example, put key points(s) in shortened form or focus question(s) on the board before the lecture. They serve as visual organizers, aid note taking and listening, and can be referred to as you proceed through your talk. The question(s) could be answered by the students at some point in the talk. Another way to use the board is to write down important words, names, phrases, and dates as you speak. However, when what you want to put on the board is long or complicated, consider another form of visual aid, perhaps handouts or charts.

   If you want to put long, complex messages on the board, consider that it is boring to watch someone writing on the board. Put the material on the board before students arrive. Material needs to be well timed. Material on the board is distracting, so cover it up until you need it. Copying a lot of material from the board is tedious. Is there a sound educational reason to use valuable classroom time this way? If the answer is "no," use handouts.

   Using the chalkboard well takes practice and requires you to monitor yourself continually with the following kinds of questions. "Can they read my handwriting?" (work on legibility, write large). "Can they see it?" Do not stand in front of what you have written, rather stand to the side and refer to it. "Can they hear me?" The voice travels in the direction it is pointed. Face the class and do not talk to the board.

4. *Pictures, Drawings, and Photographs.* A picture is probably worth more than a thousand words to students comfortable with the daily barrage of media visual images. Make sure pictures are relevant, easy to see, and simple to interpret. If they are small, consider how to make them visible to the entire class: enlarging them, making them into slides and projecting them, or doing a "walk-by" as described in item #1. "Objects."

5. *Maps.* Maps show the territory. They are used to clarify the nature of a place or event (location, movement), or context. Visibility and clarity are important. Small maps or portions of maps can be translated into handouts or projected.

6. *Charts.* Charts are useful for compressing a lot of information into an easily interpreted form. The information may be charted in the form of words or diagrams. Word charts often express the major categories of a topic accompanied by main ideas or steps in a process. Pictorial charts are often used to show how items relate to each other, such as animals in the food chain or branches of an organization.

7. *Graphs.* Graphs are used to clarify, compare, and contrast enumerative and statistical generalizations. Numbers are abstractions. Graphs make them concrete.

   Different types of graphs serve different purposes. *Line graphs* show how something has changed over time (the national debt, decline in smoking, number of home computers). A *pie graph* shows a distribution pattern with the size of each wedge representing the amount. Each wedge is labelled and shows the amount it represents (budgets, resource deployment, prevalence of a disease or behavior in a group). *Bar graphs* show the difference between two or more things. The length of the bar stands for the number or percentage involved for each thing, and the bar is labelled with the appropriate figures. Different colors can be used to make the differences stand out more.

8. *Movies, Slides, Projections, Videocassettes.* Their use requires careful consideration of availability of the source and equipment, your skill in running the equipment, and the amount of time needed. Material must be previewed for suitability. If time is a factor, specific relevant segments could be identified and excerpted for the class

There are two types of projections that are easily produced to fit your purposes. An *opaque projector* projects straight from a typed page. It easily enlarges an otherwise too small chart, graph, picture, or drawing. However, it requires a darkened room. An *overhead projector* projects images or words that have been put on transparent sheets (transparencies). Transparencies are inexpensive, the information you want to project can be easily marked or photocopied onto them, they can be reused, and they are usually provided by the school. Transparencies can be used with normal lighting and you can write or draw on them while you are talking.

9. *People Models.* You can use yourself or volunteers to give a "live" demonstration. There are three planning points to keep in mind: (1) Do not assume someone will volunteer, especially early in a term or year before relationships or climate develop. Consider the students' risk of looking foolish in front of their peers. Do not force a student to volunteer. Arrange for volunteers ahead of time (let them know what it involves), perhaps give bonus points for bravery, or be prepared to demonstrate yourself. (2) Practice the demonstration even if it involves something with which you are familiar. (3) Time it when you practice, so you realize how long it will take. Demonstrations always take longer than just describing something.

10. *Handouts.* These aids are useful when giving additional information, detailed instructions, a lot of information, a visual representation of some other type of visual aid used in the lecture (graph, charts), or for use as a learning-listening aid. For example, a handout might aid development of note-taking skills (main points with space for students to put ideas into their own words as they listen).

Execution and timing are critical. Handouts should be neat, easily comprehended, appropriately titled, and dated. Handouts should be well-timed as to when they are introduced and explained in the lecture. People look at a handout when it is given to them, which means it has a potential to distract from whatever you are then saying. If you must distribute handouts ahead of time because the class is large, tell students to turn them face down until you are ready to refer to them.

An **aural-aid** is any kind of physical representation that can be heard. Often they are a rendering of another type of support, such as an example or definition.

Recordings, Tapes, CDs. Readily available through curriculum resources and public libraries, their content includes speeches, plays, poetry, interviews, original news events, and music. Since these are commercially produced, the execution is professional. Your job is one of previewing, excerpting to fit time constraints and focus, and scheduling necessary equipment.

A **psychomotor (kinesthetic/tactile) aid** is movement done by the listeners with the speaker. Students literally *get the feel* of an idea by doing it as the teacher speaks. The movements are the support. This type of demonstration is useful when teaching students how to make something or do a physical activity. Psychomotor aids are often used with visual aids (models, chalkboards or handouts). In the lantern example, psychomotor aids were used; the students did the steps as the teacher explained and modelled them.

Guidelines for Choosing Supports

1. Each type of support is equally as good as the others. Each contributes to building explanation, clarity, and interest for its point.
2. Use a variety of types of support. Variety breaks through perceptual barriers, appeals to different learning styles, and helps sustain listening.
3. The more supports, the more depth. Each support helps build and emphasize the intended meaning. Each repeats and helps develop the idea. It is better to have too many supports than not enough. You need not use them all, but you will have them ready if students are confused, the other aids you use do not work, or you perceive a need to develop a point further. This strategy is especially helpful when you give the same talk to different classes. You can select the supports most likely to appeal to each class.
4. Decide whether a support should be translated into a demonstration. Would the information be clearer or more memorable if translated into a visual, psychomotor, or aural aid?

Step 7. Create an introduction and a conclusion: How can I prepare students for the beginning and ending?

Now that you know what you are going to talk about in the body (the substantive content) of your lecture, it is time to decide how to get your students into and out of it. Introductions and conclusions in speeches, as with discussion and small groups, give shape to the upcoming experience and pull together what has been said. To write effective ones requires, once again, referring back to your analysis of your students and *the* situation.

Introductions

The introduction signals what is coming up in the lecture. Be creative, interesting, and relevant. Earlier in the chapter I likened a specific purpose to the destination of a journey. The introduction, then, is like the orientation session before you start off. It needs to accomplish four functions, so students are prepared to listen:

1. *Focus students' attention.* Assume students are sitting there minding their own business, preoccupied by personal thoughts. Break into their perception in a way relevant to the topic. Pique their curiosity. For instance, to grab attention before giving information about an upcoming field trip, it might be enough to write on the board the destination and the scheduled date.

2. *Provide motivation.* Tell students how the subject relates to them personally either in terms of their life in the classroom, what they have done or will do, or their lives outside of school. Remember, the question is "Why should we care?" and needs an answer that relates to your students.

3. *Provide a preview.* A **preview** states the aim of the lecture (specific purpose) and how you plan to accomplish it (pattern or structure of ideas). A preview is like coming attractions at the movies or the table of contents of a book. It creates listening categories, so students know what to listen for.

4. *Clarify expectations.* There are two reasons why you need to clarify the kind of response you expect from students in each lecture: (1) Lectures traditionally place students in a passive role. They only expect to have to listen. (2) You create the shape of a lecture to fit your purpose, learning objective, and students, so lectures vary in length, how they relate to other teaching strategies, and in how they fit into parts of a lesson. For these reasons, you need to answer the question, "What do I expect students to do during *this lecture*? Listen only? Take notes? (Is there a particular format?) Participate during the lecture (ask or answer questions, work in huddles or pairs)?"

Conclusions

Lectures need to reiterate what you want students to remember and to provide a sense of closure. Since lectures are products of one author, their conclusions can be planned in detail ahead of time. Keep in mind that conclusions should be short. The danger is using them as a dumping ground for whatever you meant to say or for interesting tidbits that did not fit anywhere else. Conclusions should:

1. *Provide a summary.* "What main ideas or points do I want students to take away with them?" Review your main points and your purpose. Creatively emphasize them in your conclusion.

2. *Inspire reflective interpretation.* Emphasize the relationship between the summarized content and the specific purpose. Cre-

ate a **reinforcer** that ties the points together into a memorable ending note. An effective reinforcer leaves students thinking about the lecture and provides a hook that helps students remember what was important.

3. *Establish connectors.* "What do I expect students to do with the information that I have just given them?" If the lecture is part of a lesson, then you need a transition to the next part. If it is the lesson, then link its content to what will happen based on it.

Step 8. Create your speaking outline: How can I integrate the elements of my plan?

At this point in planning, you have the makings of your lecture. Your topical outline of main and subpoints is now filled in with the supports that you have decided to have available. You have decided on relevant ways to get students into and out of the lecture.

Integrate all these preparation elements into a speaking outline. A **speaking outline** is the record of everything that you have decided to say written in a condensed form.

A speaking outline accomplishes two functions: (1) It keeps you organized, so that points and supports are not forgotten or do not wander out of the position where they do the most good. (2) It serves as speaking notes, a visual aid prompting you about what comes next. Consider the following:

1. Organize information under the appropriate heading: introduction, body, or conclusion. Number individual functions of the introduction (4) and conclusion (3), so you do not forget to do any necessary jobs. In the body, merely numbering main points works well for shorter lectures, while creating an outline works well for longer lectures. In all lectures, numbering your supports under each point provides a good checkpoint on whether you achieved the guidelines for supports (numerous, variety).

2. Abbreviate and condense as much as possible. Nothing should be written out in sentences, except for quotations or material where wording is inveterate (formulas, axioms, laws).

   Write out citations for supports (source, author, date), so you correctly attribute credit for other people's words and ideas. Handling sources fairly models respect for other people's ideas. It also helps students develop the critical thinking skills of weighing evidence and considering different perspectives.

   This sort of brief note system supports the **extemporaneous delivery style** expected of teachers. "Extemporaneous" means the lecture is thoroughly prepared and delivered from brief notes. This format allows you to maintain a more personal relationship with your listeners because it frees you to look at them while you speak, which allows you to adjust your presentation based on their responses. Since the notes are brief, you must look down at them, pause, think of how to express the next item, and then put it into words. This process of converting notes into meaningful speech phrases as you talk to your students results in a conversational, natural sounding delivery. It makes you slow down, pause, and think on your feet just as you do in nonlecture communicative situations. This natural speech rhythm helps students listen, giving them time to think about what you are saying.

If you write your lecture out word for word, then you have opted into a **manuscript delivery style**. Manuscripts are necessary when a formal relationship exists between the speaker and the audience and precise, careful wording is required with no mistakes or omissions, and there are time limits. However, manuscript delivery is inappropriate for classrooms because it is too formal and generates problems, such as little eye contact and difficulty in noticing feedback; impersonalizes the relationship to students; and creates listening problems (speaking too fast, having little if any vocal variety or pauses).

It takes hard work to create a manuscript that has an oral-aural style and deliver it well. If you have ever experienced a teacher reading a lecture to you, then you know how deadening it can be. It is like having an invisible shield between you and the speaker. Instead of investing effort in writing an unnecessary manuscript, put your energy into creating a useful speaking outline and an interesting delivery.

3. Write "FYEO" (For Your Eyes Only) messages or personal cues to highlight reminders for yourself when you give the lecture. Use whatever symbols, abbreviations, or color coding that work for you. FYEO messages might include page numbers, handouts, material distribution, placement or timing of visual aids, and so forth.

4. Put your outline in usable, practical visual format. Make notes legible and large; for instance, double or triple space the items, so it is easy to glance down and see the next item. Leave generous left-hand margins for FYEO messages. Number the pages.

Step 9. Build in listening aids: How can I involve my students?

Attention is more like a pulse than a steady current. It normally wafts and wanes even for people who are paying attention or interested in a subject. **Listening aids** are ways you, as speaker, try to guide, sustain, and recapture attention.

The wording of your listening aids is dictated by your introduction's preview. Since the preview announces the aim of your lecture, listening aids reflect and reinforce those points. There are two types of listening aids: speaker signals and activators.

Build in Speaker Signals

There are two types of speaker signals that you can give students in the body of the lecture: transitional phrases and internal summaries. A **transitional phrase** consists of a few words that move listeners from one point to another point. It reminds students of the specific purpose and tells them where they are in the lecture and how one idea relates to another. To continue with our journey analogy, transitional phrases are like signposts along the way that point out where listeners are and prevent them from getting lost. Insert transitional phrases at major junctures within the lecture. from introduction to body, from one main point to the next, from the body to the conclusion. If we look at the topical outline of how to make a lantern, we might conclude that transitional phrases are needed to announce each step: "The first step in making a lantern is to gather the materials." Transitions might also be used within substructures to keep information organized. For example, in II. Cutting, transitions would be needed to move students from positioning paper, to cutting the handle, to cutting the lantern.

Conscientious use of clear, obvious transitions aids listening, facilitates note taking, and provides a signal that allows students to find their way back into the lecture when their attention wanes. An **internal summary** is a brief summary of material that has just been covered. It is an immediate review that allows students time to think about what they have just heard and to check their understanding. They are not needed in simple, short lectures, but they are helpful with new or complex ideas or in long lectures.

Build in Activators

Recall that teachers' lectures initiate a dialogue with students. The students' part of the dialogue is traditionally silent, although teachers may shape their lecture anyway that they want to. Teachers may invite students to become actively involved. When teachers do, they are, in effect, turning up the volume. The students' part in the dialogue process becomes vocal and active.

An **activator** is a question or a request for a response in some form that actively involves students in your lecture. Think of activators as providing thinking plateaus. Whatever form they take, they cause the lecturer to pause and engage students in *responding to what has occurred to that point.* They hook students into actively thinking about what has been said. They provide you with verbal feedback about your students' response to the lecture. This direct response assists you in several ways. It helps you gauge students' understanding, adapt the rest of the lecture (and lesson) to what is occurring, and plan more effectively for future lessons.

If your listener and situational analyses revealed that your students need to become involved, then this is where you decide *how* and *where*. What kind of activators, how many, and where you place them depend on the circumstances of your lecture, your students, and your own creativity. Consider these guidelines when selecting activators:

- Be judicious in their use. Do not use so many or ones that take so long that students lose the continuity and meaning of the lecture. Sometimes it is more effective to give the lecture and then move onto some form of active involvement, such as a discussion, individual seat work, or task group.
- Look for placement opportunities after a point (logical portion or section of the lecture) has been presented, and you want an active response from students.
- When using questions, plan them with the range of possible cognitive responses represented by Bloom's Taxonomy (chapter 7) in mind. Consider what kind of thinking you want to invite. At one point in a lecture you may want to ask knowledge or comprehension level questions. At another point, questions at other cognitive levels may be appropriate.
- If using huddles, remember to apply the mechanics for effective group experiences. Make sure students know the purpose, directions, output, and time limits before they begin.

Giving the Lecture

Step 10. Practice out loud: How does it come across?

Up to this point, you have been making decisions about what to say and how to say it based on your analysis of your students and the classroom situation. Your silent planning has focused on creating content that is clear, interesting, and memorable. However, a lecture is an oral event that is judged by what sense it makes to students when they hear it. For this reason, the so far silent, planned lecture needs to be translated into its oral-aural performance medium. Now, the task is to figure out how to present the lecture in a way to hold attention and reinforce meaning. Decisions have to be made about how you want to deliver your lecture and then tried out in practice until you are comfortable with your choices.

Review and Assess

Review the ideas that we have examined in light of your usual communicative behaviors and your analysis of your students and situation. Assess these ideas in terms of what will enhance your lecture for your students—namely, make it clearer, more interesting, and more memorable. How can you operationalize these ideas? Good choices are ones that help your students listen. Look specifically at:

Nonverbal Communication (chapter 3). Review each type and ask yourself what choices you need to make. Pay special attention to spatial arrangement, kinesics (eye and facial behavior), body movement (posture, body orientation, gestures), paralanguage (vocal variety: pitch, volume, rate, pauses), and proxemics.

Verbal Behavior (chapter 4). Review the three levels of language—phonology, semantics, and grammar—focusing on potential noises that you need to avoid.

Listening Behavior (chapter 5). Remind yourself of the causes of poor listening, especially noises, bias, and speech-thought rate disparity. Review the "Teacher as Speaker" guidelines. The third guideline, to speak in simple, short aural sentences, is especially important. Consider what kind of listening strategies you can suggest to your students, while they listen to your lecture.

Practice

Once you make decisions about the delivery, you need to coordinate them with your lecture plan and practice giving your lecture. How much practice you need depends on your skill and experience. When people first begin giving public presentations, whether lectures in classrooms or public speeches in other settings, they need a lot of practice. Experienced lecturers (and public speakers), who have honed their presentational skills and developed confidence in front of groups, need less.

The most effective practice involves you *simulating* actual presentational conditions. This means going through the lecture exactly as you intend to give it. By doing so, you become familiar with your material and confident about what you are going to say and do. As part of the simulation, make sure you:

- Practice out loud using your speaking outline. You are practicing different ways to express your notes and becoming familiar and comfortable with how they sound. Glance down at your outline, pause to think about what you want to say next, and then say what you have in mind. Experiment with different ways to express or explain each item. Think of it as building a savings account with numerous different wordings, anyone of which is clear and could be drawn on when you give the lecture.

- Practice with a *live* audience. A live audience supplies the personal responsiveness. It does not matter how many people listen to you practice. One is enough. As students in a speech class, you can practice lecturing to each other. When you student teach, you could practice with another student teacher.

    There are several dynamics that you get comfortable and familiar with through practicing with live listeners: (1) You learn to manipulate your notes while maintaining eye contact. (2) Live responses encourage you to do all the normal things people do when they communicate (smile, gesture, emphasize words). Since listeners are the best judge of appropriate delivery behaviors, the best way to find out what works is from actual listeners. Practicing in front of a mirror is not helpful because what you think of how you look is not important. What matters is how what you do and say facilitates or impedes understanding. (3) When you finish, you can ask for specific feedback about what was and was not clear and use the comments to improve your lecture.

- Practice the entire lecture several times. Make sure that you practice everything that you plan to say and do. Do not practice just the body of the lecture but also practice the introduction, transitions, demonstrations, and the conclusion.

Step 11. Give the lecture: What should I keep in mind as I speak?

The phrase "attitude is everything" applies to lecturing. How you feel about actually giving the lecture colors your delivery, which, in turn, affects the relationship you establish with your students as they listen. A person with an "Oh, let's get it over with" attitude will probably rush, look and sound bored, and pay no attention to feedback.

Positive attitudes are built on remembering the purpose for the lecture. *The aim has been a few indepth points presented in a clear and interesting way, so students understand and remember.* All of the steps lead toward the creation of a clear, informative lecture tailored to your students' informational needs. But the lecture plan is only half the process. In order to be complete, a lecture must occur as an oral event with students listening.

As you present a lecture, concentrate on your students' reactions. To return to our lecture-trip analogy, when you lecture, think of yourself as a tour guide. You are the only one who knows the destination and the route. Your goal is to make sure everyone enjoys the sights along the way and no one gets lost.

There are three guidelines that you need to remember when lecturing: (1) understand that nerves are normal, (2) make sure to monitor your students' responses, and (3) be flexible.

Nerves Are Normal

No matter if your first lectures are in a speech class, education class, or student teaching, it is important to remember that nerves are normal. New lecturers (and public speakers) usually think nervousness is a sign of weakness, insufficient preparation, a character flaw, or impending failure.

Actually, nerves are a natural, normal, and inevitable part of performing. What we call "nerves" is energy released by the pumping of adrenalin into our systems when we are faced with a situation where how we perform matters to us. We are more aware of this energy when we are performing new behaviors because we feel insecure about possible outcomes. We label the energy in a negative way as *nerves* and then become self-conscious about what we are doing.

The energy is present even when we perform old, familiar behaviors—we just perceive it differently. Since we are comfortable with our handling of the behaviors, we label the energy in positive ways, such as excitement, anticipation, or a state of readiness. Think of performances that you are comfortable with and how you handle pre-performance energy. People call it getting "pysched up" and see it as an asset that contributes to an enthusiastic performance.

However, when you begin speaking before groups, you may feel like a neon sign flashing the message, "I am nervous." Keep in mind that nerves are usually not visible to listeners for two reasons:

- There is no universal sign of nervousness. How people show nerves is idiosyncratic and personal. Some people get dry mouth, others get butterflies, others get sweaty palms, others feel their hearts pounding, to name a few signs.
- Personal indicators of nervousness are not apparent. Your friends and family know you well enough to know what you tend to do when nervousness occurs, but other people do not. Listeners cannot see, feel, or hear what your stomach, palms, or knees are doing. They expect to hear a lecture. If you are organized and interesting, they become involved in listening to what you have to say. They have no reason to think about nervousness unless you bring it up. If you begin by saying, "I am really nervous," then that is what they will focus on. You will still be nervous, but now listeners are distracted from the lecture, wondering what is going to happen.

The best advice is to prepare, practice, and understand the nature of nerves. Use the energy to give an energetic performance. Listeners will likely interpret your energy as interest in talking to them and enthusiasm for the subject. Such reactions contribute to positive listener perceptions of the speaker.

Also, realize that nerves diminish within a lecture (or speech) and over time as you gain experience. By the time they finish the introduction, most prepared speakers become absorbed in what they are explaining and forget about being nervous. As you become comfortable with lecturing, you will be less bothered by nerves because you will know how to channel the energy into your performance.

Monitor Your Students' Responses

Be responsive to your students' nonverbal cues and adjust your plan and delivery as needed. Use their responses to improve your effectiveness and to strengthen your relationship to them. Students react as most people in an audience situation do—they feel anonymous. Although they view the speaker, they do not think about the speaker noticing them as individuals. They do not think about their nonverbal behavior or how it might be interpreted by the speaker. This is true of us as adults, and it will be true of our students, regardless of their age.

Monitoring nonverbal responses gives us a rich source of feedback about what sense our students are making of what we are saying. However, as we glean nonverbal responses we need to remind ourselves that perception is always selective and the meaning of perceptions is relative. When monitoring students' nonverbal behavior, keep in mind how individual differences affect the feedback process.

- Students vary in their nonverbal expressiveness. Students who are naturally more animated will give off more nonverbal cues. Such students serve as bellwethers for the other students.
- Pragmatic background affects nonverbal behavior and meanings. Students' and teachers' backgrounds define the nonverbal behavior they have mastered as appropriate and how they interpret other people's behavior.
- Familiarity improves effectiveness of monitoring. Our ability to interpret what someone's nonverbal cues mean improves as we get to know the person better.

When you notice nonverbal responses, think of all of the possible meanings. Do not jump to conclusions. Notice if the cue is widespread or if only one or two students display it. Notice what the cues of other students are. Respond appropriately. You need to modify your plan.

For example, a number of students look confused, so you use some of the additional supports that you prepared to support the point. Or, sometimes you cannot interpret what the cues mean, so you pause in the lecture and seek verbal feedback. For example, you might say, "Some of you look like you have questions," or you might ask students to give you examples, so you can gauge whether they are following your meaning.

Be Flexible

No matter how good your plan, life happens. A lecture plan is one small element in the dynamic, fluid mix of the communication in the classroom. You cannot know, control, or plan for what is happening in your students' lives, how they will respond, or what occurs in the school the day you give the lecture. Lecture plans need to be worked out in thoughtful detail and then modified as necessary under prevailing conditions. Use your plan as a guide, not a straitjacket. Recognize the obvious and deal with it.

Let me give you an example of how one student teacher learned about flexibility. He had planned a lecture on listening, which he judged would take about twenty minutes. The plan was clearly focused, well organized, and supported with numerous, relevant examples. On the day of the lecture there was an unannounced assembly. All periods were shortened. During what was left of the period, handouts and announcements related to the assembly had to be given out. When all the unanticipated chores were accomplished, there were ten minutes left in the period. The student teacher gave his lecture as planned in ten minutes. He got through it by talking very fast, leaving out supports, and dropping time for questions and soliciting student examples. The students not only did not learn the information they needed from the lecture, but they were now also confused. At that point, the question became how to re-present the information, so students could learn it. Think about what choice you would have made in his initial situation.

After the Lecture

Step 12. Do a self-critique: What did I learn about lecturing?

While the lecture is still fresh in your mind, sit down with your speaking outline and analyze what you learned about lecturing. Recall what you did and how your students responded.

- Think about any content additions or deletions that you made during the lecture. Jot notes in the left-hand margin about changes in content that you would make if you were to give the lecture again.

- Think about the interaction between you and your students. What kind of feedback did you get as you went through the lecture? How well did you handle it?
- Assess your students' involvement in the lecture. How well did they do what you asked them to do (note taking, responding to activators, listening). How could you have facilitated the students' involvement?
- What did you learn about your students' listening skills? Note where your students responded with greatest interest and least attention. Figure out the reasons behind each response.
- Assess your nonverbal and verbal delivery. What assisted the content of the lecture and assisted listening? What distracted or interfered with the content and listening?
- Divide a sheet into two columns labelled "Worked" and "Needs Work." Replay the lecture in your mind from beginning to end, evaluating what was effective and ineffective. What you put in the "Worked" column are behaviors that you should continue to use in future lectures. Items in the "Needs Work" column should be assessed and modified. Choose items from this list as goals to work on in future lectures.

Lecturing: A Natural Process

Lectures, despite their ponderous reputation, are really only about explaining information in a clear and interesting way. They are created to fill an informational need and are adapted to the learning-listening needs of a particular group of students.

To become an effective lecturer, no matter what your subject or the age of your students, requires that you focus on your students. Every decision about a lecture—what goes in, what stays out, how things are expressed—is made with them in mind.

The twelve steps discussed in this chapter will guide you in your decision making. As you begin developing your lecturing skills, these steps may seem arduous. However, once you become familiar and comfortable with them, they will become habits of your mind, a natural way of thinking. You will think automatically in terms of listeners' perspectives, focus, patterns, supports, and listening aids whenever you are explaining to students, whether in a lecture, a conversation, or a discussion, and when answering a question.

Note

[1]Suggestions appeared in T. Good and J. Brophy. *Looking in Classrooms*, 6th edition. New York: HarperCollins, 1994, p. 380. Suggestions were not differentiated as to author.

Davis, R. and L. Alexander. 1977. *The Lecture Method*. East Lansing: Instructional Media Center, Michigan State University.

Gage, N. and D. Berliner. 1984. *Educational Psychology*, 3rd edition. Boston: Houghton Mifflin.

Henson, K. 1988. *Methods and Strategies for Teaching in Secondary and Middle Schools*. New York: Longman.

McMann, R. 1979. "In Defense of Lecture." *Social Studies* 70, 270–74.

References

Cooper, P. 1995. *Speech Communication for the Classroom Teacher*, 5th Edition. Scottsdale, AZ: Gorsuch Scarisbrick.

Fisher, W., 1984. "Narrative as a Human Communication Paradigm: The Case of the Public Moral Argument." *Communication Monographs*. LI: 1–22.

Good, T. and J. Brophy. 1994. *Looking in Classrooms*, 6th edition. New York: HarperCollins.

Kindsvatter, R., W. Wilen, and M. Ishler 1988. *Dynamics of Effective Teaching*. New York: Longman.

Kougl, K. 1988. *Primer for Public Speaking*. New York: Harper & Row.

Richmond, V. and J. Gorham. 1992. *Communication, Learning, and Affect in Communication*. Edina, MN: Burgess Publishing.

Zolten, J. and G. Phillips. 1985. *Speaking to an Audience—A Practical Method for Preparing and Performing*. Indianapolis: Bobbs-Merrill.

Suggested Reading

"Clarity: Teachers and Students Making Sense of Instruction," by Jean Civikly. *Communication Education* 41 (1992): 138–52.

This article presents an overview of the research on teacher clarity. It expands the meaning of teacher clarity by including two new variables: message clarity and student clarification behavior. It views teacher clarity as a relational process between teachers and students and not as a teacher attribute, as in past studies. The studies cited used students from elementary through college age. Implications for classroom use are suggested.

"Synthesis of Research on Explicit Teaching," by Barak Rosenshine. *Educational Leadership* 43 (1986): 60–69.

Based on research in math and reading at the elementary and junior high levels, this report explains a systematic method of instruction for presenting material in small steps with guided and independent practice, active and successful participation for students, and frequent review. The method is recommended for use when the objective is to teach performance skills or mastery of facts and concepts (in math, reading, grammar, social studies, science, and foreign languages).

Index